Her Life in Ink

Also by Sharon M. Harris

Dr. Mary Walker: An American Radical, 1832–1919
Rebecca Harding Davis: A Life Among Writers
A Feminist Reader: Feminist Thought from Sappho to Satrapi

Her Life in Ink

ELIZABETH JORDAN, JOURNALIST, EDITOR, AND MYSTERY AUTHOR

SHARON M. HARRIS

Foreword by Amy Helmes and Kim Askew, hosts of the *Lost Ladies of Lit* podcast

LP
LYONS PRESS
Essex, Connecticut

LYONS PRESS

An imprint of The Globe Pequot Publishing Group, Inc.
64 South Main St.
Essex, CT 06426
www.GlobePequot.com

British Library Cataloguing in Publication Information available

Library of Congress Cataloging-in-Publication Data available

ISBN 9781493092161 (cloth)
ISBN 9781493092178 (electronic)

Printed in India

Contents

Foreword

Nothing captures public attention quite like a gruesome double homicide—just look at how avidly today's audiences binge true-crime podcasts and investigative Netflix documentaries. In 1893, that appetite found its outlet in the work of American author, editor, and journalist Elizabeth Garver Jordan. One of the few female reporters credentialed to cover the infamous Lizzie Borden murder trial in Fall River, Massachusetts, Jordan provided readers of the *New York World* with gripping daily dispatches over the course of two sweltering weeks in August.

"Did this young woman split open her aged father's head with a hatchet as he lay sleeping on a sofa, and afterwards go back and batter his face and head with the same weapon that even the doctors who looked upon the hideous sight could hardly command their nerves?" With the sort of scintillating language modern readers might recognize from an episode of NBC's *Dateline*, Jordan's eye for detail and suspense fed the public's obsession with the trial, which ultimately ended in Borden's acquittal. This early experience in keeping a nation of readers enthralled would eventually inform Jordan's work as a writer of fictional murder mysteries on par with those of Agatha Christie and Mary Roberts Rinehart.

How did a polite and restrained Milwaukee schoolgirl trade her dreams of entering the convent for a hardscrabble life as a big-city newspaper reporter and, later, a literary editor regarded highly by the likes of Mark Twain and Sinclair Lewis? *Her Life in Ink* charts that trajectory and explores the facets of Jordan's personality that prompted her rise in the world of American media.

Like a late nineteenth-century Lois Lane, Jordan covered crime and the seedier side of New York City while also holding her own in a newsroom dominated by male colleagues and editors. Her professional moxie earned their respect, while her flair for writing human-interest stories that deeply resonated with readers established her as one of the nation's best newspaper women. Bristling at the prevalence of yellow journalism and sensationalism, Jordan eventually parlayed her prose-writing acumen into a job editing *Harper's Bazar* and later became the literary editor for the Harper and Brothers publishing house, where, like famed literary editor Maxwell Perkins, she identified and helped mold the works of emerging literary greats. In correspondence with Henry James, she was no passive disciple. Their intellectually charged exchanges reveal a woman unafraid to challenge him, winning his admiration in return.

Cognizant of the uphill career path she had forged for herself with scant assistance, Jordan took it upon herself to mentor and champion other women writers—quietly building the kind of professional support network that has only recently become more visible in the age of women-in-media coalitions and #MeToo-era newsroom equity efforts. Another cause close to her heart, women's suffrage, led Jordan to spearhead and edit *The Sturdy Oak*, a charming, comedic (and still very relevant) "composite" novel on the subject of women's rights, written collaboratively as a chain-story of sorts by well-known authors of the day, including Fannie Hurst, Anne O'Hagan, and Dorothy Canfield (Fisher).

Though immensely private about her personal life (which included an intense, long-term relationship with *Secret Garden* author Frances Hodgson Burnett), clues to Jordan's existence are readily available through her writing. Her popular May Iverson novels for young adults give insight into her convent school girlhood, while stories featuring female reporter Ruth Herrick could have been written only by a woman who'd "been there, done that."

Jordan herself exemplified the concept of the "New Woman," with a life spanning the Victorian mores of the late nineteenth century and the freewheeling freedoms of the Roaring Twenties flapper. Having never considered marriage, she financially supported herself—and later several members of her family—by negotiating professional contracts that placed a high value on her worth. She frequently traveled abroad—including a stay in Bermuda with Burnett—reflecting the kind of cultural mobility and personal freedom that few women of her time enjoyed. Jordan clung fiercely to the independent life she created for herself in New York City and refused to compromise her desired aims to appease the expectations of others.

Just like *The Sound of Music*'s Maria von Trapp, Jordan was destined to "never be a nun." Rather, her ever-evolving career plans led her through the realms of investigative reporter, magazine boss, literary editor, novelist/mystery writer, Broadway playwright, and Hollywood book-to-screen broker. Jordan's influence and impressive professional network would, in today's world, make her "kind of a big deal." As with so many other women authors who made a mark on their generation only to be forgotten with time, her legacy and her own literary output deserve a closer look.

As podcasters, we've learned that following the thread of a forgotten name can often lead to an extraordinary story—and Elizabeth Garver Jordan's life is no exception. More than a century later, she still leaps off the page: sharp, charismatic, incisive, and utterly modern in her ambition. In *Her Life in Ink*, Sharon M. Harris offers a thoroughly researched, deeply readable portrait that brings Jordan's remarkable accomplishments back into view.

Amy Helmes and Kim Askew
Creators and hosts of the Lost Ladies of Lit *podcast*

Acknowledgments

There are many people who have encouraged me in relation to this biography. I hope that I have thanked you along the way, and I do so again, especially for your heartfelt enthusiasm. Scholars interested in Jordan's life and work have been particularly helpful, including Karen Roggenkamp, Lori Harrison-Kahan, and Jane Carr. I cannot thank Lori and Jane enough for their thoughtful reading and astute comments relating to an earlier draft of this biography.

Two other people stand out for their diligence and generosity:

First, Chris Wolak, freelance researcher extraordinaire, has been of invaluable assistance. I could not have completed this biography without her thorough and thoughtful research over the past years and especially for delving into all the quirky, seemingly unsolvable mysteries that emerge as a project nears the end. Everyone should be so fortunate as to work with a researcher who is also a library archivist.

Second, my sincere thanks to Betsy Devine, Elizabeth Jordan's goddaughter and Clothilde Reo Devine's daughter. Betsy has been a model of generosity in sharing privately held materials relating to Jordan (the Betsy Devine Collection). I appreciate her contributions more than I can say; they have enriched this study of Jordan's life.

In addition, sincere thanks to my editor, Brittany Stoner, as well as everyone else at Lyons Press.

Preface

Elizabeth Jordan's life (1865–1947) crossed many of America's most important eras—from the Civil War to the Progressive Era and Jazz Age to World War II—and, as a writer, she influenced public opinion on many of the major issues of the day.

Whether as a journalist, a magazine editor, or a newspaper columnist, Jordan gained fame not only for her own work but also for her pattern of giving a hand up to talented young journalists and authors. While serving as an editor at Joseph Pulitzer's *New York World*, she gathered around her a staff of women assistants—Anne O'Hagan, Grace Margaret Gould, Marie Manning, Olivia Howard Dunbar, and Harriet Hubbard Ayer—who became influential in the field themselves.

Considered by critics among the best short-story writers of her era, not only did Jordan help shape this broad period of American literature through her own writing, but her work as a literary editor was also instrumental to the successful careers of writers such as Sinclair Lewis, Fannie Hurst, Dorothy Canfield Fisher, and others. She likewise aided the late career of Henry James, publishing his work and organizing a lecture tour for his return to America after years in Europe. Equally important, she used her position as a national figure to promote the idea of women's suffrage and argued that women working at home or in any profession were essential to the national economy. Jordan was like a brilliant flame, illuminating the world around her through her art and guiding other artists on their way.

It would be enough to warrant recovery of her life and work if Jordan had only been an early journalist, an influential editor of *Harper's Bazar*, literary editor for Harper's books and for Goldwyn Studios, an independent newspaper columnist, and author of thirty-three well-received novels as well as four edited books. But Jordan was also an important mystery writer. Fifteen of her thirty-three books were mysteries, published between 1919 and 1943. When she began, there was a small group of American women who were finding success in the field of mysteries and detective fiction. Anna Katherine Green was nearing the end of her career, but Mary Roberts Rinehart, Carolyn Wells, Jordan, and others were emerging. Agatha Christie would join the ranks the year after Jordan's first mystery appeared.

Jordan's mysteries were critically acclaimed and popular in her own time and deserve recognition today. They are fascinating psychological mysteries in a variety of subgenres (locked room, country estate, gothic, based on a true crime, etc.). Jordan also added another level to her mysteries. In addition to her amateur detectives having to stop or solve a murder, each detective must uncover something about themselves in the process—their own mysteries that, once understood, will allow them to move forward in their own lives.

Surprisingly, Jordan has been written out of histories of mystery writing, in spite of being acknowledged in her day as one of America's best writers in the genre. Her mysteries warrant comparison to those of Agatha Christie, with a sustained body of high-quality, innovative stories. The study of Jordan reveals that we are only beginning to understand the extraordinary way in which women writers before and during World War I modernized the genre and forged the path to the Golden Age of mystery writing.

Jordan gave her audience years of exciting and enduring entertainment through her indelible mysteries and detective stories, and, as a journalist and editor, she became a major influence on the literature of her day. Her success was largely shaped by the great optimism that defined her life and helped shape the talents of others. This is her story.

Sharon M. Harris

Chapter 1

Life in Milwaukee

Only a month after Robert E. Lee surrendered at Appomattox on April 9, 1865, Elizabeth Garver Jordan was born on May 9, 1865. She was the first child of Margaretta Garver Jordan (1843–1931) and William Francis Jordan (1841–1901), a middle-class family soon to be on the rise. The Jordans named their firstborn after Margaretta's mother, Elizabeth Moore Garver (1821–?), who was of Spanish descent and taught her granddaughter her native tongue at a young age.

Being an only child for the first eight years of her life allowed Elizabeth to develop especially close, but quite distinct, relationships with her parents. Jordan said her mother "was the most independent woman I have ever known."[1] Margaretta had been an honor student at Mendota Female College and studied medicine at Rush College in Chicago for two years until her father's death, when the family could no longer afford the tuition.[2]

Elizabeth's father was an astute businessman. He took every opportunity to expand his meat and grocery market in the postwar years. Within a few years, his property investments would catapult him into the ranks of Milwaukee's wealthy up-and-coming men. He modeled the value of hard work for his daughter while offering his family a life of privilege. Elizabeth would learn the lesson well and craft for herself a life of extraordinary industriousness and social status after she left home.

Elizabeth's bond with her father was deeply rooted in their shared "undying sense of humor. It has been my most precious possession," she observed late in her life, "and up until the time of [my father's] death it held us together like a steel cable."[3] Elizabeth was able to draw on the strengths of both parents. Her seriousness and willpower, garnered from her mother's example, helped her forge the life she wanted, and the personal magnetism and sense of humor inherited from her father drew an amazing array of people to her, many of whom became lifelong friends.

When Elizabeth was still so young that her hands could barely stretch across the keys, her mother insisted she begin taking piano lessons. To Margaretta's joy, Elizabeth demonstrated exceptional talent. By the time she was old enough to start school, she was playing Beethoven,

Elizabeth Jordan's mother, Margaretta Garver Jordan
BETSY DEVINE COLLECTION

Bach, Chopin, and Mozart and performing in public for benefits. Margaretta began to form a dream that she would never relinquish—her daughter must become a concert pianist.[4]

Elizabeth loved the piano, but at a very young age she also began to harbor a hunger for words. Her parents followed the prevailing philosophy that it was best to protect a young child's brain through "slow development in a safe environment."[5] *Slow*, however, would never be a part of Elizabeth's vocabulary. Perhaps nowhere was her determination to get what she wanted out of life as evident as when she decided she must learn to read. She developed a Plan to gain what she wanted—the first of many Plans that would direct her life.

Before Elizabeth turned five, she formed a pact with the family cook: Nora would teach Elizabeth to read, and Elizabeth would select books from her parents' extensive library and sneak them into the kitchen so they could read together.

This surreptitious act of rebellion was rooted less in resistance than in a great love of intrigue and mystery. She would slip into the library and quickly select a book whose contents remained a great secret until she and Nora cracked its pages in the shelter of the kitchen. In many ways, it was not at all surprising that Elizabeth would become a talented mystery writer in the 1920s and 1930s. The love of intrigue and a gripping story had been bred into her at the ripe age of five.[6]

When Nora had to work, young Elizabeth spent many hours in the library, lying on her stomach in front of the fireplace, reading a multitude of volumes.[7] One day she surprised her father by reading aloud to him from the Christian tract *The Sweet Story of Old*. After his shock subsided, William decided he must take charge of his daughter's reading. He subscribed to several children's periodicals—*Cock Robin*, *Chatterbox*, and *St. Nicholas*—but he had grander ideas for her education, starting with Charles Rollin's classic *Ancient History*.[8]

In 1873, at age eight, Elizabeth enrolled in St. Mary's Institute, a boarding school at Milwaukee's Convent of Notre Dame with nearly one thousand nuns and a student enrollment of several hundred.[9] The five-story, fortress-like convent occupied an entire block, with the school taking up nearly half of the north wing.[10] In the summer before Elizabeth's enrollment, a miracle was documented at the convent. The news was reported widely that a young woman severely afflicted with consumption was healed by the appearance of the Virgin Mary.[11] The impact of this event, mysterious and otherworldly, undoubtedly aided in Elizabeth's fascination with being a part of the convent—as a student, but also with a secret desire: to become one of these pious nuns who could fathom such mysteries.

Although Margaretta Jordan was not Catholic, she agreed when she married William that their children would be raised in his faith, and she appreciated the educational opportunities the convent school offered her daughter—not least of which was its music department. Though the Convent of Notre Dame was cloistered, students were allowed to offer public recitals and receptions in the Exhibition Hall. Elizabeth was one of their best students, musically and academically, and she was already used to performing. As she recalled, in these years "Milwaukee was saturated with music, and its pet method of raising money for its charities was by concert. . . . I played at many such concerts" while at the school.[12]

Convent of Notre Dame, in which St. Mary's Convent School is located
THREE ROUSING CHEERS

In the meantime, the Jordans had been trying to expand their family. After the loss of two children in infancy,[13] finally on December 29, 1873, their daughter Alice was born. Elizabeth and her sister "Allie" would remain close throughout their lives, but it was never a relationship of equals and certainly not always an easy alliance. The Jordans loved their second daughter, but she was an average child with few distinctions, forever overshadowed by her exceptional older sister. William and Margaretta had the wisdom to send Alice to a different convent school than Elizabeth so she would not be forever compared to her talented sister.[14]

School was a joy for Elizabeth. Her charismatic personality drew students and nuns alike to her, and she loved to study. Sister Ethelbert, who taught writing, was her favorite teacher, and Elizabeth remained close friends with her long after she left St. Mary's—indeed, until Sister Ethelbert's death.[15]

In addition to her studies, Elizabeth continued to practice piano for two hours a day; this pattern of daily practice would continue throughout her life. Sister Cecilia headed the music department and encouraged her pupil's love of music and of performance. Years later, Elizabeth would declare that Sister Cecilia was "by far the best musician and teacher of the piano I have ever known."[16] Studying with her for many years enhanced Elizabeth's expertise—and her mother's hope that her daughter would pursue a career in music.

By the time Elizabeth was in her early teens, however, she was torn between dreams of becoming a writer and of taking vows as a nun. In those reading sessions with the cook Nora, Elizabeth had talked often of her desire to be an author, so at thirteen she developed a new Plan—she would start her literary career by keeping her efforts secret until she had achieved her goal. She took a breath of courage and submitted a story to the *Evening Wisconsin*.

To her delight, it was published. Her plan for presenting this exciting news to the family reflected her love of drama. The night of its publication in the newspaper, she joined her family in the living room. She had a larger than usual audience on this particular evening since her grandmother and two aunts were visiting. They gathered together when Elizabeth announced she wanted to read them a love story she had discovered in the newspaper. She did not reveal that she was the author of "Caleb Green's Affinity." Her plan was that she would read it to her family "and watch them fall dead, so to speak, when at the end the author's name was revealed."[17]

"I read it with love and fire," she recalled. "To me it seemed a remarkable tale." To her dismay, her aunts yawned, her grandmother nodded off, and Alice stretched out on the rug in front of the fire and went to sleep before Elizabeth finished. There was no applause when she concluded. Her mother wondered why newspapers wasted space on "anything so trivial"; her father admitted he had stopped listening early on; her youthful aunts acted out a burlesque of the main scene. Finally, her grandmother asked what had interested Elizabeth in the story. When she confessed that she had written it, everyone tried to revise their assessment of its merits, but Elizabeth knew she had already received their accurate evaluations.[18]

She burst into tears. "I wanted to die. Or at least to go into the convent, without an hour's delay."[19] Her father finally assured Elizabeth that "while the story would be very slight as the production of an established author it was highly promising as the first effort of a little girl."[20] The humiliation faded but was not forgotten. Twenty years later, she would publish "Olive's First Story" based on the experience.[21]

As painful as these responses were, they served as an impetus for Elizabeth. She had never failed at anything, and she would not do so now. She set about honing her writing while she continued her schooling.

At the head of St. Mary's was Reverend Mother Mary Caroline, and Elizabeth adored her: "She had the beauty and graciousness and charm an Archduchess should possess, as well as personal magnetism that drew even the unwilling into her orbit."[22] Elizabeth did not know that Sister Cecilia had informed the Reverend Mother of Elizabeth's musical talents and of her mother's desire that she become a professional pianist. Mother Caroline was herself a pianist and appreciated Elizabeth's talents. When Elizabeth was fifteen, she and three other music students were granted special dispensation for a rare opportunity to hear the *Der Ring des Nibelungen* at the Milwaukee Opera House. The students and an escort were driven to and from the performances in the convent bus with its curtained windows. For Elizabeth, the experience was "pure rapture." The experience honed her love of opera, which would last a lifetime.

It was not until Commencement Day, when Elizabeth stood in the wings waiting to be announced as valedictorian, that Mother Caroline revealed her belief that Elizabeth was fit for the habit of Notre Dame. No more was said, and the excitement of the day consumed Elizabeth's attention. But when she returned home that evening, she found "Mother Caroline's words burning in my mind and heart."[23] Becoming a nun

Elizabeth Jordan, age seventeen, graduation photo
THREE ROUSING CHEERS

had been her unspoken ambition for several years. She had tried more than once to express such an idea to her schoolmates, only to have them respond with loud laughs. "They said I was not the material nuns are made of . . . and they were right. I was a high-spirited and irrepressible young person" whose curiosity frequently led her into escapades resulting in discipline by the nuns.[24] At commencement, however, she heard only Mother Caroline.[25]

In addition to being valedictorian, Elizabeth was awarded the coveted Cross of Honor, which was given only to a graduate of exceptional religious studiousness and character. For the remainder of her life, the Cross granted her access to any convent in the United States, where she could expect to be welcomed like a sister.[26] Throughout her life, Elizabeth would take full benefit of these privileges, finding peace and rejuvenation at convents away from her hectic life.

But she knew she would meet with firm resistance from her mother if she declared she wanted to take vows. When the family returned home that evening after commencement, Elizabeth decided to tell her father about her desire. She chose a moment when her mother was busy with a house full of relatives and friends. William listened carefully and then, to her surprise, said that it would be unwise to give up a life that she had not yet experienced. She could commit seriously to becoming a pianist or she could pursue a writing career, as she had once dreamed. William suggested she consider the newspaper business, which he thought might be an exciting field. He suggested Elizabeth try that path over the next four years. Then she could decide whether she wanted to return to the convent.

She struggled with her father's proposition. Always strong willed, she was used to having her own way, but after considering the idea of becoming a journalist and then author—which would be her ultimate goal—Elizabeth spoke with Mother Caroline, who agreed it was a good plan to try the outside life before making any decision. Elizabeth, who always had "a Plan" (she insisted on the capital *P*), began to craft a path toward a career in writing.

Chapter 2

The Plan

Despite Elizabeth's disastrous experience with the publication of her first story, she continued to write and submit her work. A year after her first publication, she had a short story accepted by *Texas Siftings*, a humor magazine, for which she received $5.[1] This achievement reinforced her belief that a writing career was not out of the question. Her father had envisioned a career in newspaper writing for his daughter, but he was distressed when Elizabeth made it clear from the beginning that, if she was going to be a newspaper woman, she would need to go to New York.

William Jordan was not at all ready to have his seventeen-year-old daughter move to New York on her own. He had his own plan. He approached his friend George W. Peck, a famous Milwaukee publisher and humorist, about taking Elizabeth on at his weekly newspaper, *Peck's Sun*. William also promised his daughter that after six months or a year in such a position, he would pull some strings and secure her a position in Chicago; if she made it in that market, she could go to New York. Further, he promised to support her financially until she made it on her own.[2] He tried every way to make life outside the convent enticing without acquiescing to the idea of his daughter leaving immediately for New York.

Elizabeth had a Plan of her own, however. She would be delighted with his help, but first she wanted to develop skills she felt would be necessary for success in New York. She enrolled in a special course at the University of Wisconsin[3] and, the following year, was admitted to the Spencerian Business College, considered one of the best educational institutions in the city for its offerings in secretarial, accounting, and other business courses.[4] There, Jordan studied shorthand as a necessary and practical skill to master if she were to become a reporter.[5]

As Elizabeth learned more about the newspaper business, she realized that she would not be able simply to move to New York City and land a job. While the various New York newspapers were hiring women in increasing numbers, they largely relegated female reporters to the role of space writers who were paid by the word for filler items. Jordan wanted to be an investigative reporter *and* to be able to support herself in as comfortable a lifestyle as possible. So, in 1886, when she completed her course at the business college, she took her father's advice and went to work for a number of local papers, beginning with *Peck's Sun*. The weekly newspaper had a national circulation of 150,000 and advertised itself as "The Funniest Paper in America."[6]

George Peck offered her the position of editor of a new woman's page he wished to add to the *Sun*. For an inexperienced journalist, it was a notable opportunity, but Jordan soon learned the position would offer her no avenue for the tough-minded reporting she had envisioned for herself. Peck insisted on calling the department "Sunshine" and, to Jordan's dismay, "conveyed the impression that I would personally supply light and warmth to the universe. . . . I myself was not a sentimentalist. It is a miracle the stuff I had to carry in 'Sunshine' did not permanently destroy my interest in newspaper work."[7]

Despite Jordan's disappointment in the kind of light journalism the position offered, she gained experience and began writing a few items for other local newspapers as well, including the *Milwaukee Journal*, the *Milwaukee Sentinel*, the *Weekly Wisconsin*, and the *St. Paul Globe*. After a year, she left *Peck's Sun*, hoping to parlay her experience into a position writing for a Chicago newspaper. Her father had other ideas, however. He felt she was still too young to move to Chicago on her own and informed her that he had found her another position—as secretary to William E. Anderson, Milwaukee superintendent of schools. Her father, a member of the school board, was again able to call on an important friend to hire his daughter.

Jordan was not happy, but she had already learned that sometimes it was necessary, at least for a short while, to make the best of a difficult situation, an attitude that would serve her well in the coming years. She bit back her disappointment and stepped into her new role with the idea that it would allow her weekends for her writing. In these years, she developed the habit of being a "workaholic," though the term hardly does justice to the level of productivity she would maintain over the next sixty years.[8]

Finally, Jordan felt she had enough experience to try the Chicago market, and her parents could not deny she had earned the opportunity. Within a short time, she was freelancing for several of the major newspapers in Chicago—the *Times*, *Tribune*, *Herald*, and *Inter-Ocean*, making her greatest mark with the *Chicago Tribune*. That paper's managing editor, William Van Benthuysen, was especially encouraging to the young reporter and assigned her several special features.

Her mother often traveled by train to spend weekends with Jordan. Margaretta knew the city well, having lived there while attending medical college. They spent many Saturday afternoons at recitals and operas. The bond between mother and daughter grew in these years through their mutual love of music. Yet, as much as Jordan enjoyed her work for the Chicago papers, she had a new Plan brewing in her mind, assuring herself "the next move on life's chess-board . . . was to be made by me, not by my Father."[9]

In the late summer of 1889, she told family and friends that she was off on a holiday to visit friends in Boston. She did spend a week there, but her real destination was New York City and the newspaper offices of Joseph Pulitzer's *World*.

When Jordan arrived in the city, it was early September and the heat was intense. She went straight to the *World*'s offices. They were housed in an old, rundown building on Nassau Street, but its appearance didn't matter to Jordan. She wanted to be a part of its inner world.

Joseph Pulitzer
LIBRARY OF CONGRESS

Joseph Pulitzer had purchased the *World* in 1883, and he followed what was known as "the new journalism"—which included the initiation of reporters having bylines, increasing respectability of newspaper work, and independence of thought.[10] When Pulitzer purchased the *World*, there were almost one hundred reporters, editors, compositors, and other employees in the firm. He would greatly expand that number as he shaped the daily publication into the most influential paper in the city. Pulitzer intended to create a truly democratic newspaper and asserted that the "keystone of *The World*'s arch of triumph is public service."[11] These were the values Jordan embraced as she envisioned joining the paper.

Audaciously, with no appointment or letter of recommendation to present, Jordan entered the offices of the *World* and asked to see the editor in chief. Fortuitously arriving at a slow moment in the day's usually frantic work pace, she was admitted to Colonel John A. Cockerill's office. The impression he made on her lasted a lifetime: "He was a big man, six feet tall, and . . . about two hundred pounds. He had a massive head with graying hair, an expression suggesting power combined with a valiant kindliness, and strained, tired eyes that usually held a friendly twinkle."[12] When an office boy interrupted them one too many times, however, Cockerill let out a torrent of curses—not at all unusual for him, as Jordan would learn. Cursing and drinking excessively would soon become his most obvious traits.[13]

At first dubious about the young woman who asserted herself without hesitation, Cockerill listened to Jordan detail her experience and her proclamation that she wished to work as a reporter for the *World*. Cockerill seemed amused at first. The more they spoke, however, the more interested he became, recognizing the spark of intelligence, determination, and ambition that suggested the makings of an excellent reporter.

Jordan made certain demands even as she asked for a job: "I warned Colonel Cockerill that I was not up to 'stunt' reporting and that I did not like it."[14] This was an extraordinary demand. Stunt reporting was the means by which many of the handful of full-time women reporters on the big papers had made their names. "Girl stunt reporters," as they were known, included the *World*'s Elizabeth Cochran. These young women were typically given catchy names—for Cochran, it was "Nellie Bly," the name under which she had feigned insanity and spent ten days in a "mad house" and would soon take off on her "around the world in eighty days" adventure. Stunt reporting may have been the name given to women's reportage, but in its early days it was actually investigative reporting that required talents of detection that paralleled Pinkerton's own agents.[15]

By the 1890s, when Jordan met with Cockerill, however, there was a backlash forming that viewed this form of stunt reportage as "gutter" journalism that would damage a woman's morals and "desex" her because of the places she would have to go and the degrading language and actions she might experience. If gutter journalism was a highly conservative perspective, stunt reporting had changed from social justice assignments to trite escapades.[16] Jordan did not want to engage in stunts or use an assumed name, but she did want to report on the city's ills and its most needy inhabitants, which were a large part of the focus of the new journalism newspapers.

To the surprise of everyone at the *World*, Jordan was hired. She and the colonel agreed with a handshake that she would start in April 1890. Her Plan was coming to fruition.

In January 1890, Nelly Bly made her famous trip around the world and then, to continue the sensationalism of her endeavor, made a triumphant tour from New York across the Midwest. When Bly arrived in Milwaukee, she was greeted by an appointed welcoming committee—the *Milwaukee Sentinel* city editor, Charles Ledlie, and Elizabeth Jordan. They were to meet her at the train and take her to a reception planned in her honor.

Jordan was thrilled. Not only would she meet the remarkable Miss Bly, but she also would be able to inform Bly that she would soon be joining the staff of the *World*. The meeting did not go as expected, however. When Jordan shared that she was about to be employed by the *World*, "Miss Bly remarked briefly that she had just resigned from the *World* and that she was sorry for any one who was going to work on that sheet." Stunned, Jordan's expectations for Bly crashed. "The entente between us took on a delicate layer of frost."[17] Jordan could not have known that Bly had left the paper because, after creating an extraordinary level of publicity for the *World*, they refused to pay her what she felt she was worth.[18] The experience did not, however, dull Jordan's excitement about joining the elite group of the *World*'s reporters.

Bly was a sharp, creative entrepreneur of her own career and reputation, but she did not at this moment offer to give a young admirer a hand up. It was an error Jordan would not make. Her skirt tails would carry many a new reporter or author to a successful career.

Little could Jordan know in these exciting weeks of anticipation that her arrival at the *World* a few months later would be met with a similar "layer of frost." She may have won over Cockerill, but his star was fading and Jordan was about to be caught in his downfall.

Chapter 3

A New Kind of Education

Margaretta Jordan was not at all pleased with her daughter's success in securing a position in New York. It took a great deal of William's gentle persuasion to bring his wife around to the idea. Eventually, the three of them agreed that Elizabeth would stay in New York for a year or two at most.[1] Margaretta remained dubious about the move, even more so as she realized that this opportunity signaled the end of her dream that her daughter would become a concert pianist. The best she could manage was to secure a promise from Elizabeth that she would practice the piano every day.

Margaretta's worries proved well founded: Elizabeth Jordan fell in love with New York City and lived there until her death fifty-seven years later.

Throughout her life, Jordan maintained a series of Plans tucked away in her mind and rarely shared with anyone until she had accomplished her goals. So, despite agreeing to a short New York stay, she had determined that literature held the premier place in her future, over music and newspaper work. She planned to devote five years as a reporter to hone her writing skills and then find magazine work, which she felt sure would "open the door to the world of literature."[2] And that world was in New York. Her predictions may have been slightly off timewise—she would remain with the *World* for ten years—but her career in literature as an author and editor would be notable. When Jordan made up her mind regarding a Plan, she followed its path to the end.

She arrived in New York in mid-April 1890; the following month, she would turn twenty-five. It was a time when newspapers were thriving. When Pulitzer had purchased the *World* seven years earlier, there were forty-three daily newspapers in the city, and the *World*'s circulation in 1883 was flagging at fifteen thousand, a number that did not begin to compete with the more than one hundred thousand subscribers for the *New York Times* and the *New York Tribune*.[3] Pulitzer had a vision, however, and he promised staff and readers that the *World* would be truly democratic: inexpensive and "dedicated to the cause of the people rather than that of purse-potentates." Its goal would be to expose "all fraud and sham, fight all public evils."[4]

Partly a true desire and partly good advertising, this goal captured Pulitzer's intention to garner the greatest circulation New York had ever seen. Seeking to break away from the staid traditions of his competitors, Pulitzer emphasized human-interest stories presented in prose that sounded more like a good story than a newspaper article.[5] This attitude about newspaper stories offered Jordan the perfect school for learning to become a magazine writer.

When Jordan arrived, the *World* had become home to more than six hundred reporters, editors, and other staff, and it had a circulation of around 185,000.[6] Ready to begin her reporting adventures, Jordan fully expected to be welcomed into the bosom of this hotbed of reporters that defined the city and its people. Instead, she was stunned to land in the middle of an in-house battle for management of the paper. Joseph Pulitzer rarely came to the office these days, due to worsening eyesight problems. She met him face-to-face only a few times in her decade of work at the *World*, but he kept in close contact with his employees through the use of cables and telegrams.

Pulitzer's frequent absences led to infighting among his editorial staff as they jostled in what Jordan called "a life-and-death struggle for supremacy."[7] One of the most heated of these battles when Jordan arrived—which she termed "Homeric" in its intensity—was between John Cockerill, editor in chief, and Ballard Smith, managing editor but clearly rising in the firm.[8] Due to Pulitzer's long absences, editorial roles were not as clearly defined as they were in most newspapers, and the battle between the numerous men holding these positions lasted throughout the 1890s while Jordan was at the *World*.

She appreciated the traits of both editors: "Colonel Cockerill was a born newspaperman, a great worker, a great leader, but of the old school. Ballard Smith . . . was young and dynamic. He was a really brilliant newspaper man, and he carried his ambition like a flaunting flag."[9] Soon after Jordan arrived, she realized that Cockerill was clearly losing the battle—and he was the man who had hired her. Smith resented that decision, since he had not been consulted and believed he alone had the right to hire reporters.

None of which was obvious or explained to Jordan; she simply knew that there was a very cold wind blowing in her direction. She was given only trivial assignments, and even when she crossed paths with Smith in the hallways, he ignored her.[10] Still, she tried to embrace the joy she felt every time the bell rang signaling the start-up of the press and the thunderous thumping that meant news sheets were being cut, printed, and folded, ready to bring the news to the world.

She was not to be thwarted: "My optimism was indestructible. I set my jaw and took what came, though my pride was a tattered flag."[11] She trusted that her work would prove her talents.

To improve her skills, she studied the star reporters in the city room, learning their styles and methods. She read every item in the *World* each morning and many other newspapers' major stories. Over the next two months, she also observed enough to understand the feud between Cockerill and Smith and to realize her supporter would not win. Fortunately, she received a good salary and, at this point, Smith did not have the power to change that, but he could try to force her out by making her life miserable.

She worked fourteen to eighteen hours a day (a schedule she maintained throughout her years at the *World*), which should have given her the opportunity to produce some excellent articles, but she was assigned nothing of importance while being sent all over the city on leads that rarely developed into anything worthy of publication. When Cockerill stepped in and offered her a real story to cover, Smith would strike the assignment from the reporters' schedule board. The city editor sided with Smith in the feud, so he did not intervene. No one was going to risk his position for a cub reporter, especially a female, who many felt had no place in the profession. When she tried suggesting topics for specials, they were rejected out of hand.[12]

To Jordan's dismay, Cockerill came up with what he believed was an excellent solution. Without consulting her, he arranged for her transfer in June 1890 to the staff of the Brooklyn edition of the *World*. The change meant she would no longer be in the Manhattan office, at the heartbeat of the paper. It broke her heart and humiliated her. It was exile.

When she arrived at the regional office, she learned that her assignment was to cover the local resorts. Brooklyn Heights had become a favorite summer community for New York professionals, especially since elevated railways now made the commute into the city relatively easy. Jordan understood only too well that her assignments were fluff pieces meant to promote the resorts and thereby create more advertising for the paper.

She was bored in no time, even when the Newport and Lenox resorts were added to her coverage. Two good things came out of these months of misery, however. She became friends with the Brooklyn edition's managing editor, Vincent Cook, and together they were successful in increasing the edition's circulation and advertising, which earned her a raise and pleased Ballard Smith. The second benefit was personal. Just after she was assigned to Brooklyn, her mother decided to visit in order to see what kind of life her daughter was truly leading in New York. Margaretta went to some of the resorts with Elizabeth, and "the jaunts were healing and soothing to us both."[13] If Margaretta still lamented her daughter's choice of a career, she returned home believing it was a safe and genteel occupation. Had she arrived a few months later, she would have feared for her daughter's safety, but, for now, Margaretta was appeased, even if her daughter was not.

Jordan knew there was little chance that she could cover a story at the resorts that would be her ticket back into the Manhattan office, but an unexpected opportunity did arise. President Benjamin Harrison and his wife, Caroline, were spending the summer in a cottage at Cape May, along with their daughter, Mary Harrison McKee, and her three-year-old son, Benjamin. Caroline Harrison was notorious for refusing interviews. Ballard Smith told his star reporters he wanted to know what that cottage was like and how the family was spending the summer. The Harrisons had, of course, expected such interest and refused all interviews. Smith was unhappy with his crew, as were newspaper editors across the country who had sent reporters to Cape May.

By July, infuriated at his Manhattan reporters' failure, Smith remembered "that girl over in Brooklyn" and sent for Jordan. His instructions were short: get the story. She left for the shore that night and the next morning was on the doorstep of the Harrisons' cottage. Jordan dressed judiciously in "a fresh white linen tailor-made suit, white canvas shoes, a white sport hat, and white wash gloves," so that when the butler eyed her at the Harrisons' front door, he would assume she was a friend.[14]

He led Jordan into the hallway, farther than any other reporter had gotten so far. Fortuitously, at this moment Caroline Harrison entered with her grandson. Jordan knew if she had been announced, she would have been turned away, and she was not going to lose this opportunity. She stepped forward, explained that she was a new reporter and that she had been ordered to get an interview. Wisely, she turned her attention to the child, known to the public as "Baby McKee." It was the way to a grandmother's heart. Mrs. Harrison invited Jordan to join her and the baby as they headed down to their private beach.

Jordan had Harrison to herself while little Benjamin played in the sand. During the hours she spent with the First Lady, Jordan was introduced to her daughter, Mary Harrison McKee, who instantly took a liking to the young reporter. The two women became lifelong friends. Meanwhile, Harrison described the family's daily routine while in Cape May, noting how nice it was to escape the pressures of Washington, and told Jordan about the books she was reading.[15]

When Jordan's article appeared the next morning with intimate details about Harrison's summer months, it was considered the most important news story of the moment. After the publication, Mrs. Harrison sent Jordan a note, indicating she appreciated the way Jordan had presented her. Even more important for Jordan's future, Ballard Smith was thrilled. He reassigned her to the New York office immediately, raised her salary, and appointed her to his personal staff of reporters. Her real life as a journalist had begun.[16]

Chapter 4

Making Her Way

THE NEW SALARY JORDAN RECEIVED WHEN SHE RETURNED TO THE NEW York office was large enough to cover her living expenses.[1] She was proud of this fact, as it meant she no longer had to rely on her parents for financial support. She had gained an important position of trust within the upper hierarchy of the newspaper, and her future seemed secure.

In September 1890, Jordan published a notable item that embodied the *World*'s new philosophy for its articles: stark reality and genuine sympathy. Pulitzer eschewed vagueness, wanting as many shocking, poignant, enlightening details as possible while maintaining his insistence on accuracy.[2] Jordan's article, "The Death of Number Nine," traced the tragedy of a poor woman who, because she had no money, was forced to carry her child through the streets of New York to Bellevue Hospital, only to discover when she arrived that the child had died en route. When Jordan arrived at the morgue, she found the child's body had been placed in a small pine box with "Number Nine" written on it. "I was determined," she wrote, "that he should have proper burial." She returned to the office and wrote her story with a conclusion asking for contributions to bury the child properly. By the next day, "enough contributions had been received to bury almost every dead child in New York that day." The excess funds were given to the mother so she and her remaining children could be brought out of poverty.[3]

"The Death of Number Nine" impressed the city editor, Morrell Goddard, who awarded the piece one of his rare "model story" recognitions. When Goddard thought a piece was exceptionally well written and effective, he cut it out of the paper and pasted it on the newsroom wall as an example to other reporters. Jordan liked that Goddard possessed sentiment but "absolutely no sentimentality," which was what she strove to achieve in her newspaper writing and later in her fiction. The distinction was important: sentimentalism was exaggerated and often self-indulgent emotion; sentiment allowed for genuine feelings combined with facts. In this distinction, Jordan drew on a lesson she had learned from Sister Ethelbert during her senior year at St. Mary's. "Let your readers shed their own tears," Sister Ethelbert had penciled at the end of one of Jordan's stories. She felt it was the best literary criticism she ever received.[4]

After being granted Goddard's recognition, Jordan was invited by the other reporters to celebrate at Mouquin's, a nearby restaurant where reporters from numerous papers often gathered after work. Receiving such recognition after less than six months on the paper brought about some good-natured teasing by fellow reporters, including Bayard Veiller, with whom Jordan remained friends long after they both left the *World*.[5]

Her colleagues took advantage of the moment to tease her about the one flaw they had found in her: she had a "convent manner"—reserved, formal, never using bad language.[6] Though she joined in the fun on this occasion, as a woman in a man's world, Jordan could not participate in all of the buddy-buddying of the newsroom or in the saloons after hours. Harassment of women reporters by their colleagues was not uncommon, and she felt alone and unsure how to handle such situations except to maintain a staid presence. It would be years before she could admit to anyone what she actually experienced in these early days of her career.

Jordan's success with her "model story" led Ballard Smith to come up with another special assignment for her. It was popular in magazines at this time for Northern writers to travel to the South and report on the region—either as an inferior section of the country or to capture the changes in the "New South."[7] Smith wanted the *World* to run a similar kind of story. He had read an item about an old preacher in Appalachia who he thought would make good copy, and he assigned Jordan to write it.

Her colleagues understood that the area into which Jordan had been ordered to travel constituted some of the most isolated mountain regions of Virginia and Tennessee, but Jordan was "enchanted. This was real adventure. It was a dream come true."[8] She caught a train from New York City to Bristol, Tennessee, and then traveled by wagon to Big Stone Gap, Virginia. With the discovery of ore in the region, the town was teeming with men, but only one other woman resided in the boarding-house where she found a room for the night.

From there, it was pure wilderness that could be navigated only on horseback. Fortunately, Jordan was a skilled rider, but finding a guide was more difficult than expected. The husband of the other woman in the boarding-house recommended an African American man to serve as Jordan's guide, with the assurance that he was more reliable than any of the white riffraff in town. Off they went, relying on the hospitality of locals for a place to sleep and eat. She soon realized, however, that while her guide was trustworthy, he had no knowledge of the mountain area beyond Big Stone Gap. After a few days, she paid him and sent him home, though she knew how dangerous it could be for a woman to travel alone in an isolated area.

The weather had not yet turned cold, and Jordan could bathe in the many streams running through the mountains or use a basin outside one of the many cabins she visited. Along the way, she stopped to peruse the mines and moonshiners' camps; at night she found a bed in one of the mountaineers' homes, if one was close by, or she slept in the open air wherever she found herself. She loved the comforts of her middle-class life, but to get a story, she would put herself through any hardship. She was careful to report to her readers that "not once in all this time did [this reporter] receive a word or look which a brother could have resented had he been with her."[9] Such an assertion was questionable, but it was important for the projection of the modern, capable female journalist.

After several days, Jordan located the preacher, Joseph Wells, who proved to be the model of mountain hospitality. She stayed in his hut, sharing a bed with his daughter and two of her children, and spent hours interviewing Mr. Wells. From there, she spent two weeks in the saddle, roaming the mountains to learn about local feuds, which Smith wanted her to include in her coverage. A severe case of rheumatism in her right arm and shoulder finally sent her back to Bristol.

She was in such bad shape when she arrived in the town that the idea of days on a rattling, rocking train seemed impossible. No doctor was available, but a local woman took Jordan home, where one of her servants proved to be the best nurse possible. For three nights, Jordan remained with the family, until she was well enough to catch a midnight train back to New York.[10]

Smith was so pleased with the Appalachian story that he decided to place it on the front page. First, however, he handed Jordan the proofs and directed her to create the news headline and subheadings. She had never done such work before, but Smith insisted she learn by doing. She did not guess from this last-minute assignment that Smith had a major change planned for her.

Chapter 5

True Stories

A MONTH AFTER JORDAN RETURNED FROM THE APPALACHIAN TRIP, Ballard Smith approached her with a unique offer—to write a new column in the paper, "Stories of the News." While most Americans thought of New York as the height of sophistication, where high society defined couture and manners, a completely different world marked the character of the city as well, and that is what these articles were meant to emphasize. She published nearly sixty items in this column over the next year. They were rife with blazing headlines and enticing subheadings, just like those Smith had insisted Jordan create for her Appalachian story. The "Stories of the News" were half-page specials and prime examples of the new journalism—true stories culled from every corner of the city but, as Smith demanded, written like a fictional tale with dialogue and drama.

This combination soon led the *World* to change the column's title to "True Stories of the News." For Jordan, it was strenuous, sometimes brutal work, but it could not have been better training ground for a reporter who saw journalism as a stepping stone to fiction. In fact, the *World*'s advertisements highlighting the new column described it as depicting "the Romance, Pathos and Humor of Every-day Life in New York." Even in these early newspaper pieces, the inclination toward mystery writing is evident as Jordan kept readers on edge until the end in her true crime entries.

Readers were shocked daily by accounts of New York's slums that appeared in most of the city's newspapers, and Jacob Riis had published his famous exposé about New York slums, *How the Other Half Lives*, just months before Jordan's column began. The initial twenty-five pieces for her column were numbered like book chapters, so readers felt drawn to continue reading day after day to uncover the notorious mysteries of the city. The first column, "Jessie Adamson's Suicide," appeared on November 25, 1890. Like most of the items in the "True Stories" series, there was an edge of irony and indictment against an uncaring city that offered no hand to a struggling citizen. Jordan recounted Adamson's desperate search for work while viewing "the wealth of a great town spread everywhere before her eyes." In such accounts, Jordan perfectly captured the irony of the Gilded Age—the disparity of visible wealth, philanthropy, and great monuments to art and culture versus the achingly poor existences of thousands in tenements or living on the streets.

The "True Stories" column was unsigned, but, in no time, word spread among readers and city officials about this new reporter. Jordan began receiving tips about possible stories from people at the Tombs (the jail), Bellevue Hospital, the Charity Hospital on Blackwell's Island, police courts, city prisons, and elsewhere. Some paid off, most did not, but she followed them all. Her long hours increased, as did the danger of her work. She said it was a blessing that her mother had visited when she was in Brooklyn covering resorts and not during these months of divining stories in what were often dangerous locales.

Years later, in her autobiography, Jordan remarked on the talented and courageous young people who worked as reporters during her years with the newspaper: "A fascinating group—young and cheerful, high-spirited and ready to die at their posts if need be. Some of them did. Many of them risked doing it."[1] Though she preferred to downplay this aspect of her own work, she did reveal an instance when she visited an asylum and talked to a "charming-looking patient." When Jordan prepared to leave, the woman asked whether she could kiss her goodbye. Fortunately, Jordan hesitated. The woman became insistent—until a nurse intervened and told Jordan that the woman was a "biter," who liked to "take an occasional mouthful from the faces of those around her."[2]

Not all the stories in Jordan's series were about deaths. Joseph Pulitzer, like other publishers of the era, had quickly recognized the potential increase in circulation that came with covering crime stories, and criminals played a significant role in Jordan's "True Stories" columns—the bigamist who tried to murder his first wife, the embezzler who was traced by detectives and brought to justice.[3]

Also in line with Pulitzer's promise to expose crime and corruption wherever he found it, Jordan wrote about criminality that circulated within genteel homes—from spousal abuse to fashionable young women addicted to opium (which would figure in two of her later mystery novels). Her articles placed an "imprint on crime reportage by exposing the unsavory activities of the 'better' class of people," not merely the poor.[4] A call for social reform pervaded these articles.

In the midst of her work on the "True Stories" columns, Pulitzer's new building for the *World* was completed, and their offices were moved to the grand structure in the center of Manhattan on "Newspaper Row." Rising thirteen stories high (making it the tallest building in the world at that time), the Pulitzer Building towered above the city.

When Jordan first arrived at the new World Building, she entered a cavernous lobby that was guarded by bronze torchbearers symbolizing art, literature, science, and invention. Crossing the entry, she stepped into one of the elevators that ran the height of the building. The first ten stories were leased by lawyers, stockbrokers, and other businesses. The *World*'s offices began on the twelfth floor, a high-ceilinged area that was home to more than two hundred compositors and thirty proofreaders. In the reporters' area, rolltop desks were crammed close together and placards hung all along the walls that read, "ACCURACY, ACCURACY, ACCURACY!" and "WHO? WHAT? WHERE? WHEN? HOW?" In several spots the *World*'s credo was repeated: "THE FACTS—THE COLOR—THE FACTS."[5] This arena was Jordan's new workplace, though not for long.

The most impressive aspect of the building, however, was the four-story golden tower that topped the building. The editorial offices of the *World* were located here. The area had been designed so that Pulitzer and his editors had quick access to one another—from Pulitzer's office there

New York World Building on left with its golden dome
LIBRARY OF CONGRESS

extended three interconnected rooms for his editors.[6] Legends quickly emerged about the building and its elite golden dome arena, including one oft-told tale in which a visitor rode up the elevator to Joseph Pulitzer's office. When he stepped out and looked around, he asked, "Is God in?"[7]

During the winter months, Jordan trudged through rain-soaked streets and snowy pathways to track viable stories for her column. When the rest of the city was ending its day—"amidst the clatter of 'L' trains and the monotonous tread of home-going work-people and the cries of newsboys"—she continued.[8] The hours were long and arduous, and at the end of the day she was exhausted. But she never reneged on her promise to her mother to practice piano for an hour a day. Doing so proved to be a soothing reprieve after the sadness and tragedy of so much of what she observed every day.

Being out of the office most of the day allowed her to avoid the tensions that were growing once again between John Cockerill and Ballard Smith. She was torn between her loyalty to the man who had hired her and the man who was pushing for more progressive ideas for the paper and under whose wing she now worked. The editors' differences finally came to a head at the end of the year. Cockerill was out, and Pulitzer named Smith acting editor in chief. It was a triumph for Smith, but it was not the last major change to occur at the *World*. Smith's tenure would soon be tested.

Chapter 6
Sections Editor

Jordan's "True Stories" column ended in April 1891 with Ballard Smith's decision to promote her to editor of a daily and of the *Sunday World*'s women's page. After only one year as a reporter, she was moved up to an office in the coveted golden-dome editorial space and was given appropriate staff assistance. This would be her workspace for the next nine years. Her office was crescent shaped with ample windows and two balconies as well as a view of the river.[1]

Women's pages had become the hottest commodity in progressive newspapers, due in large part to the growing national women's club movement, and "club notes" became a standard column for many women's pages. In addition to such news, Jordan's page included special features about women who represented newfound freedoms and work opportunities, and women writers found an increased ability to publish their work in this part of the paper. Equally important from a journalistic perspective, the women's page was one of the premier sections for producing advertising revenue. It featured the expected fashion and society discussions, but Jordan followed the progressive track and developed the *World*'s women's page into much more.[2]

While some newspaper women eschewed the club movement, Jordan embraced it, not only in the pages of the *World* but in her own life as well. In addition to the New York Women's Press Club, she was a member of Sorosis, an organization largely made up of professional women interested in social reform, including women's suffrage. Jordan recognized that women's clubs were a prime breeding ground for the suffrage movement's organizing efforts. She would join many other professional clubs during the coming years, not only as a means of spreading the suffrage word but also for her personal benefit. Clubs offered her space for intelligent conversations with like-minded professional women. She built the women's page at the *World* into an integral base for advancing women's lives, her own career, and the fight for equality.

Jordan had a notable staff of assistants who helped build the page into the advertising winner it became.[3] She wanted to advance other women in the profession, so she selected a talented group of assistants: Anne O'Hagan, with whom Jordan would have a long professional association after they both left the *World*; Grace Margaret Gould, who went on to become fashion editor of the popular *Woman's Home Companion*; Marie Manning, a talented reporter who later became famous as the advice columnist "Beatrice Fairfax" for the Hearst papers; Olivia Howard Dunbar, who went on to become a successful short-story writer; and Harriet Hubbard Ayer, a beauty specialist who helped establish the cosmetics industry. Once this group of journalists began working together, they remained supportive of one another for the rest of their careers.

Jordan quickly became famous not only in New York but also nationwide. Washington, DC's *Evening Star*, for example, included an item about her work as a reporter. As would so often happen in the earliest national coverage she received, her youth (she was twenty-six at the time) and attractiveness were given as much attention as her professional skills. In another article, *Godey's* even titled their piece "Some Handsome Newspaper Women,"[4] and the *Evening Star* described her as "one of the prettiest young women in newspaper life." Fortunately, they added, "She is young, energetic and brilliant to her finger tips."[5]

All the accounts of her rise focused on her rare position as an editor. Margherita Arlina Hamm's article "New York Newspaper Women," for example, asserted that it was "through her splendid work and rare ability" that Jordan rose rapidly to the position of editor. "She is a woman of powerful character and many accomplishments. She has a great aptitude for languages, which has been of vast use to her in her profession."[6] Jordan was fluent in Spanish, having been taught the language as a child, but admitted to being only passing in German and French.

In spite of Jordan's professional skills, it was difficult in this era to escape the image of a genteel woman "playing" the role of journalist. Ishbel Ross wrote about Jordan's many accomplishments but fabricated a portrait that would be hard for the public to shake: Ross insisted Jordan worked as a reporter while dressed in "her elegant costume and ostrich

New York World reporters, 1890 (back: Elizabeth Jordan; front from left: Marie Manning, Grace Gould, Olivia Howard Dunbar, and Harriet Hubbard Ayer)
MARIE MANNING PAPERS, SOPHIA SMITH COLLECTION, SSC-MS-00385, SMITH COLLEGE SPECIAL COLLECTIONS

feathers."[7] Although Jordan rarely reacted to reported details about her life (some of which were taken from interviews with her and others drawn from the air), she did respond to Ross's image: "I was at that time and for many years afterwards one of the most severely tailor-made young persons in New York. It would no more have occurred to me to do my newspaper work in 'elegant costumes and ostrich feathers' than it would have occurred to me to do it in no clothing at all."[8]

In an era of what came to be known as the "cult of celebrity," the public clamored for information about the personal lives of people in the news. Being the subject of so much public attention created complications for Jordan as a lesbian. It was an era of contradictions. Many women openly lived together in what had long been termed "Boston marriages"; some of these arrangements were for convenience, while many were love relationships. In Jordan's time, "Wellesley marriages" came to define professional women such as the academics at Wellesley College who openly lived together. At the same time, however, same-sex love was increasingly viewed as deviant or a sexual perversion, as psychiatrists Richard von Krafft-Ebing and Jean-Martin Charcot claimed homosexuality was an inborn deviance.

Jordan managed a surprisingly effective balance in this era between seeming to share her personal life and maintaining a distinct privacy. She willingly gave magazines a resume that included her education, her work on Midwestern papers before coming to New York, her love of music, and the like. But as these details became known and journalists wanted more to report to their readers, Jordan created a tactic that she would use throughout her life: giving reporters amusing anecdotes about herself—some foible of hers, a silly mistake she made. These anecdotes seemed to allow the public into her life without revealing anything truly personal. For nearly fifty years, Jordan lived a life in the public eye without her readers or even some of her acquaintances knowing that she was lesbian. Had she done otherwise, she risked losing her job and any future position of note that she sought.

One of the smartest decisions Jordan made in her early years at the *World* was joining the Women's Press Club of New York City, founded in 1889 by the dean of early women newspaper reporters, Jennie C. Croly. In its early years, the organization offered women journalists a support system as it focused on civic projects and offered lectures and literary events. In the latter instance, it became an important conduit between women journalists and authors.

Within a year of starting at the *World*, Jordan had become an active participant in the Press Club. Not surprisingly, she accepted the position of chair of the Committee on Literature and Journalism. Typically, around one hundred women attended the meetings, and as chair of this committee, Jordan presented lectures on topics such as "Does Newspaper Writing Spoil Literary Style?"

It was not long, however, before Jordan's generation of newswomen found the Women's Press Club too much like a social club. When it was founded, any woman who had published a sketch or a poem in a newspaper was admitted. As the investigative journalist Ida B. Tarbell lamented shortly before Jordan started at the *World*, "'Real' newspaper women need a professional organization of their own, not a club devoted to 'tea and tattle.'" The younger generation of reporters would reshape the monthly meetings into a far more progressive, professional organization, and Jordan would play a significant role in professionalizing journalism for women.[9]

At this time, Jordan was living in a residential hotel at 221 West 44th Street, west of Broadway. One of the nine other boarders was Harriet "Hattie" Beardslee Prescott. A graduate of Mount Holyoke College and Melvil Dewey's School of Library Economy at Columbia College (later Columbia University), Prescott and Jordan became friends—a friendship that lasted until Jordan's death.

Residing nearby at the Hotel Gerard was Varina Davis, widow of the Confederate leader Jefferson Davis. Joseph Pulitzer had married into the Davis family, and in 1891 he invited Varina to write a column for the

World.[10] The Pulitzers introduced Jordan to her, and she came to admire the living symbol of the Confederacy, in spite of their extraordinarily divergent political views.

Davis was neither the first nor the last of Jordan's wide circle of friends who represented her ability to form alliances with people from different backgrounds and of varying political and social spectrums. She did not merely tolerate people's differences; she had an uncanny ability to accept a person on her or his own terms, without caveat. From the famous Confederate widow to Bohemian artists such as Rose O'Neill, from priests to theosophists, laborers to presidents, Jordan quite simply found people fascinating. It was a trait repeatedly remarked on by anyone who knew her. She was far more interested in delving into an individual's self than in judging them. So many of her friendships lasted a lifetime precisely because of her acceptance of differences.

This trait also led Jordan to assist many up-and-coming journalists and authors. In 1892, for instance, the burgeoning novelist Gertrude Atherton arrived at the *World* to ask Ballard Smith whether she might sit in the newspaper's offices in order to gain background for her next novel. Smith directed her to Jordan, who provided Atherton with a desk in her editorial office and suggested the California author feel free to observe and roam at will.[11]

As soon as Atherton settled into the city, Jordan hosted a dinner party for her as a means of introducing the Californian to some of her favorite people at the *World*.[12] Atherton became very fond of Jordan and reciprocated by introducing her to many of her friends in the city, including actors and playwrights. The two women became lifelong professional associates and friends.

It was not unusual for these connections to lead to layers of favors and assistance. At one point, Jordan extended a hand to the new journalist Zona Gale, who had come to New York from Wisconsin and who would later receive the Pulitzer Prize in drama, and Gale introduced Jordan to another journalist—Kate Field.[13] Field was considerably older than Jordan and had already founded her own successful newspaper in Washington, DC (*Kate Field's Washington*), when Gale wrote the letter of introduction for Field; however, their age difference did not matter.

Gertrude Atherton
LIBRARY OF CONGRESS

Just as political or social backgrounds never swayed Jordan, the same was true of a person's years. If they were of keen intellect, an engaging conversationalist, and committed to whatever profession they chose, they fit Jordan's criteria, and she and Field quickly became friends.

Field spent as much time as possible in New York at this point in her life, and she was a notable horsewoman, so she and Jordan frequently rode together in Central Park. With their long work hours, the only way they managed the time was to meet at six in the morning and ride along the park's bridle paths in the early hours when dew was still on the grass and the park was relatively isolated. During these morning rides, they developed a bond that lasted until Field's death.

Kate Field
BOSTON PUBLIC LIBRARY

The two women also bonded over their passion for the theater and attended numerous opening nights together.[14] To Jordan's dismay, Field would live only another few years. After Field died in 1896 from pneumonia, the *Los Angeles Herald* would proclaim that the two had been "chums almost inseparable" and that Jordan was the person to write her biography: "Miss Jordan has bundles of letters that Kate Field wrote to her at all sorts of odd moments. The publication of these, with the facts and comment that Miss Jordan would be able to add, would present the journalist of Washington in a light that all who knew her would appreciate."[15] Jordan never undertook such a project, but she did mention her admiration for Field in her autobiography years later.

Jordan also made many lasting friendships with a group of male colleagues. Perhaps none of these relationships was as enduring as that with Frederick A. Duneka, city editor of the *Evening World*. Originally from Kentucky, Duneka was more than a decade Jordan's senior, but, as usual, the age difference did not matter. Jordan had a renowned sense of humor and was always drawn to people who could make her laugh, and Duneka had just such talents.

An additional special friend was Bayard Veiller, four years Jordan's junior and a particular favorite. He would become far better known as a playwright than a journalist. His love of theater and creative instincts formed the basis of a bond with Jordan that lasted throughout their lives. When he published his own jaunty memoir several years later, he recalled what a remarkable journalist Jordan was: "For the steadfast, earnest and astounding work, give me Elizabeth Jordan." The *World* had a good number of outstanding reporters at the time, he noted, "And there wasn't one of them who wasn't eager and proud and happy if Miss Jordan would work on a story with him."[16]

Veiller continued: "She was cool in emergencies, resourceful always. I have never seen her excited, and how our managing editor and the bosses loved her. There never was any question about her accuracy. When she said something was so, it was so, and you could gamble on it. And a great many times the *World* did gamble on it."[17]

Late in life, Elizabeth Jordan recalled her years at the *World* as "the most interesting and educational of my life."[18] In large part, this was due to her refusal to have her journalistic life limited to editing other people's reporting. Shortly after she accepted the position of editor of a daily and of the women's page, she negotiated an understanding with Joseph Pulitzer and his editors that she must still be allowed to cover occasional major stories: "Whenever a really big 'story' came along—especially a famous murder—I cheerfully accepted an assignment to cover it."[19] Those special assignments would indeed lead her from journalism to literature and especially mystery writing, since the majority of her special assignments would be to cover murder trials.

Jordan negotiated this flexibility because she realized that "one's reputation has to be made anew every day in newspaper life."[20] It was a very smart move, considering how many editors Pulitzer hired and fired;

outstanding reporters were rarely let go. The idea of reinventing oneself anew mattered to Jordan, as she constantly developed new Plans and new avenues to pursue. Change was her elixir. And for the public, it added to her mysterious nature. Women were supposed to marry and have children, but here was a woman who not only defied convention but also did so over and over in her life.

Managing editor Ballard Smith supported Jordan's request that she not be tied to her editorial desk, but his idea of getting away from the desk and hers were sometimes at odds. When an infamous murder occurred in early 1892, he assigned the breakthrough story to Jordan. Helen Potts had died in her early twenties, and her mother soon became suspicious of the cause when she went to her daughter's room in the city and discovered that Helen had been secretly married to Carlyle Harris, a medical student, and that he had been giving his wife "headache tablets," including on the night she died.

The bereaved mother took some of the tablets to the district attorney, who had his office investigate; they discovered that morphine had been substituted for quinine in some of the pills. Ballard Smith was a friend of the district attorney, and he was told, before any other newspaper man in the city, that Harris would be arrested on the night of March 20, 1891.

At six o'clock that evening, Smith handed Jordan "a great mass" of notes he had taken during the weeks he worked with the DA on the case; he wanted a page-one headliner finished by midnight. While Smith went home to dinner, Jordan worked through the material, formed her ideas about motives, and prepared the story that would run over seven columns for the compositors. Smith returned at midnight and went over the proofs. When Jordan's front-page story of Harris's arrest broke the next day—a story none of the other New York newspapers had yet—it created a sensation that lasted throughout Harris's trial.[21]

Jordan received no byline for the story, but everyone in the business soon knew she had written it. She felt, however, that she did not deserve recognition for her coverage because Smith had gathered the information from the DA during their prearrest investigation.[22] She wanted to do her own investigating.

Jordan's next murder case would be the most sensational criminal trial of the century, with reverberations into the present. But before she was assigned to Lizzie Borden's case, Jordan faced another significant shift in management at the *World*, one that would impact her life for years to come. Ballard Smith became editor in chief, and Pulitzer hired a new man to become managing editor, George Harvey, which meant Harvey would be Jordan's direct supervisor. Only a year older than Jordan, Harvey was a distinguished figure but more conservative than most of the *World*'s staff. He began his journalism career as a reporter for the Springfield, Massachusetts, *Republican*, and by the time Pulitzer sought him out, he was making a name for himself in the Washington, DC, news market. Harvey would serve as managing editor only until 1894, but his impact was notable, and he and Jordan would continue to interact professionally and personally for many years to come.

In the midst of these transitions, a small news article appeared in the Boston newspapers about the axe murders of a couple in Fall River, Massachusetts. If the means of death was not sensationalistic enough, a national frenzy emerged with the news that the couple's daughter, Lizzie Borden, had been arrested for the brutal killings.

Chapter 7

Lizzie Borden's Trial and a Shocking Aftermath

On the afternoon of August 3, 1892, the bodies of Abby and Andrew Borden were found brutally slaughtered in their home in Fall River, Massachusetts. It was soon determined the murder weapon had been an axe, and before too long the Bordens' daughter was arrested for the murders. It would be nearly a year before Lizzie Borden's murder trial commenced in early June 1893, and the interval allowed the horror of the events to magnify in the imagination of Americans from Boston to San Francisco. Borden spent more than 280 days in the women's section of the Bristol County Jail in Taunton, Massachusetts. As newspaper readers hungered for news of when the trial would begin, Kate McGuirk, a reporter for the *New York Recorder*, managed to secure a jailhouse interview with Borden. The two had been friends years earlier when they worked at the Fall River Fruit and Flower Mission.[1]

McGuirk's article based on that interview painted a sympathetic picture of a stoic Borden enduring her days of imprisonment.[2] When McGuirk told Borden that people were concerned about her seeming lack of emotion, Lizzie replied, "They say I don't cry. They should see me when I am alone or sometimes with my friends."[3] Details from McGuirk's article were picked up by other reporters and excerpted in newspapers. The image McGuirk presented resonated as Lizzie Borden was transferred to New Bedford for the trial months later.

In June 1893, every major newspaper on the East Coast sent their star reporters to cover the sensational case that had shaken the nation. For most Americans, it was impossible to believe that a demure, middle-class, white woman could kill her parents and certainly not in such a manner. The idea sent chills through households across the country, and a salacious frenzy of speculation about whether Lizzie Borden could have been so deranged made it the top news story of the era.

While almost all other papers sent male reporters to New Bedford, the *World* sent Elizabeth Jordan to cover the trial. The paper gave her articles front-page coverage. Jordan was assigned not only to report the details of the case but also specifically to lead readers to one or the other conclusion as to Borden's guilt, whatever she determined once on-site.[4] The assignment was a coup, and her coverage of the trial would make her a household name and impact her life in ways she could not have imagined at the time.

This assignment came just as Ballard Smith appeared to be unceremoniously removed from his position as editor in chief because Pulitzer was dismayed by editorial commentaries that had appeared in the paper. Smith learned of his fate only when he heard that a farewell dinner was being planned for him.[5] These constant shifts in Pulitzer's moods made for an extremely volatile atmosphere among the management team that quickly filtered down to reporters and everyone in the building. It was just as well, then, for Jordan to be out of the office during these fractious weeks.

Like the majority of reporters and most of their readers, Jordan proclaimed an inclination to believe in Lizzie Borden's innocence when she arrived on June 3, 1893, in New Bedford.[6] The minority who thought Borden was guilty saw her as a spinster who was angered over her "abnormal" unmarried status. Perhaps, they speculated, she had killed her parents so she could inherit the house and have a home of her own.[7]

Jordan's first report emphasized the defendant's good character—well respected in the community, known for her religious interests, kind and generous. But readers wanted more than a simple account of Borden and her trial, and Jordan, like all the reporters covering the event, gave the public (and their editors) what they wanted: shocking language and possibilities. Jordan asked, could this young woman have

> *split open her aged father's head with a hatchet as he lay sleeping on a sofa, and afterwards go back and batter his face and head with the same weapon . . . ? Did this same young woman, just before or just after this deed, strike down her step-mother and chop and hack her head and face until it was beaten almost out of human resemblance? Did she do at least one of these horrible deeds within twenty minutes' time, and was she at the end of this interval able to appear before the neighbors she had summoned without a spot of blood on her clothing, without a sign of derangement or hasty adjustment of her dress, with the weapon concealed beyond discovery, and not even a scrap of direct evidence to connect her with the deed?*[8]

Jordan went on for three columns detailing the upcoming trial and emphasizing details to support her impression that Borden could not possibly have committed the murders. It was what readers hoped to hear, but Jordan seems at this point to have truly believed in the young woman's innocence. As the days of the trial exposed additional details, Jordan would give readers a graphic picture of each day's proceedings and then her assessment of how they fit Borden's claim of innocence. In total, she published more than twenty articles about Lizzie Borden during the two-week trial, though only near the end of her time in New Bedford was she given a tagline (her name at the end of a story) but never a byline, which was reserved for the well-established reporters—although her name was occasionally used in advertising that another special edition would soon be printed with Elizabeth Jordan's latest report.

When Lizzie Borden entered the courtroom on the first day of the trial, Jordan presented her readers with the sight they would have met if they had been able to attend: "At precisely 10:58 Miss Lizzie A. Borden, the prisoner, came slowly into the room . . . and was shown her seat in the dock. She was attired in a very becoming costume of black brocaded stuff, and wore a pretty shade hat, relieved by a touch here and there of blue."[9] The idea of Lizzie's impeccable nature long remained with Jordan as a marker of the woman's character. "She was the neatest human being I have ever seen," she recalled years later. "She radiated cleanliness like an atmosphere."[10]

With the significant number of reporters assigned to cover the trial, the courtroom was packed. On the second day, Jordan identified for her readers each juror and gave background for all of the major participants conducting the trial. Of great interest to everyone was the question of whether Lizzie Borden was insane. Some reporters asserted that her eyes made her look so or that her rational appearance under such circumstances was itself a sign of insanity. Every aspect of Lizzie's life on the day of the murder was exposed to examination in the courtroom. When she admitted she had fleas (not unusual at this time in hot New England summers) and was menstruating at the time of the murders, her purportedly immodest comments were deemed confirmation of insanity by some reporters. However, a Pinkerton detective, O. M. Hanscom, insisted that Borden's composure suggested a sane, controlled woman. While Jordan agreed, she cast her assessment in terms of how a jury would respond: "No jury will believe that woman, with her firm face and steady intelligent eyes, ever did any important thing she had not subjected to the unobscured light of . . . reason."[11]

A notable day of testimony occurred on June 9 when a friend, Alice Russell, offered damning testimony against Borden. Russell claimed Lizzie had burned a dress right after the murders. Jordan took an instant dislike to the young woman, who seemed so willing to betray her friend, and scathingly reported that Russell seemed like

> *one of the strange women characters in which Wilkie Collins delights, and which flit like ominous specters through deep shadows. . . . Today she took the witness stand and not only testified to what will come nearer to putting a rope around her girl friend's neck than anything yet brought out, but she did it with a vicious snap in her voice and a cruel compression of her thin colorless lips, which suggested anything but sorrow for the fact that she was compelled to do this.*[12]

The next day presented a bit of a reprieve for Borden. Several police officers had made different claims already at the trial, but this day was to see an extraordinary moment in Borden's favor. When the prosecution called a patrolman to testify that he had seen an axe handle in the Borden cellar, they were shocked as the patrolman denied having ever stated such a fact, and the district attorney was unable to produce evidence of any handle having been recovered from the scene. Jordan reported, "It was upon the three and a half-inch edge of this useful little household tool that the case for the commonwealth would split."[13]

On that note, the court adjourned for the weekend. When the trial resumed, it was evident that sympathy was building for Lizzie Borden, much to the prosecution's dismay. At one point, when the judges ruled in Borden's favor on a disputed point, she began to cry. Jordan interpreted this reaction as a sign of innocence: "It would seem that she had become so accustomed to nothing but cruelty from the fates as to be almost callous to all other injuries they have in store for her, but that too much kindness on their part had been quite too much and the spark of relief had quite unstrung her."[14] Unfortunately, the jury had been removed from the courtroom during the deliberation and was not present for Borden's tears, but the newspapers reported the event with vigor.

If there had not been enough dramatics in the trial so far, the next day offered a horrific scene. Surprisingly, it was the defense that brought the severely damaged skull of Andrew Borden into the court for jurors and spectators to see. The intention was to argue that "the terrific force of one blow that had split the head diagonally from the top down through the left jawbone" would have required strength beyond that of any woman.[15] Lizzie was allowed to be out of the courtroom at the time. Her father's skull was set on a stack of law books when suddenly its jaw rocked back and forth for a moment as if trying to speak from the grave. Gasps could be heard throughout the courtroom.[16]

On June 14, prosecutors called to the stand a witness whom Jordan deemed another betrayer of Borden. Anna Borden was a distant relative. When she took the stand, Anna recalled an event from three years earlier when she and Lizzie were returning from a trip to England. According to Anna, Lizzie had declared she did not want to return to her "unhappy home." Jordan conveyed to readers her perspective on this comment:

> *After this first glimpse [in Europe] of real sunshine Lizzie had had in her narrow, cheerless life, she had lamented the fact that she was coming back to the dreary gloom of her Puritan home. She had confided this much to her cousin on some cosy evening at sea and in the unbosoming intimacy which the close contact of shipboard life breeds, and now, two years later, those words spoken in confidence away off somewhere in the solitude of the North Atlantic, were coming home to her to weigh in the balance against her.*[17]

Jordan's anger at this betrayal was still evident decades later when she wrote about the trial in her autobiography: "I could have strangled the creature as she sat in the witness chair, feeling important and smugly manufacturing her little strand of the rope that might hang her fellow-passenger."[18] For Jordan, a failure to promote solidarity among women said more about these "friends" than it did about Lizzie Borden.

The prosecution rested after nearly two weeks of presenting their case. Jordan openly conveyed to readers her sense that Hosea Knowlton, the prosecutor, was losing: "Knowlton, after another and final parade of the dismal paraphernalia of the crime, sat down in the ruins and rested his case."[19] The defense's case began on June 16 with the swearing in of Emma Borden, who defended her sister. Jordan reported on Emma's testimony, but it was Lizzie who drew readers. Therefore, in the evening edition of the *World* for June 17, an advertisement appeared promising that the next day Elizabeth Jordan's nearly full-page assessment of the "real Lizzie Borden" would appear. It would be "the first exhaustive and accurate presentment of a strange type of the New England woman."[20]

The piece was an extensive and highly personal analysis of Jordan's impression of Lizzie Borden after days of intimately observing her actions during the trial. It began with the overall theme: "There are two Lizzie Bordens. One of them is a very real and very wretched woman who is now on trial for her life. . . . The other is . . . a human sphinx, a thing without heart or soul." But the latter had been created by unscrupulous reporters, she insisted, to "dangle before the eyes of the American people." Every aspect of Borden's appearance—from the shape of her mouth to the way in which she presented herself on the stand—was analyzed by Jordan, and the article concluded that however much some reporters had presented the "human sphinx" image of the defendant, Lizzie Borden was a dignified lady and Jordan was among the majority of reporters who believed she was innocent.[21]

The courtroom was packed with reporters on June 20 when Lizzie Borden was acquitted on all counts of the murders of her father and stepmother. Applause broke out in the courtroom when the decision was announced. Borden burst into tears. Jordan recounted the evidence, much of which was circumstantial, and concluded with the assertion that the jurors had honorably done their duty: "There were men who entered the jury-box biased from their reading against her. They left it convinced to a man of her absolute innocence."[22]

While working at the *World*, Jordan had started writing short stories, and the following summer she published her first story in a major literary magazine, *Cosmopolitan*. In "Ruth Herrick's First Assignment," the title character, a young reporter, interviews an accused murderess in her jailhouse cell, during which the woman confesses she committed the crime, but her motives are so tragic that the reporter decides to keep the confession secret. The woman is acquitted. Unwittingly, this piece became Jordan's first mystery—not because of its content but because of how it was read by the public and Jordan's own subsequent actions.

As soon as the story appeared, readers interpreted it as Jordan's revelation that Lizzie Borden had confessed her guilt when Jordan interviewed her in jail. The only problem was that Jordan claimed never to have interviewed Borden; she had no direct contact with the defendant and no opportunity to have a personal exchange. Kate McGuirk had interviewed Borden long before the trial started, but the sensation of the fictional story and perhaps Jordan's lengthy account of the "real Lizzie

Borden" during the trial apparently conflated the two women reporters in people's minds.

Readers wrote to Jordan, reporters questioned her, and her own managing editor at the *World* was furious with her for withholding the confession.[23] No matter how many times she insisted that her short story had nothing to do with Borden and that she had written it before the Bordens had been murdered, no one believed her. For the rest of her life, people tried to wheedle from Jordan her own confession that she was Ruth Herrick and the woman prisoner Lizzie Borden.

In her 1938 autobiography, Jordan still proclaimed shock at the reaction to this short story. She might well have been shocked at the time "Ruth Herrick" first appeared, but it was specious to proclaim such surprise in 1938 when she had since published a second story, this time as an episode in *May Iverson's Career* (1914), a highly autobiographical collection of stories, in which she again presented a female reporter interviewing a woman accused of murder who confesses her guilt to the reporter; having promised not to report the confession, the reporter must stand by as the woman is acquitted of her crime.

So, did Jordan write the second story knowing what a sensation it would create and most likely again draw national attention to the issue? By the time *May Iverson's Career* appeared, Jordan was a well-known author, not a new fiction writer who might have needed to seek such attention. Or was she haunted by the possibility that Lizzie Borden might have been guilty? Or . . . ?

When Jordan's autobiography, which included a chapter on the Borden trial, appeared in 1938, public opinion had turned and suspicion of Borden's guilt had blossomed once again. Jordan received a letter from Alexander Woollcott, a famous member of the Algonquin Round Table and a self-proclaimed expert on the Borden case. He tried to push Jordan to admit Borden's guilt.

Jordan took care to give her considered opinion on the events but also to challenge Woollcott, who was too young to have known about the trial at the time:

The Borden case has always been, and will always be, I think, as long as it is remembered at all, a subject of passionate disagreement and argument. You must have been a babe in arms when those murders were committed, yet your interest in the case is still intense. And after the baking days in that New Bedford courtroom during the trial the overworked bunch of us who had to report it sat up for hours and hours every night, unwearyingly discussing it. We did not, then, disagree as to Lizzie's guilt or innocence. Most of us believed her innocent. . . . What we were discussing was the identity of the real criminal. Who was it? I don't know yet. Neither do you, though you feel so certain of Lizzie's guilt. Neither does any-one. That old house lay open that day to any visitor who cared to stroll in. The time was noon. The neighbors were eating their dinners, or washing their dishes or, as the Bordens were doing, taking a nap. Half a dozen persons could have strolled in and out during that half hour when Lizzie was in the barn. The crimes seemed the crimes of a maniac. Those rooms in which the killings occurred were slaughter houses, in effect. The blow that split the old man's head was delivered with a force and power only a giantess among women could possess. Yet while the bodies were still warm Lizzie Borden discovered them, or said she did, and led her neighbors into the house to see them.

Lizzie Borden's leading lawyer, Judge Robinson of Boston, told a bunch of us the prosecution was convinced that Lizzie was nude when she committed the murders. IF she committed them, she certainly was. I saw photographs of those rooms taken the day of the murders. And Lizzie, as always, was immaculate when she brought her neighbors in to see the dead bodies. Much was stricken from the records, you know. I could not swear now, though I thought I could, that the prosecution advanced the theory of nudity in cross-questioning a witness. Of what witness would or could it have been asked? But I know that the theory was constantly discussed, that those who believed in Lizzie's guilt were convinced that it alone could be considered plausible. What bloody murderer crept across lots after the crime and vanished in the near-by woods? "I dunno." Neither does any-one else.

> *Even during the trial we argued constantly about details. We got conflicting impressions and we wrote conflicting reports. That always happens, to a degree. It was a striking feature of the Borden case. One man's guess was as good as another.*[24]

The letter was Jordan's last recorded comment on the trial, but, as much as she might have wished otherwise, it was not the last word on the subject.

The issue blew up again when her friend Bayard Veiller, who had worked with Jordan at the *World* at the time of Borden's trial, published his autobiography in 1941. He claimed that many people would like to know "the things that Jordan has never told. Those of us who remember the case will recall that she spent an entire night—I think it was Christmas Eve—in the cell with Lizzie Borden. What did they talk about?"[25]

Did Veiller mistakenly recall Jordan's short story rather than the real trial? There is nothing in the story about it having occurred on Christmas Eve. Or did Jordan secretly visit Borden in jail months before the trial began? Did Veiller know something about this meeting that Jordan never recorded? Was there a true basis for "Ruth Herrick's First Assignment"? If not, why did Jordan create Herrick so much in her own image? In both the short story and the episode in the May Iverson novel, the young reporter's work was greatly admired by her editors, and she was assigned to cover a major murder trial, echoing Jordan's own experience. Years later, Jordan re-created Ruth Herrick as a character in her play, *The Lady from Oklahoma* (1910), in which Ruth moved from being a reporter to a magazine editor, just as Jordan had. Why did Jordan continue to tease the public with the possibility that Ruth Herrick's jailhouse interview might well have been a shadow of Jordan's own interview with Lizzie Borden?

It remains one of the great mysteries of Jordan's life.

Chapter 8
Assistant Editor

Despite the aftermath created by Jordan's stories about a woman murderer's confessions and the persistent belief that Jordan knew more than she had revealed, the Lizzie Borden case secured Jordan's reputation in journalism circles. She would enhance that reputation as a crime reporter as she continued to cover major murder cases in the coming years.

The volatile state of the *World*'s management had not eased in Jordan's absence, however. Although George Harvey worked night and day, Pulitzer was not satisfied. Without notice to anyone, he hired Charles H. Jones and gave him complete control of the paper.[1] Harvey resigned. It was during this turmoil that Pulitzer surprised the vacationing Ballard Smith, who was preparing for his farewell dinner, with the news that he had not been fired, instead appointing him the *World*'s correspondent in London. Jones would prove to be a disastrous choice to run the *World*, but fortunately for Jordan, the Lizzie Borden case cinched her value at the paper.

With the growth of newspaper syndication, women journalists like Jordan gained fame, but a national readership also offered women of her standing a new benefit—the ability to wield power over their own publicity and to use that opportunity to promote their favored projects.[2] Jordan quickly embraced this power, not only for her newspaper writings but also for her entrance into the world of literature.

Part of that power came from recognition by other women journalists. A reporter for the *New York Letter* detailed Jordan's accomplishments, noting that she had worked her way up to her current position: "She deserves her success. For my part I hope to see her managing editor yet. . . . Practically the whole machinery of the Sunday edition is under her control." Margherita Arlina Hamm, a freelance reporter covering the emergence of increasingly accomplished women journalists, declared that Jordan was "a very important and influential personality in the newspaper ranks."[3] As Ishbel Ross wrote several years later, Jordan "affected young newspaperwomen as Hemingway did young writers; her style was much copied, and she was greatly admired within the craft."[4]

Jordan's reputation provided an avenue through which she met many famous, industrious, and talented people. Her growing interest in politics and the suffrage movement was strengthened in the fall of 1892 by a meeting she had with Frances E. Willard, an internationally recognized force through her leadership of the Women's Christian Temperance Union. Willard was visiting New York and sought an introduction to Jordan.

Jordan felt an instant rapport with Willard, but she also realized that the suffragist's interest in her during several conversations over tea or dinner was driven by her desire to "tactfully [draw] from my little reservoir such information as she needed." Willard understood that Jordan was plugged into the "subterranean current of news" that circulated in the *World*'s editorial offices but was never printed. Jordan was not offended by Willard using their meetings to gain information; she viewed the older woman not as insincere but as practical.[5] That attitude extended to a subject that Jordan would certainly have appreciated—Willard's attitude about same-sex love:

> *The loves of women for each other grow more numerous each day, and I have pondered much why these things were. That so little should be said about them surprises me, for they are everywhere. . . . There is no village that has not its examples of "two hearts in counsel," both of which are feminine . . . thus clasping hands, they have taken each other "for better or for worse."*[6]

In spite of the enjoyment both Jordan and Willard found in their acquaintance, they did not meet again after this short interlude. Willard died nine months later.

There were two male colleagues at the *World* who deeply influenced Jordan in various ways at this point in her life and who remained lifelong friends. Arthur Brisbane admired Jordan and respected her talents and efficiency; she respected his work as a journalist and his erudite nature. They would soon be partnered as editors of the *Sunday World*, and their paths would cross in several ways long after they left Pulitzer's newspaper.

The other fellow traveler was of a completely different ilk. John "Jack" à Becket was the dearest of her male friends. They had much in common. He had planned to enter the priesthood but eventually realized he was unfit for that profession. They went to Mass together on Sunday mornings at the convent chapel on East Fifteenth Street. He was also an ardent lover of music, and they often attended the New York Philharmonic together. Further, Jack, like her friend Charles Conant, willingly served as an escort when one was needed.[7]

The debonair Jack had many talents as a reporter and magazine writer, but he had no real ambition. As Jordan defined him, he was a classic playboy and a friend who depended on her whenever he ran into trouble—which was often. She loved him and enjoyed his lively manner, but she had no illusions about his waywardness.[8] Years later, he would be the model for her novel *The Play-Boy*.

In spite of the long hours that came with her daily work schedule and the exhausting months of covering the Lizzie Borden trial, Jordan never lost sight of her Plan. Journalism was to be a stepping stone to becoming an author. She had begun publishing short essays in 1891 with "Approaching the Editor" for *The Writer*, in which she addressed the question of how to become a reporter.[9] Her next major publication also grew out of her experiences in journalism, with the 1893 release of *The Submerged Tenth*, a collection of articles she had published in the *World* in recent months focusing on the harrowing conditions in New York's East Side tenements.[10]

The term "submerged tenth" had been coined by William Booth three years earlier in his study of British poverty, *In Darkest England*, and referred to the percentage of a population living in permanent poverty and typically invisible to the rest of the populace. It was a term that would be used throughout the 1890s by authors as diverse as W. E. B. Du Bois and Edward Everett Hale. Although Jordan would become known for her humorous children's literature and her many novels and mysteries about upper-class Americans, she founded her career on exposing the horrendous conditions of the impoverished, a group she never forgot and would write about in later years as well, even as she climbed the social ladder.

But it was another essay—"The Newspaper Woman's Story," published in *Lippincott's Magazine* in March 1893—that moved Jordan more fully into the literary world. *Lippincott's* was one of the top five literary magazines of the era. In this article, Jordan took the position of the seasoned reporter offering advice to hopefuls. She observed that, though their numbers had increased, women's standing in the profession remained as tenuous as it had been years earlier. It was imperative, therefore, that the woman journalist of the future "lay the foundation of her own work by training up to it, and by familiarizing herself with all the details of 'the business,' as her male associates have done. Then, and not until then, will her position be assured." She commended her predecessors such as Jennie June and Middy Morgan for following such a pattern and noted several more recent women who were doing the same, including Margaret Sullivan in Chicago and Kate Field in New York.

Jordan cautioned young hopefuls, however, that "the good work of one day will be overshadowed by failure on the next, for her record begins anew each morning that she reports for duty, and on that day's work she must stand or fall back. . . . Her sex will hinder her one hundred times to once that it helps her . . . her best work will be taken as a matter of course, and anything less than her best as a deliberately-planned and personal injury."[11] She admitted in the article's conclusion that she had given "the dark side" of the profession, but it was necessary for prospective journalists to understand the realities of such a career. She concluded with a more upbeat assertion that she continued to be fascinated with her life as a reporter.

During this time, Jordan had been publishing some sketches under the pen name "Jean Memy."[12] Her family began to call her "Jean," and it stuck as a pet name for the rest of her life. Wisely, she then turned to short stories about life in a newsroom under her own name with the hope of compiling a sufficient number for a book collection. But just as she seemed to have achieved everything she had dreamed of, her world—and that of most Americans—came crashing down with the financial panic of 1893.

Jordan was making a notable salary at this point and no longer needed assistance from her parents to live comfortably in the city, but she had always had the security of knowing that if anything changed, she could fall back on her well-to-do family. That refuge collapsed in an instant. William Jordan had continued to accumulate considerable wealth and was poised to become extremely wealthy with property he had purchased on Lake Michigan. To his utter devastation, every bank in the city failed in the panic, and he lost everything he had worked a lifetime to accumulate.

In the span of a moment, everyone in Jordan's family became dependent on her. She had been at the *World* for less than three years and was only beginning to feel her own financial independence. Her father, always an honorable man, insisted on paying off all his debts after the crash, which left the family with very little to live on. Jordan initially tried to assist them from a distance but finally determined it would be easier and more economical if they joined her in New York.

She had moved to the Windermere Hotel on West 57th Street, in an "old but roomy and comfortable" apartment, and her family joined her there.[13] Jordan did her best to give her family anything they needed during this transition. William, Margaretta, and Alice spent the winter of 1893 with her, but her father descended into a depression from which he would never fully recover. New York City was an alien territory to her parents. By spring, the situation had become untenable, and together they determined it would be best if her family moved back to Milwaukee, where they could be in a familiar environment. Alice was to be married in the spring, so this was the last time the Jordans were together as a family. Shortly after their return home, William's health collapsed, leaving him an invalid for the remainder of his life.

Jordan drew deep into herself, tapping into the optimism that had buoyed her through earlier difficult times, and recognized, "My job had become a necessity. From that time till my parents' death—my mother lived to be eighty-eight—I had the privilege and happiness of supporting them."[14] She had a good salary at the *World*, and she periodically received bonus checks from Joseph Pulitzer when he found her work notable. But she realized that she had been very free and foolish with her money—having expensive suits made for her by the city's leading tailors, attending the theater and opera whenever she could find the time, dining out at expensive restaurants, never saving money.

In spite of this realization, she had no intention of forgoing the lifestyle she had come to love. Instead, she decided that she must make more money. Her first effort was to approach her the managing editor about a raise. She was ready to defend her request, but he agreed without protest.[15] He undoubtedly knew she could readily move to any other newspaper after her coverage of the Lizzie Borden trial.

Jordan's second effort would take a bit more time, but she was determined now to make an additional living by writing fiction. She began in earnest to write the tales she had envisioned for her short story collection.

High notes that helped sustain Jordan against the winds of economic disaster for her family were renewing her acquaintance with Gertrude Atherton and meeting the illustrator Rose O'Neill. Like Jordan, Atherton was feeling the pinch of the slowing economy. In 1893, she arrived at Ballard Smith's office seeking work, with a letter of introduction from a mutual friend. He offered Atherton an assignment of visiting mountain and seaside resorts and writing a series of letters about them for the *World*. As Atherton admitted, "I had not much faith in myself as a newspaper woman, but accepted the offer as it seemed a godsend at the moment."[16] Atherton was indelibly drawn to Jordan: "Miss Jordan had a masterful personality, and a Juno-like beauty that would give any girl confidence—she could hold her own."[17] They remained friends long after Atherton left the *World*.

At this time, Margaret Sangster, editor of *Harper's Bazar*, wrote a letter of introduction and sent a nineteen-year-old woman to meet Jordan. Rose O'Neill had just moved from the Midwest to New York City, where she hoped to expand her burgeoning career as an illustrator. Like Jordan, she had been educated at a Catholic school, and her family selected lodging for her in the city at the Sisters of St. Regis convent. Jordan liked O'Neill instantly, and a great affection developed between them. O'Neill recalled her impression when they first met: Jordan "was two or three years older than I was and with the shape of a goddess with brilliant wide-apart dark eyes and perfect upper lip."[18] Throughout the years, O'Neill sent notes and sketches to Jordan (to whom she referred as "darling"), painted her portrait, and gave her one of her exquisite sculptures. It is likely that the cryptic dedication—"To R"—of Jordan's play, *The Lady from Oklahoma*, was for Rose O'Neill.

O'Neill would become famous as an illustrator for newspapers, magazines, and books and especially as the creator of the Kewpie comic strip and subsequent Kewpie Dolls modeled on the character. Even when O'Neill moved to Paris, she would never forgo her rapturous assessments of Jordan. Years later, O'Neill told Jordan that she had "put her upper lip into my novel *The Lady in The White Veil*."[19] The character of Doris van Cleve is repeatedly defined as being alluring and having a "perfect upper lip."

Rose O'Neill
LIBRARY OF CONGRESS

Rose O'Neill's charcoal portrait of Jordan
BETSY DEVINE COLLECTION

As these friendships sustained Jordan, her family had a moment of reprieve from their economic problems when Alice Jordan married Edward C. Beyer in April 1894 and settled in Racine, Wisconsin. It seemed to Jordan that she could now count her sister as well taken care of and no longer her financial responsibility. For a few years, that would remain true, but, as the family would soon learn, Beyer was not an industrious man, and he and Alice would need periodic help from Jordan later in life.

For now, however, the future seemed to brighten, even as yet another editorial change took place at the *World*. George Harvey's departure from the paper had left a notable gap. During his short tenure, he had earned Jordan's admiration for having made "a spectacular success" of the newspaper. She "mourned him deeply" when he left.[20] But, as with so many of Jordan's relationships, workplace proximity was not necessary for their continued association. She had become close with the Harvey family and adored his wife, Alma. The three of them remained friends.

In the summer of 1894, Arthur Brisbane was promoted to editor and Jordan to assistant editor of the prestigious *Sunday World*. The appointment of two relatively young editors to these major positions created a sensation among the professionals on Newspaper Row.[21] Brisbane would remain as editor of the *Sunday World* for only three years, but in that short time, he and Jordan reshaped the Sunday edition into an unequalled success. She had been doing much of this work without the title, so she slipped into her new position with ease. After ten weeks at its helm, the duo had increased circulation by eleven thousand per week.[22]

Jordan was required to work Wednesday and Thursday nights because that was when "all the various supplements of the *Sunday World* were fully made up. I had a big office by that time, and it was well filled on those nights," as special writers and illustrators, coming in at the last minute (usually around three or four in the morning), needed her to edit the copy and send it to the composing room as well as approve illustrations and pictures before forwarding them to the art department.[23] She was one of the few women who held such a position in the world of New York journalism at the time.

With Jordan's newfound influence, she began to push even more for suffrage advocacy in the pages of the *Sunday World*, even though Pulitzer himself did not support the cause. She contacted Lillie Devereux Blake, a novelist and nationally recognized suffrage advocate. At the time, Blake was president of the New York State Suffrage Association, to which Jordan also belonged. Jordan understood how many women looked to New York socialites as models not only in style but also in social and political customs, so she asked Blake to write an article about socialites' involvement in the suffrage movement. Knowing how in demand Blake was at the time, Jordan offered her three times the usual fee for a column.[24] Jordan could not know at the time that focusing on the "gilded suffragists" would be important to her own future connections as well.[25]

Jordan loved her role as assistant editor of the *Sunday World*, but it left her at times in a precarious—indeed, dangerous—position. Several nights a week, she worked until anywhere from midnight to 3 a.m. when the edition went to press. The late hours meant that when she finished for the night, she had to walk several blocks alone because the elevated train did not go as far as the block where she lived. Many of the blocks between the office and her home were poorly lit, and one night she was approached by the driver of a cab who said he would give her a lift and not charge her. When she looked in the back of the cab, she spotted a man in evening attire; he had his faced pressed against the window, staring at her.

She refused the cabbie's offer and hurried on, but he continued to cruise next to her, insisting it would be worth her while and finally demanding she get in. With no one else on the street to whom she could appeal for help, Jordan began to run. The cab driver kept pace with her until they hit the lights of Broadway; then he stopped and turned away. Jordan did not rest easy until she was inside her apartment with the door barred.[26]

There were dangers within the workplace as well—dangers that she had to face alone and did not always know how to address. Harassment by male colleagues was a topic never openly discussed by the women working at the *World*. Jordan felt her upbringing had not prepared her for this aspect of work life: "Against the background of my convent life the stares and winks and 'passes' I occasionally encountered seemed horribly degrading. There was a period when I was wretched over them." Like so many women, she condemned herself first: "I felt that they not only smirched me but that, in a way, I might be responsible for them, possibly something in me drew them out!"[27]

It was *Harper's Bazar* editor Margaret Sangster who helped Jordan better understand the situation. They were lunching at the Hotel Astor on lower Broadway when Jordan noticed Sangster seemed somewhat ruffled—an unlikely state for the usually stalwart woman in her sixties. Sangster explained that she had been harassed in her office that morning by a man she had known for several years but who had "suddenly gone amorous." A third member of the luncheon, also in her sixties, confirmed similar experiences.

At first, the far younger Jordan found it amusing and could not picture anyone being passionate with women of their age, but then she understood: "If those two wonderful women, at their age, were still subjected to these experiences, surely I need not blame myself when such shocks came to me. After that, I didn't. I learned a special technique in meeting and checking them."[28] This account painted the issue of sexual harassment in the workplace with a relatively light brush. She would offer a much clearer depiction in 1914 when she used her own life as a model for *May Iverson's Career*. There, her details of harassment and of being assaulted were shockingly explicit for the time, as was the psychological impact of such acts.

Despite the long hours required as an assistant editor of the Sunday edition, Jordan made sure she found time here or there to work on her short stories. After she published "Ruth Herrick's First Assignment" (the story that caused such a sensation following the Lizzie Borden case), William Dean Howells invited her to contribute to a collection he and Henry Mills Alden were editing, *Different Girls*. Howells was considered one of the major figures in nineteenth-century American literature, primarily for his years of editorial work with the *Atlantic Monthly*, and Alden was then editor of the prestigious *Harper's Magazine*. These were men who knew the best and brightest of American writers, and having a story accepted for one of their collections was a coup for such a new member of the field.

Jordan contributed "Kittie's Sister Josephine," narrated by a Catholic schoolgirl, a figure who would dominate Jordan's fiction in the early years of her literary career. Though a rather conventional story of how Kittie helps her sister and the man she loves find a way to marry, the story rises above the norm with the delightful narrative voice of the Catholic schoolgirl who sounds every bit age-appropriate in her comments about her friends at school and her desire to be a writer.[29] The Holmes and Alden collection would appear in five more editions over the next decade.

While this initial foray into the world of fiction supported Jordan's never-forgotten Plan to move from journalism to literature, within a few months a radical change would occur in the New York newspaper world, a change that engulfed Joseph Pulitzer and ultimately everyone at the *World.* A brash, young newcomer, William Randolph Hearst, purchased the *New York Journal.* Hearst immediately set about making the *Journal* a true competitor with the *World*, using similar tactics of low pricing, vocal editorial campaigns against corporations and monopolies, and sensational feature stories.[30] It was an audacious move by Hearst, since Pulitzer's brand of journalism had increased his newspaper's daily circulation to 580,000 by this time.[31] But Hearst, just two years older than Jordan, was fed by his initial success with the *San Francisco Examiner* and by his family's extraordinary wealth as backing.

The presidential election of 1896 set the two newspapermen at odds. The *World* had been the leading Democratic newspaper in the city for many years, but when the Democrats nominated William Jennings Bryan, Pulitzer refused to officially endorse the candidate, though he did not support the Republican nominee, William McKinley, either. Hearst picked up the banner, endorsing Bryan in the *Journal.* Though McKinley won, Hearst garnered the credit for sticking with the Democrats, and his paper's circulation grew while the *World*'s declined.

Shocked, Pulitzer immediately focused his attention on a circulation war with Hearst—a competition that would alter both newspapers and impact their reporters for several years to come.[32] Pulitzer began to demand more sensationalistic stories—especially around the atrocities occurring between Spain and Cuba, not only endorsing the call for America's involvement in the conflict but also encouraging his reporters to detail the atrocities and at times make them up if they were not shocking enough in reality.[33]

One of Hearst's early coups against the *World* was luring away city editor Morrell Goddard and ten additional members of Goddard's staff. It sent a ripple of shock through the *World*'s newsroom. Brisbane and Jordan tried to ignore the tensions and worked to build the Sunday paper into a powerful edition that held its own in competing with the *Journal.*[34]

Another murder case that drew headlines a month after Hearst purchased the *Journal* became one of the first stories over which the two papers fought for dominance, and Jordan used the competition to promote women's rights by raising the question of an all-male jury for the trial. Evelina Bliss had been murdered in August 1895, and her daughter Mary Alice Fleming was arrested for the crime. Reporters for each paper became increasingly ruthless in their exploits to one-up the opposition. The *World*'s credo of accuracy and facts was trampled in the desperation to beat the *Journal*. It was the beginning of Jordan's increasing dissatisfaction with what was becoming known as "yellow journalism." She loved being a reporter and editor, but, over time, the changes that were occurring at the paper would dim her enthusiasm.

For a year, the two newspapers ran front-page headlines and lengthy inside stories about every possible sordid detail of Mary Alice Fleming's life. In 1896, Fleming finally came to trial, and another major issue arose: Would a jury be willing to electrocute a woman for the first time? Jordan saw an opportunity for the *World*. She established a "woman's jury" and insisted another question needed to be considered: Could a woman defendant receive justice from an all-male jury, hardly a "jury of her peers"? As the case had been covered over the last year, many Americans had raised the concern that Fleming was being charged not for murder but for a scandalous private life.[35]

Jordan's jury was not an official deliberative body, but she ran articles about its constituents and their qualifications and assessments throughout the long trial. She organized a distinguished panel of jurists, not least of whom was the attorney Clara Foltz. The jury and the idea of an alternative perspective was first presented in a full-page announcement in the *Sunday World* on June 21, 1896: "These Twelve Clever Women Who Think for Themselves Are Considering the Evidence and Will Render a Verdict from the Woman's Standpoint When the Case Is Closed."[36]

In addition to Foltz, jurors included the Countess Ella Norraikow, who wrote about Russia's political and social conditions; Elizabeth Grannis, publisher of the *Church Union*; Dr. Sarah French Batty, a New York physician; Alice E. Ives, a playwright; Rev. Phoebe Hanaford, nationally renowned for her religious leadership and women's rights activism; Miss

Barcalow, a political activist; Rosalie Loew, an attorney; Catherine Terhune Herrick, former editor of the *Springfield Republican*; Florence Sutro, an attorney and suffragist; Genie H. Rosenfeld, journalist and author; and Jordan herself.

After all the witnesses had been heard and the final statements were given, the woman's jury presented its verdict: seven voted for acquittal, three for conviction, and two voted "not proven."[37] This decision by the woman's jury indicated that women could be fair minded and not influenced by a bias toward women. The all-male jury found Fleming not guilty.

Chapter 9

Transitioning

WITH THEIR TURN TO YELLOW JOURNALISM, BOTH THE *WORLD* AND THE *Journal* saw an exceptional growth in circulation. By 1897, the *World* was bordering on one million readers.[1] Still, many felt that Hearst had managed to drag the *World* into gutter journalism, and Jordan lamented the direction the paper was taking. That disappointment swelled when Arthur Brisbane accepted the editorship of Hearst's *Evening Journal* in the fall of 1897. Jordan and Brisbane remained close even as they worked for competing newspapers. She would lunch with him often and visit his home on Long Island.

Nor were colleagues leaving only for the *Journal*. Her friend Frederick Duneka accepted a position as secretary at the esteemed publishing firm Harper and Brothers; he would quickly move up the ranks to become vice president of the firm.[2] Jordan missed these colleagues and felt her time as a journalist was coming to an end. So she began earnestly to shape a new Plan for the future in the field of literature.

In the new year, Jordan set her Plan in action. She published one of the short stories she had been writing, "The Wife of a Candidate," in the February 24, 1898, issue of the *Independent*. As with most of the romances Jordan would write over her lifetime, she eschewed sentimental love stories, preferring stories that delved into the poignant truths of life. Jordan's stories presented characters who faced great challenges or moral dilemmas. Realism and hardship pervade these narratives, but, as an optimist, Jordan wanted her characters to gain something through experience—if not their desires, at least an awareness of the benefits of effort. The majority of Jordan's short stories and most of her novels included some element of this style of a touch of romance in realistic works.

Finally, Jordan had ten stories collected for a volume she titled *Tales of the City Room*, and she went to Charles Scribner's office without an appointment—just as she had entered the *World*'s editorial offices when she was a cub reporter looking for a job—and asked to see the editor. This time, however, she was a famous figure in the city, if not yet a notable author. After talking with her, Scribner agreed to read her manuscript, and a fortnight later he accepted it for publication. However, he advised her that it would be financially more beneficial to first publish the stories in magazines and then in book form. It was a pattern Jordan would follow in the future, but at this time the thought of waiting months to see

Elizabeth Jordan, 1895, age thirty
THREE ROUSING CHEERS

her book in print was too disheartening. She insisted they move ahead with publication,[3] and the collection appeared in May 1895.

The stories gave readers a sense of having the curtain pulled aside in the newsroom and its vast machinations revealed. Most unusual, however, was that the entire group of stories was from the perspective of women reporters. Readers always saw a hint of the autobiographical in Jordan's stories about women reporters, and reasonably so. She used events from her own life, as well as names of people she had known (such as Sister Ethelbert), and embedded her impressions of journalism into the stories.

Reviews were mixed, not because of the collection's quality but because it focused on women in the world of yellow journalism, which some reviewers insisted gave them "a moral shock."[4] The book received international attention as well. England's *Dover Express*, for example, referred to Jordan as "one of the best newspaper women in America" and found the stories in this collection "exceedingly entertaining and novel."[5]

Overall, the stories were a hit, and they made a lasting impact on many hopeful or established journalists who read the book. Mary Elizabeth Prim, later a star reporter for the *Boston Transcript*, remarked that *Tales of the City Room* was her favorite book as a young girl, and H. L. Mencken, soon to become a highly influential newspaperman, named it as one of the important books in his journalistic education.[6] The moral issues about newsrooms that Jordan raised in *Tales of the City Room* would have an even longer impact as they were carried forward by later authors such as Miriam Michelson, Edna Ferber, Katherine Anne Porter, and Martha Gelhorn.[7] As Theodore Dreiser, Stephen Crane, Frank Norris, and others shaped literary history through their initial and often continuing commitment to journalism, so, too, did Elizabeth Jordan. In particular, she used newsrooms and women journalists to explore questions not only about the practice of journalism but about contemporary culture as well.

The success of *Tales of the City Room* encouraged Jordan to continue writing fiction in any spare moment she could find, but in April 1898 the world took another spin with the declaration of war. If Jordan had been dissatisfied with the move toward yellow journalism prior to the Spanish-American War, she would now face an extraordinary shift in this direction at the *World* that altered all the values Pulitzer had so proudly proclaimed for his newspaper.

The *World* and the *Journal*'s cutthroat competition led the publishers to endorse America's entry into the dispute with numerous articles about the atrocious acts being committed by the Spanish, and Hearst coined the rallying cry of "Remember the *Maine*" after the explosion of the US battleship in Havana Harbor.[8] There was nothing too sensational—in some cases created by the newspapers themselves—to be reported. A level of falsity crept into the pages of both newspapers that Jordan found deeply disturbing.

Her determination to enact her Plan to move toward the world of literature was not changed when, on November 28, 1898, every *World* reporter was called to a meeting in the city room. This had never happened in all her years at the paper. The various editors spoke about the excesses of the last two years—by which they meant the extraordinary costs that had been entailed in the competition with the *Journal* to cover the war. They explained that their publisher now desired to return to being "a normal newspaper." Sensational stories would still be acceptable if the occasion warranted, but never at the expense of truth.[9] It was a promise that came too late for Jordan. She would hang on for another year, but she had already decided on an alternate future.

In November 1899, the *New York Times* ran a front-page announcement of a major reorganization at Harper and Brothers Publishing. Though the public and most of Jordan's friends did not yet know that the story had significance for her future, she sent her letter of resignation to Pulitzer, fully expecting a nice letter in response since she had worked for him for ten years and was assistant editor of the highly successful *Sunday World*. However, to her dismay, she received no response. This reaction was highly unlike Pulitzer, who, in Jordan's experience, typically wished his editors success in whatever new endeavors they undertook.

Jordan was about to join the reorganized Harper and Brothers family—and she was stunned to find that when Pulitzer learned about her move, he sent a letter to George Harvey, now president of Harper's, admonishing him for stealing Jordan away. This was too much. She wrote Pulitzer again, indicating that she deserved "a better feeling from him." Again, Pulitzer did not reply, but he did send his live-in physician, Dr. George Hosmer, to meet with her and question whether she really was making the right decision in resigning.

Furious at the suggestion that she did not know her own mind, Jordan replied that she was indeed happy with her decision—in fact, she "felt as if I had died and gone to heaven," which Hosmer reported to Pulitzer. Outraged, Pulitzer broke one of his own rules. He had a will that left $10,000 to any employee who worked for him for ten years or more. Jordan's name was removed from the will.[10] It was an unfortunate end to a successful ten-year association in which Jordan had been instrumental in developing the *Sunday World* into one of the most important and influential editions in the country.

Chapter 10
Harper's Bazar

Jordan's decision to move to Harper and Brothers as editor of *Harper's Bazar* offered both opportunities and risks. The reorganization of the company included George Harvey taking over the position of president and managing director of the publishing firm, with John and Henry Harper as vice presidents.[1] The reorganization was in fact due to a financial crisis at the company—the brothers had gone bankrupt. Harvey took control of the firm, and he intended to modernize the entire enterprise, with Jordan's hire as part of that goal.[2]

She entered a situation in which she had many friends already in the business. Jordan's colleague from the *World*, Frederick Duneka, was Harper's corporate secretary.[3] In addition, Margaret Sangster, editor of *Harper's Bazar* for the past decade, had long been an admirer of Jordan's work and of her personally. She had the generosity of spirit to welcome the changes Jordan envisioned for the *Bazar*.

In Jordan's capacity as editor, she was introduced to an important figure within publishing and soon within her life. Years earlier, Henry Mills Alden, editor of *Harper's Magazine* for the past forty years, had published one of Jordan's stories in the collection *Different Girls*. The imposing man with his loosely cropped hair and hefty beard would be instrumental in introducing her to many of the famous authors who became her close friends. Jordan's personal fondness for Alden was unending; she described him as "the kindest, the gentlest, the most benignant of human beings."[4] She soon became close to his entire family.

The news of Jordan's appointment to editor of *Harper's Bazar* exploded across the pages of newspapers and magazines throughout the country and internationally. New York's *Fame* magazine declared that Jordan's selection as editor "is regarded by those best fitted to judge as a display of sound sense. Miss Jordan's strength lies in the fact that she is without 'fads,' having received her training in a daily newspaper office."[5] Catholic periodicals celebrated a woman of her faith having been chosen for such a prestigious position,[6] and the *Los Angeles Herald* spoke aloud what others implied—the *Bazar* had become "moribund" and bringing Jordan's "brisk, decisive personality" to bear on the magazine was just what it needed.[7]

Of course, Jordan had a Plan—many plans—to reinvigorate the *Bazar*. Her thirteen years as editor of the *Bazar* would enact major transitions for the periodical, moving it forward to become a leading fashion magazine, but also bringing explicit calls for women's suffrage to its pages and shaping it into a magazine in which both established and up-and-coming writers sought to be published.

The first five months of Jordan's employment with the magazine were spent coordinating upcoming issues with Sangster, who had already commissioned material that would fill the pages of *Harper's Bazar* for several months. The first issue that was fully Jordan's appeared on May 5, 1900. She took to heart Harvey's promise that she could run the magazine as she wished without interference.[8] Of course, this could never be totally true—she would have her most stringent arguments with her employers over the costs of illustrations, the number and quality of which she wanted to increase significantly—but Harvey's promise set the tone for her independence as editor.

In these months of transition, Jordan undertook another major life change that would impact her in the most generous ways for the rest of her life. Her new position came with a significant advance in salary, and she planned a move from 44th Street to a more upscale neighborhood. Her salary at the *Bazar* would go a long way toward ensuring that possibility, but she was never one to deprive herself of the luxuries she enjoyed, such as fine clothing, nights out at the theater or the opera, hosting luncheons and dinners at the city's finest restaurants, and summer travels. She realized that moving into a nicer neighborhood and maintaining the lifestyle she enjoyed could be accomplished only if she had roommates.

Jordan found a large apartment in Stuyvesant Square at 17 Livingston Place. She had become friends with another boarder at the 44th Street house, Harriet Beardslee Prescott, who was a year younger than Jordan and a graduate of Mount Holyoke College and of Columbia University's studies in library economy. In 1900, as Jordan took on the editorship of *Harper's Bazar*, Prescott was appointed head of the Cataloguing Department at Columbia University Library, supervising twenty associates.[9] Though close in age to Jordan, Harriet was quite different in temperament. She was quiet, studious, a talented librarian who marched on and got her work done without fanfare.

Harriet Beardslee Prescott
MOUNT HOLYOKE COLLEGE ARCHIVES AND SPECIAL COLLECTIONS

Once they had agreed to share an apartment, they decided it would be best to have a third member to ensure a comfortable lifestyle. One of Prescott's close friends at Mount Holyoke had been Louisa Salome Cutler, who had died in 1895; Harriet suggested Louisa's youngest sister, Martha Hill Cutler (1874–1951), as their roommate. Born in Northampton, Massachusetts, Cutler had graduated from Smith College in 1897 and was currently enrolled in the New York School of Applied Design. Though nearly a decade younger than her roommates, she fit in perfectly with a dedication to her work and dreams of advancing in her profession. All three were active club women and belonged to numerous organizations popular with modern women at the time.

Still, Jordan had never shared living space with anyone but her family, and she worried about what that experience would be like. So the three women created a set of rules: each would live her own, independent life; if one of them wished to host a dinner party, the others would dine out

Martha Hill Cutler
SMITH COLLEGE SPECIAL COLLECTIONS

or remain in their rooms; if, after nine months, any or all of them wished to separate, they would do so with equanimity.[10]

It was a challenge they never had to face. The rules of separate living were abandoned well before the nine-month trial ended. Elizabeth, Harriet, and Martha became the best of friends—"adopted sisters," as Jordan termed it—and remained roommates for more than forty years.[11] This was not a gathering of spinsters; it was the modern world of the early twentieth century in which three professional women evolved into a family in the best and strongest sense of the word. Living with Harriet and Martha grew into a sacred commitment to Jordan, not to be eclipsed even when she fell in love.

Jordan's new status as editor of a top-flight magazine meant she was subject to constant public scrutiny; however, there was surprisingly little questioning of her choice to form a household with two other women. The "bachelor girl" was one of the most popular cultural subjects of the day, which emphasized the choice of career over marriage. Unlike the many hand-wringing pieces that appeared in newspapers and magazines about the "masculine" New Woman, the "bachelor girl" who worked and often lived with other women was largely embraced by the public. In 1898, journalist Neith Boyce's series on "The Bachelor Girl" in New York had appeared in *Vogue* and helped popularize the idea.

Still, Jordan limited access to her private life as much as possible, refusing to participate in the popular style of interview that invited readers into a famous woman's home to be photographed and to demonstrate her lifestyle. Jordan did not hide her friendships with Harriet and Martha, however; they entertained, went to restaurants and theaters, and traveled together. But she had been raised behind convent walls, and she liked that kind of seclusion for her personal life. It was necessary that she manipulate her public image, legitimately becoming the hardworking journalist and editor whom everyone admired but also sheltering her sexual life. Like many women writers and professionals of her era, Jordan's lesbianism was both known and secret—unknown to the general public, but recognized by some of her friends. It was a balancing act maintained by many homosexuals in this era, and Jordan handled it expertly.

Chapter 11

Fashioning Literature

OVER THE THIRTEEN YEARS OF JORDAN'S EDITORSHIP OF *HARPER'S Bazar*, she expanded its publication of fiction, established an editorial page, created new columns, and added many other features. Her changes constituted "an hour of renascence" for the *Bazar* and for Harper and Brothers as a whole.[1] The magazine continued to be at the forefront of presenting the latest fashions, and Jordan was instrumental in shaping the magazine's recognition for "literary brilliance" and for "the beauty of its art nouveau covers."[2]

Fashion remained the heart of the *Bazar*, and Jordan embraced that goal. She was herself a clotheshorse and more than willing to ensure that her attire was always appropriate for the editor of a high-class fashion magazine. She expanded the number of pages focusing on fashion during her tenure as well as the number of illustrations accompanying the latest designs and other articles, including fiction. Color plates highlighted clothing, and hued illustrations appeared elsewhere in the magazine to create a visual wonder around fashionable styles for women of any age.

One of the major changes Jordan made was making the magazine a weekly, which meant she needed a large cache of material for the increased space. Henry Harper sent her a list of seven serials for her consideration, but she rejected several of them because she felt they were rather old-fashioned pieces about social life in the Middle West or the history of early Massachusetts.[3] These were the stodgy kind of pieces that she intended to weed out of the magazine.

She had unending ideas about what she would do with the *Bazar*, but she had her own transition period as well. She jumped into editing as if she were still a reporter, working day and night, expecting everything to happen immediately and for her staff to work in a similar style. It took a while to adjust to the idea that this was a different work environment, one in which she could have evenings and weekends to herself or, in reality, could use those times to socialize with authors and publishers in order to build the necessary connections for making *Harper's Bazar* one of the most sought-after places of publication in the country.

At first, people already working at the magazine were taken aback by Jordan's pace, but she attempted to find a balance and so did they. Before long, she could say she was "doing work I loved, in an atmosphere of harmony; and I was meeting frequently and intimately many of America's most luminous literary figures."[4] It felt like nirvana.

But there were challenges. Edward Bok, editor of the *Ladies' Home Journal*, had cautioned Jordan against taking the position because the company required each of its magazines—*Harper's Bazar, Harper's Monthly*, and *Harper's Weekly*—to cover the entire budgets of the firm's technical and editorial departments, which included its book publishing business, and to be responsible for one-fourth of the expense of the overall firm and its production factory. Bok was right. This was, Jordan quickly realized, a "lump sum I was expected to accept without comment," assessed from on high; she worked diligently to shape a profitable budget for the *Bazar*, but she had no control over that lofty amount, having to factor it into her budget and make adjustments elsewhere.[5] It remained a constant thorn in the side of all the Harper magazine editors.

There was also an awkward situation with the magazine's office space that had been arranged without her input. When George Harvey undertook leadership of the firm, he negotiated new contracts with two of the most recognized authors of the day—William Dean Howells and Samuel Clemens ("Mark Twain")—with the expectation that they would publish in all the Harper magazines. Harvey had arranged with Howells, then sixty-three, to have a small office in the *Bazar* suites. While Jordan admired Howells's accomplishments, she discovered he had little interest in working with a new, relatively young editor. Clemens, by contrast, would not appear in the office for some time, but when he did, they would form a warm friendship.

Within days of joining the firm, Jordan contacted Howells and asked whether he had any stories ready for the *Bazar*. She needed to have a sense of when authors would be submitting material so she could plan each issue, a more arduous task than usual given that she would need a considerable increase in submissions in all departments of the magazine to enact the shift to a weekly by May.

Howells, who was traveling in Italy at the time, responded by thanking her for "your very kind and explicit letter" but declined to submit anything at present.[6] Although he had arranged with the higher-ups to write a series on nineteenth-century heroines for the *Bazar*, he resisted Jordan's desire to have it start in May—her initial issue. He declared that he could not produce work on such short notice as five months, and it would be the following January before he would have anything for her.[7]

This reply was not at all to Jordan's liking; through gentle cajoling, encouragement, and sending a stenographer to assist in the preparation of his manuscripts, she persuaded Howells to produce his first "Heroine" article for her inaugural issue. This solution did not, however, end the challenges Howells presented. He had a habit of going directly to the Harper brothers rather than to her when he had any concerns about his submissions to the *Bazar*.[8] To their credit, the Harpers and George Harvey always made sure Jordan saw any correspondence relating to her magazine. Over time, as Howells gained confidence in Jordan, he stopped going over her head and worked directly with her. Eventually, they became friends and would work on other projects together in the future, but it took a great deal of effort on Jordan's part to achieve that balance.

Howells was not the only author who would repeatedly ask for delays or simply not submit on time. In the newspaper business, reporters never questioned editorial demands. It was their job to meet whatever deadlines and parameters editors set. But authors were another breed altogether. This complicated not only the content of each issue but also advertising. Magazines gained readers by announcing with great fanfare the well-known authors who would be appearing in the next issue and over the coming year. Jordan quickly discovered that the most sought-after authors were booked for a year or more in advance. For instance, she contacted the investigative journalist and lecturer Ida Tarbell in the early months of her tenure only to have Tarbell reply that she wished she could submit but felt "overwhelmed with the number of things I have undertaken."[9] At the same time, authors expected decisive, prompt responses to their queries. Such differences between journalistic and literary publishing required a quick and rather steep learning curve.

Another new aspect of the literary field that confronted Jordan was that many authors now had agents. Stephen Crane was someone Jordan very much wanted for the magazine, and she contacted him shortly after beginning at the *Bazar*. He responded warmly with ideas about what he could submit. He published two stories in the *Bazar* in Jordan's first year, but her negotiations with him had to be coordinated with his London and US agent, James B. Pinker.[10] Pinker was one of the most powerful agents of the era, representing everyone from Crane to Henry James and Joseph Conrad. Over the course of their negotiations (especially in relation to James), Jordan would develop a congenial working relationship with Pinker.

In Jordan's inaugural May 5 issue, an announcement appeared that the magazine was under new management, but one of the most mysterious aspects of Jordan's years as an editor was that she was *never* named as editor in the pages of the *Bazar*. *Harper's Monthly* had the editor's name on the magazine's cover; almost every literary magazine had a notation in each issue about who held the major editorial and staff positions. Everyone in the country and many abroad knew that she was the new editor, so extensively had her acceptance of the position been discussed in newspapers and magazines, but not a note of recognition appeared in the *Bazar* itself. When she published a short story in the magazine, her name would appear as the author, but if subscribers had somehow managed to miss the newspaper coverage of her new position, they would have no idea that Jordan was editor. This was a pattern she would employ more than once in her life, apparently seeing editorship as a behind-the-scenes job, which did not require her name to be attached, and her fiction writing as her career in which she very much wanted recognition.

In Jordan's initial issue, fiction received an honored place at the front of the magazine, a pattern that would continue for many years, with the fashion sections and regular departments following. Articles and stories in this issue were by well-known writers, including Howells and Elizabeth Stuart Phelps. Essays suggested the range of topics that the new *Bazar* would cover: "Settlement Work in London," "The Problem of the Young Person," and a poem by Edith M. Thomas, whom Jordan admired and whose poetry appeared in the *Bazar* throughout Jordan's thirteen-year tenure.

After an article about women and golf and another illustrated short story, the reader came to more familiar territory with an article on club women. The remainder of the issue intermingled the magazine's traditional kind of articles with newer perspectives—how to create an attractive dining room, an essay on "The Outlook for College Women," cooking articles, baby care, summer fashions, patterns, readers' correspondence, and a continuation of the humorous illustrated column, "In Jocund Vein." The issue ended with a new column: "Editorial Comment."

The unsigned "Editorial Comment" column became an important outlet for Jordan's own opinions. She covered some fashion issues but emphasized "the news of the day," on a national and international basis, as it related to women. Politics should not be outside the range of "women's issues," to Jordan's mind. The impact of war on American women was a topic that drew her consideration in several editorials. Following the recent Spanish-American War, with the Boer War close behind, and the country's current engagement in the Philippine-American War, she studied the impact of conflict on women. These pieces situated American women in relation to their "sisters" in China, India, Italy, and South Africa as well as the changes war created between men and women.[11] The editorial "When Johnny Comes Marching Home" was an extraordinary indictment of the costs of war for soldiers: "The irony of war appears in the wrecked manhood that survives."[12]

After expressing her own opinions, Jordan concluded by asking readers for answers: "Are the minds of women satisfied that the sacrifice involved in the solution attempted by the government is reasonable and just?"[13] This technique of asking readers to consider questions ranging from the political to managing household finances marked her years as editor. Rather than dictating opinions to readers, she presented her own and then encouraged readers to consider their thoughts on the subject as well.

Other editorials Jordan wrote during this first year addressed issues relating to women and work, rural regeneration, child care issues, and women's colleges. The editorials overall reminded women that while their love of fashion and beauty was a strength, and though they might spend the majority of their time within the home, their lives were not separate from what happened in the broader world. Everything they did, everything their country did, impacted their lives and those of their loved ones.

This was the new *Bazar*.

Chapter 12
Editor and Author

Jordan threw herself into an effort to attract new writers to the *Bazar*. In 1900 alone, she brought on board Stephen Crane with his "Cora Stories"; Alice Brown, novelist and poet; Octave Thanet (pen name of Alice French), a leading local color writer and political essayist; Charlotte Perkins Gilman, the distinguished author and social reformer; and Margaret Deland, who wrote fiction and essays and began a series in the *Bazar* on "Studies of Great Women." Novelist and poet Harriet Prescott Spofford also became a frequent contributor; the Irish feminist Sarah Grand serialized a novel in the magazine; and Frank Stockton, humorist and author of children's literature, appeared in early issues edited by Jordan, as did Mary E. Wilkins Freeman, a famous author of realistic short stories and supernatural tales who had contributed to the magazine under Sangster's editorship as well.

Additionally, Jack London was an author Jordan admired, and she succeeded in having him contribute "Housekeeping in the Klondike" and short stories to the *Bazar*. Jordan had a keen eye for spotting up-and-coming writers. By the following year, London would be one of the most sought-after authors in American magazines after the success of his novel *The Sea Wolf*. International writers were also sought out by Jordan, including Madame Wu, wife of the Chinese minister to the United States, who wrote an article on "Chinese and American Women Contrasted."[1]

Old friends became part of her stable of writers as well. She brought several former colleagues from her *New York World* days into the pages of the *Bazar*. Jeannette Gilder began in June to write a column, "Books and Writers," for each issue. Jordan's beloved pal Jack à Becket became a frequent contributor of wide-ranging interest with short stories, essays on art and children's theater, and commentaries to illustrate for women what men were really like at their clubs or at work.

On occasion, a new friend emerged from Jordan's association with authors at the *Bazar*. One such figure was Josephine Daskam (Bacon). A writer in diverse genres, including satire, who had graduated from Smith College in 1898, Daskam began publishing in the *Bazar* in the early months of Jordan's tenure. Theirs was not an immediate connection. They politely exchanged correspondence as Jordan took over, but her trait of pushing authors to produce work as soon as possible sent Daskam over the top by October. She was working on a novel, and Jordan's demands for material sooner rather than later led Daskam to rant that even the producer of a baby is granted nine months![2] In spite of their rough beginning, Jordan and Daskam became lifelong friends, supporting one another through difficult and joyful times.

Another enduring friendship she began to develop in these months was with the novelist, poet, and playwright Alice Brown, although it would take years for the reclusive Brown to fully clasp the offered hand of friendship. Though Brown was only eight years older than Jordan, the two women could not have been more different. Theirs was a relationship largely established through correspondence; Brown lived in Boston, rarely visited New York if she could help it, and had a very sheltered life. Over the years the two women would share ideas about authors, religion, politics, and especially their different life choices. Jordan embraced "playing the game," as Brown called modern urban life with its rushed lifestyle and emphasis on production, production, production, while Brown increasingly became more reclusive. Their differences did not matter. Theirs would evolve into a lasting friendship.

In December, Jordan was especially pleased to bring Henry James to the *Bazar*, publishing his short story "The Faces." James's agent, James B. Pinker, had submitted the story to the *Atlantic Monthly* the previous year, but the editor rejected it. Pinker tried several other places of publication over the intervening months, to no avail. As James lamented, his story had "gone a-begging."[3] It was a dark tale, a revenge story of a woman who humiliates her unwitting rival by conniving under the guise of guidance to attire her rival in unfashionable clothing and thus to embarrass her socially. The theme hardly seemed attuned to the *haute couture* by which the *Bazar* made its mark, but Jordan wanted James as a contributor and liked the unusual nature of the story.

James would publish three more stories in the magazine over the course of Jordan's years as editor of the *Bazar*. When the two finally met in person, they formed a deep and lasting bond. James liked intelligent, talented women like Edith Wharton and Constance Fenimore Woolson, and Jordan was another such figure in his life. They would reconnect through other projects over the years.

When Samuel Clemens finally began to spend time around the *Bazar* office, he, too, would become another important figure in Jordan's life. Unlike with Howells, Jordan and Clemens immediately liked one another. They delighted in each other's senses of humor. "I can see him still," Jordan later recalled, "dark eyes shining with mischief."[4] In these days, they also met often at Jorjalma, the Harveys' New Jersey country home where Jordan spent many weekends.

Unlike most of the Harveys' guests, Jordan had to take an early train back to New York on Monday mornings in order to be at work. On these occasions, she typically breakfasted alone, though the mischievous Clemens began to join her—once he learned she did not like to talk in the morning. He would joyfully pummel her with conversation, delighting in her mumbled responses until she could escape back to New York.[5]

The issue of illustrations in the *Bazar* was dear to Jordan's heart. Her ability to hire illustrators of the caliber she desired and to increase the number of illustrations, especially with color plates, was a constant point of contention between her and Harper's management, which exposed the limits of the "total control" over the magazine she had been promised. Throughout her tenure, Jordan fought for what she thought was right for her magazine. Sometimes she won; more often Henry Harper did. But she persevered and brought some highly talented figures to the magazine.

Women illustrators were rare in the magazine when Jordan took over, but she remedied that gap immediately. Fannie Y. Cory was one of the earliest women illustrators brought on board; Cory illustrated many children's articles and stories over the years during which Jordan was editor and would soon become a syndicated comic strip artist. Within a few years, the number of women illustrators on the magazine was notable, including Charlotte Harding, whom Jordan chose to illustrate one of her own stories in the *Bazar*. Harding had a unique style in which the manipulations of the body often took precedence over the face of a character.

One of the most important women illustrators that Jordan brought to the magazine was Rose O'Neill, whom Jordan had met while at the *World*. The opportunity to exchange ideas about illustrations for a variety of authors' works kept them in constant contact throughout the years that Jordan edited the magazine. O'Neill's depictions of children were delightful. They always had very round, chubby bodies and equally round heads with a dollop of hair on the top and at the back. Most important was the fact that in almost every depiction of children, O'Neill had one child who would look directly at the reader with an impish grin or the cast of an eye, as if the child were sharing a secret directly with the reader. With such talents, O'Neill would soon gain a national reputation for her illustrations.

In addition to notable illustrations, one of the complicated themes Jordan brought to the pages of the *Bazar* early in her editorship was women's rights, with an early interview with Elizabeth Cady Stanton on the progress of the suffrage movement. The alliance of temperance and women's rights was captured in the *Bazar* as well, including coverage of the WCTU convention in the fall. In the early years of Jordan's editorship, these articles were occasional; in 1909, when the women's suffrage movement heated up again, she would increase the coverage, negotiating the delicate balance between readers who were pro- and anti–female suffrage.

Jordan also wanted to suggest to *Bazar*'s readers that new opportunities were emerging for women, and she published several articles on college women throughout her years as editor. They included essays about friendships made while at college, the importance of "self-government" for the college woman, and articles by Mary E. Woolley, president of Mount Holyoke College, that extoled the benefits of higher education for women. The message of the *Bazar* was clear: home life, fashions, children were significant aspects of a woman's life, but in the changing world of the twentieth century, women's education ranked equally high in life's necessities for the modern woman.

While Jordan was editing the *Bazar*, she seriously considered her own development as an author. She was an advocate of the "write what you know" school, beginning with her collections of stories about women

Elizabeth Jordan, 1901
THREE ROUSING CHEERS

journalists. She looked further back for her next collection of stories, *Tales of the Cloister*, in which she explored the lives of nuns at St. Mary's.[6] In March 1901, she published "Between Darkness and Dawn," a story that would appear in the collection. The story was the first piece she published in the *Bazar*.

Due to the newer practices of magazine syndicates, this story and most of those she would write over her career not only appeared in magazine and book form but also were syndicated in dozens and sometimes hundreds of newspapers. The syndicates negotiated with the papers to give them "exclusive" use of the story *in their region*. Thus, every paper in which the story appeared could claim it was being published "exclusively" in their paper.[7]

Syndicates were integral to an author's establishment of a national reputation, but they also typically copyrighted the material as a means of enhancing their profits. Jordan learned a great deal from these early years of seeing her work syndicated, and when she later returned to writing a newspaper column, she was one of the few women who knew to insist on maintaining copyright of a column in order to advance her own earnings in syndication. In the interim, she worked diligently at writing fiction, publishing her stories in a variety of magazines and newspapers. Her Plan to enter the field of literature was blooming.

Chapter 13
Retreats

As Jordan's first year as editor passed, she and the officers of Harper and Brothers discussed the benefits of returning *Harper's Bazar* to a monthly. The weekly had been a success as a means of reinvigorating the magazine. It had allowed for increased fashion and fiction sections, but after a year's experience, Jordan had several ideas for how she would like to change the magazine again, including expanding its physical size and adding new columns, and a monthly format would give her the time to enact these changes more easily. With the May 1901 issue, the *Bazar* returned to its original monthly publishing schedule.

In the summer of 1901, Jordan gave herself a well-earned reward for having accomplished so much in her first year as editor—five weeks in Europe, her first trip abroad. Ocean travel at this time took a week's journey each way, eating up much of her summer break, so she focused on visiting France, England, and Germany. She fell in love not only with these countries but also with travel, and this trip marked the first of thirty-nine journeys abroad she would make in her lifetime. Wherever she traveled on these sojourns over the years, she always tried to spend a week each summer in Munich, where the music offerings were incomparable.[1]

After Jordan had settled back into her work routine in New York, *Tales of the Cloister* appeared in the fall of 1901. The opening scene in the collection depicted the sadness of two nuns who must confront the fact that the older one is dying, but the tales evolved into tender and amusing stories of life in a convent. The irrepressible May Iverson, a young student at the convent school who would become the subject of a series of subsequent books by Jordan, gave readers a jolt of sympathy, humor, and warmheartedness in the midst of the older nuns' sorrow.

What was particularly notable about this book was the way in which it challenged the anti-Catholicism rampant in America in this period. Jordan opened the door onto a world of religious, cultural, and educational refinement—the world she had known all her life. The collection's dedication captured how deep and long-lasting friendships from that time had been: "To Sister Clare / with the friendship / of twenty years."

Dozens of reviews praised the collection. *Current Literature*'s assessment was typical:

> *Miss Jordan, in her Tales of the Cloister, has disclosed a vein of remarkable wealth and beauty in the mine from which short stories are dug. A convent school is not the place in which many authors would seek material, but Miss Jordan has produced from within the closed precincts some tales of surpassing beauty and merit. She has shown that in the consecrated life, often supposed to be the grave of withered affections, there still exist depths of pathos, humor even, and sympathy with humanity, of which the outside world has but little conception. No one will lay down the book without a feeling of reverence for the Cloisters of St. Mary.*

The *Evening World* asserted that Jordan "has found an absolutely unworked vein of literature. . . . We are admitted for the first time in fiction to the real life that lies behind convent walls."[2]

Such reviews were decidedly welcome, but writing the stories had deeper importance for Jordan: "The tales . . . helped to keep alive my own interest in convent life—not that any help there was needed. I sometimes eased the increasing strain of an overfull professional and social life by taking the midnight train for South Bend, Indiana, and passing Saturday and Sunday with two new convent friends I had made—Sister Mary Rita and Mother General Perpetua, both of the Order of the Holy Cross." Jordan had been able to make these new acquaintances because she had received the Cross of Honor when she graduated from St. Mary's, granting her access to a convent whenever desired. Sister Mary Rita and Mother General Perpetua "were wonderful women, and I needed those quiet days in a convent atmosphere," in part because the "New York professional and social games were strenuous. I was rarely at home over week-ends. I passed most of these at Jorjalma, and the rest with other hospitable friends who had country homes near New York."[3]

Most weekends were spent among friends with whom she could relax and be herself, but there were other kinds of invitations: "One week—the record week—I had eighteen Friday-to-Monday invitations. . . . The great majority, as always, were from generous and gregarious couples who enjoyed entertaining and liked to be surrounded by cheerful guests. I was a cheerful guest."[4] Against such constant social interaction, nearby convents offered rare moments of quiet and contemplation.

The various weekend gatherings she spent with friends, however, would have a future value. When Jordan began to write mysteries, she set many of her early works in country estates where weekend visitors gathered. While these brief stays seemed like genteel getaways on the surface, Jordan drew from them the social games that went on behind the lunches and dinners and strolls in the garden—an undercurrent of tensions, feuds, and mysterious ways in which some guests who became hangers-on, staying for months, seemed to have a strange hold on their hosts.

But the social games Jordan faced at this time were not only weekend jaunts and being the ever-cheerful guest. The more successful and internationally recognized she became as an editor and author, the more scrutiny fell on her private life. One piece that appeared during these years demonstrated just how invasive such scrutiny could be. After detailing her life and work, the *Catholic Advance* writer observed, "Privately, Miss Jordan lives in what one of her admirers has called 'a splendid isolation.' She has many friends, including noted men and women on both sides of the ocean, but no intimates. It is said of her that she 'has neither nerves, love affairs nor headaches,' but this is probably not true for she is very human, very feminine and full of understanding and sympathy."[5]

Constant scrutiny meant Jordan always had to veil that part of her life. She worked hard to find a balance in doing this—trying to be honest with those she felt it was safe to confide in and skirting questions from reporters and others that felt too intrusive. It was a delicate balance, but she had two avenues to relieve the stress of a hidden life. The convent sojourns were one avenue; they afforded her a literal wall between herself and unending scrutiny.

The second avenue was her roommates, her New York family. When she returned home to their apartment after work, she could relax behind closed doors and be herself with Harriet and Martha. Rumors would always circulate about whether there was an attraction between her and some male friend, but, with the help of these two sheltering influences, she managed to live a remarkably comfortable life. And in a few years, when Jordan truly fell in love, she would become more open about her relationship.

Just as everything seemed to be falling into place—the magazine was thriving, her old and new friendships were flourishing, she was financially better off than she had ever been—Jordan received word that her father was seriously ill. She returned home immediately and was at William Jordan's bedside when he died on November 17, 1901. The shock and all the mundane legal and social arrangements that had to be made filled her life for the remainder of the year. Jordan's grandmother had died earlier, and she and her mother decided that Margaretta should move to New York to live with Jordan and her roommates.

This decision required a larger apartment, so early in 1902 Jordan, Harriet, and Martha found a large apartment in the Gramercy Park area of the city. A few years later, they moved into a lovely place on the tenth floor at 36 Gramercy Park in Manhattan, where they would reside for the next thirty years. This section of the city was known for its literary residents, past and present, which earned it in later years the title of the "American Bloomsbury." Gramercy Park housed the National Arts Club and the theatrical Players' Club, and famous authors and actors from across the country became members of one or the other and spent time there when in the city. Authors such as Herman Melville, Stephen Crane,

Edith Wharton, Nathanael West, and O. Henry lived in Gramercy Park at varying times,[6] and now so did Jordan.

Margaretta Jordan was nearly sixty when she moved to New York, in very good health, and an independent woman in her own right. She fit in comfortably with the three younger professional women and quickly embraced Harriet and Martha as "daughters."

Once they were settled into their new home, Jordan returned her attention to enacting the changes she envisioned for the new monthly *Harper's Bazar.* With the changing culture of the early twentieth century, Jordan wanted the magazine to enhance its role as a trendsetter. While the clothing illustrated in the *Bazar* was decidedly high fashion, the audience was from both the elite and the middle classes; the latter were readers who wanted to be dressed as finely as the best-dressed ladies in Europe.

Thus, as Jordan turned the magazine's attention to political and cultural issues, one of her greatest challenges was balancing a readership in which some embraced the conservatism of the past and others delighted in new, progressive ideas. In this light, she reinvigorated the magazine's interest in girls, with an emphasis on girls nearing adulthood and college-age women. Typically, parents wanted their daughters to follow traditional social paths. The girls and young women themselves often sought new and different roads to their vision of ideal womanhood, and Jordan wanted to retain the older reader and lure the younger.

In the spring, she invited Henry Van Dyke, an author and literature professor at Princeton University, to write an article for the magazine. Van Dyke presented "The Strenuous Life for Girls" for the July 1902 issue. The idea of the strenuous life had first been projected by then New York governor Theodore Roosevelt to express his idea of a life well lived—which required overcoming hardships and embracing "toil and effort" to live a better life, one that would benefit the individual but equally so the nation. Roosevelt's vision explicitly rejected the idea of "ignoble ease";[7] ease was, of course, what the *Bazar* promoted on every page.

Van Dyke admitted that he did not actually believe in a "strenuous life" for girls, a perspective that would appeal to many among the magazine's readership when he concluded that he did not like the militant style of women's actions, which he defined as hysteria, but thinking about the issue made him realize that the leeway Jordan had given him to write as he wished rendered it difficult to make such a statement without adding that he was also "no advocate of a narrower life for woman."[8]

It was hardly the kind of article one might expect from an editor who advocated suffrage and all forms of new rights for women, but in fact it was a clever choice: Van Dyke's article became the touchstone from which many favorable articles about a strenuous life for girls would diverge.

Especially noteworthy were the articles embracing women's athletic endeavors in golf, basketball, tennis, and field hockey. This year Anna Parmley Paret also took over editing the "Books and Writers" column at the *Bazar*. Paret reviewed a wide array of books in her column, some of which appealed to traditional readers, while others looked to new horizons. Paret included selections for readers interested only in fashion and household issues, but far more widely covered were new and innovative literary works, from H. G. Wells's *Anticipations* to Hamlin Garland's *The Captain of the Gray-Horse Troop*. Factory girl stories received attention as well, including Marie Van Vorst's *Philip Longstreth*. New authors were frequently reviewed, including the well-regarded actress turned author Clara Morris, whose *A Pasteboard Crown* (1902) was set in the world of the New York stage. New social concepts and nontraditional authors also found fair play in "Books and Writers," from Jane Addams's *Democracy and Social Ethics* to Onoto Watanna's *The Wooing of Wisteria*.

In terms of her own fiction, Jordan was anxious to build on the success of *Tales of the Cloister* and worked diligently on her next collection of stories, *Tales of Destiny*, which appeared in April 1902 with a dedication to her sister Alice. The collection signaled an important shift in Jordan's writing. She moved beyond the convent and focused on adult relationships in the broader world. The collection included deeply moving moral tales, such as the shame that could come from mocking another human being and of cowardice in war, but there were also upbeat tales, such as one about a society woman who decides to change her life and finds happiness living a simpler existence in Japan. Perhaps most interesting, however, were the stories about women reporters that revealed just how disheartened Jordan had become with yellow journalism.

The reviews for *Tales of Destiny* were uniformly strong, and it became one of the best-selling books published that summer.[9] The *Chicago Tribune* described the stories as "uncommonly good," while *Literary World* asserted, "This collection of short stories is the best we have received for some time."[10]

In the midst of her ongoing editorial work, social commitments, and the publication of *Tales of Destiny*, Jordan enjoyed a break in the summer via her annual trip to Europe. This year included a unique experience, as she undertook a special course of study at the Sorbonne in Paris.[11] Jordan never grew tired of visiting the City of Lights. Its beauty, intellectual atmosphere, and love of the arts made it one of her favorite locales. Years later, in her novel *Faith Desmond's Last Stand*, she described what she loved about Paris: the favorite haunts that could be found by wandering through the city, the delight at discovering odd little out-of-the-way places that seemed to be one's own find, and, most of all, a city devoted to concerts, theater, and grand opera.[12]

After returning to New York, Jordan immersed herself in the *Bazar* again, continued to publish short stories, and began working on her next collection. By the beginning of 1903, Jordan could boast considerable success at increasing the advertising in the *Bazar*. Each volume now included forty pages of advertising at the end, creating an impressive revenue stream for Harper and Brothers. Within a few years, she would double that number, with advertisements moving from appearing only at the end of the magazine to the more modern-day style of being interspersed among the last third of the issue where the regular columns appeared.

She also continued to seek out new contributors. This year she added Dorothy Canfield (Fisher), who would become a noted author and social activist in coming years. Canfield was writing her dissertation at this moment, and her *Harper's Bazar* story was her first published short story.

She would contribute several stories to the magazine over the next few years, and her and Jordan's paths would cross in many ways in the coming years.

Jordan also drew on her connections from her days at the *New York World*, adding Anne O'Hagan to her roster of contributors. O'Hagan wrote a wide variety of essays for the *Bazar* in these years, as well as some short fiction. In a few years, she would become known for her studies such as "The Shop Girl and Her Wages" that focused on the exploitation of working women.[13]

Jordan had always admired Frances Hodgson Burnett's work, so she wrote the popular author in April, inviting her to contribute to the *Bazar*. Burnett replied with a standard author's rejection of such requests: "My dear Miss Jordan: Thank you for the compliment implied by your note. I am however so much engaged with dramatic and other work that it would not be possible for me to undertake anything more. Yours sincerely, Frances Hodgson Burnett."[14] It would be a decade before they met again and discovered how much they cared for one another.

At the *Bazar* this year, Jordan explored the implications of cultural attitudes toward the spinster. She published a range of perspectives on the subject, from Lillian Bell's series on "Talks to Spinsters" (which fell into the conservative camp of assuming unmarried women were unloved and lonely) to Agnes Repplier's lead article in the February 1904 issue, "The Spinster." Repplier had publicly let it be known that she chose not to marry, and in this essay she surveyed the varying types of spinsterhood and concluded that women select marriage or spinsterhood based on what they see as a life of content. Repplier's perspective was that which Jordan addressed throughout her years as editor of the *Bazar* in the editorial column, in her short stories, and later in her novels as well. She was having none of the doom and gloom of the single life.

The following year, she turned her readers' attention to theatrical issues. She had begun earlier to touch on the theater with articles such as Jack à Becket's remarks on children's theater and other reviews of current stage productions. To add to this compendium, Jordan began to publish one-act plays and monologues in the *Bazar*. First was a play by a readers' favorite, Elizabeth Stuart Phelps. Her short piece, "The Joy Giver," appeared in the January 1904 issue and was followed the next month by Edith V. Brander Matthews's "At the Eleventh Hour: An Episode of Life in One Act." Thereafter, a play appeared in the *Bazar* at least once a year. The selections included monologues by Saidee Vere Milne, Ruth McEnery Stuart, and Margaret Lattimore; dialogues by Dorothy Canfield and Jordan herself; one-act plays by William Dean Howells and John Kendrick Bangs; and a "Tri-A-Logue" by Myra Emmons.

Attending the theater had always been a passion for Jordan, and her contribution to the *Bazar*'s theatricals, "A Confidence," was an amusing "dialogue" that examined a friendship in which one woman is so self-absorbed that she keeps up a running monologue of her own concerns as her friend tries but can never get a word into the conversation. "A Confidence" would not be Jordan's only foray into playwriting.

In another venue, a notable new contributor joined the magazine this year: Jordan's roommate Martha Cutler, who had graduated from the School of Applied Design in 1901. Cutler had begun to contribute articles to a few magazines when Jordan brought her on board at the *Bazar* to write about fine arts. Cutler's first article for the *Bazar*, "New Designs in Wall Paper," appeared in the October issue and included several photographs illustrating the subject. However, the next month, when she published "Chairs Past and Present," Cutler included her own sketches with the article, a practice she would continue for nearly a decade.

Cutler published an illustrated article in the *Bazar* every month for the next ten years, covering every imaginable design issue from drapes to furniture to bric-a-brac. She had a delicate hand as an illustrator, creating detailed images that made it seem as if the piece of furniture was right before the reader. Her articles were a success from the beginning, and, in April 1910, Cutler added a new fine arts column to the magazine, "Home Decoration," in which she responded to readers' questions about home design. The column ran for two years. If Jordan gave Cutler a hand up, Cutler more than fulfilled the obligation and produced essays that appealed to the *Bazar*'s readers.

In addition to the many demands on her life as an editor, Jordan was already at work on her next book, a novel that would bring back the irrepressible May Iverson who had appeared as a secondary character in *Tales of the Cloister*. At the same time, Jordan was working as a go-between for Frederick Duneka as he sought from Margaret Deland the right to publish a novel that she had serialized in *Harper's Monthly*. Duneka wanted the manuscript earlier than Deland wanted to produce it. The negotiations between the two broke down soon thereafter, and he enlisted Jordan's help because Deland had made it clear to everyone at Harper's that she liked working with Jordan. A visit to Deland's home proved successful, and Jordan bought all rights to *Awakening of Helen Richie*, a powerful novel about spousal abuse, women's rights, and what constitutes an "unfit mother."[15] Gaining the signed contract proved to be a very profitable accomplishment for Harper and Brothers, as the novel sold well and was soon adapted for the stage and a silent film.

Chapter 14

The Whole Darn Family

In the early summer of 1904, Jordan and Henry James were working together on several projects during which they forged a deep friendship. James, who had been living abroad for several years, wished to return to the States and give a series of lectures to women's clubs as a means of making money and renewing connections with his American audience. James insisted it should not be considered a lecturing *tour*. William Dean Howells, who in the early stages acted as an intermediary, conveyed to Jordan that James did not wish to lecture more than a "very, very few times, and *not* at any towns of public vastness. He should read, as I have done, in drawing-rooms, country clubs . . . and the like, and the audience should be more or less invited, and made to feel itself privileged."[1]

Jordan had met James on several occasions when she traveled to England and felt a rapport with him, so she immediately responded in the affirmative and began planning what would be needed for such a venture. James sent her a letter of appreciation in response and reminisced that "our meetings in London have already dropped back into the particular perspective that makes half the effect of romance. But please believe with what pleasure I think of their being subject to no distant newal."[2] James's quixotic reference to "romance" about their earlier meetings would be echoed in a different way in newspapers' speculation about the two when James came to the States and met frequently with Jordan. Neither was interested in the other sex romantically, but they admired one another and felt a bond through their lives as writers.

After much negotiating, Jordan and James decided that he would present a lecture, "The Lesson of Balzac," at exclusive venues, thus defraying the costs of his travel to America.[3] It had been more than twenty years since he had been in the States, and Jordan willingly undertook the project, contacting the best women's clubs and other groups before which she thought it most suitable for James to appear.

Jordan was delighted with the success of her next book. She dedicated *May Iverson—Her Book* to her beloved roommates, Harriet Beardslee Prescott and Martha Hill Cutler. Set at the fictional St. Catherine's convent school, the novel took readers back to when the narrator, fourteen-year-old May (who appeared briefly in *Tales of the Cloister*), began her writing career. May's writing instructor, Sister Irmingarde, was based on Jordan's favorite teacher at St. Mary's, Sister Ethelbert.[4] The fictional May, like the young Elizabeth, could not seem to adhere to Sister Irmingarde's advice to "go ahead and tell the story, and never mind the rest,"[5] but May's repeated and lengthy asides gave readers access to the delightful machinations of the convent student's mind, her friendships, crushes, relationships with the sisters—everything that made the May Iverson books one of the most delightful young adult series of any era.

May Iverson—Her Book received excellent reviews. Several critics agreed with Jeannette Gilder, who referred to May Iverson as "a new type" of girl "and an entertaining one." The reviewer for the *Literary World* also proclaimed that Jordan had "tilled a new field in the vast estate of fiction with delightful results in these 'extracts' from the diary of May Iverson . . . the whole book is distinctly clever and irresistibly funny."[6] May was active, sentimental, emotional as only a fourteen-year-old girl could be, and she had great ambitions to be a writer.

The success of this story about a convent schoolgirl was notable, since it appeared during one of American literature's extended anti-Catholic periods. Infamous books, such as *Awful Disclosures of Maria Monk, or The Hidden Secrets of a Nun's Life in a Convent Exposed* (1836) and *Amy's Probation: Six Months at a Convent School* (1880), had permeated the public's

[See p. 260

"THE BIG, BRIGHT STAR WE ALWAYS LOOK FOR IS SHINING ABOVE THE CROSS"

Illustration from *May Iverson—Her Book*

reading experiences for decades. Jordan, with humor and a thoroughly realistic depiction of a teenage convent student, countered the long history of stories denigrating her faith and presented a nuanced vision of that experience.

Although Jordan wanted to publish more novels, the time demanded to edit the *Bazar* meant she turned most often to short stories. She had met Charles Hanson Towne, editor of *The Smart Set*, a year or so earlier, and he had positively reviewed one of her books. She was pleased when he sought her as a contributor to the magazine, which was committed to the world of elite New Yorkers. Towne published two of her stories in the magazine in 1905. Most notable was "Van Dorn's Home" which satirized the racially inflected attitudes of the wealthy as a Mrs. Crosby brings a young East Indian man to London with her "with a characteristically vague impression that he would be a picturesque feature of her new London home."[7]

Throughout her years of writing fiction, Jordan had a significant retinue of standard places in which she published—the various Harper magazines, the *Chicago Tribune*, *Ladies' Home Journal*, and so forth—but she tried to add a new place of publication on a fairly regular basis, as a means of growing her audience and of finding new venues for her ever-expanding exploration of various genres, from romance to satire to realism to comedies or poignant tragedies.

As the summer approached, Jordan was delighted to receive an invitation from Alma Harvey to go abroad with her for three months. Jordan had never taken that much time off from the magazine, but since Alma was married to Jordan's boss, she did not hesitate to accept. They spent six weeks in Paris, including side trips through the château country, and another six weeks at Claridge's during the height of the London season.

George Harvey was already in London and had arranged a dinner for the night they arrived—with twenty-four guests. He seated Jordan next to Henry James, as he wanted them to have a chance to talk. "That evening was," Jordan declared, "the most interesting of my literary life." It was one thing to correspond with James but quite another to have a long, engaged conversation with him. In spite of the many famous guests, it was only James whom she remembered.[8]

Jordan returned to New York thoroughly refreshed. To her delight, she finally convinced Samuel Clemens to contribute to the *Bazar*. His article, "A Helpless Situation," was the lead for the November 1905 issue. It presented the dilemma of every well-known writer—the novice author who asks whether Clemens will hand her manuscript to a publisher. He replies with an imagined conversation between himself and the publisher—all the ways in which he could not speak to who the author was or the quality of the work since he knew neither. Jordan was thrilled to at last have Clemens as a contributor.

The following month, she joined a vast array of literary figures (including Willa Cather, Mary E. Wilkins Freeman, Kate Douglas Wiggin Riggs, William Dean Howells, and Richard Watson Gilder) at Delmonico's to celebrate Clemens's seventieth birthday. She wore a beautiful satin gown in the latest fashion with elaborate ruffles along the back and down the side. The dinner was covered by newspapers throughout the country, and a souvenir booklet was prepared with photographs of many of the attendees, including those at Jordan's table.[9] The fact that Clemens now published in her magazine went a long way to enhance Jordan's standing as an editor.

In January 1906, Jordan expanded her own sources for publication by placing "Assiduous Anne's Career" with *Success Magazine*. The periodical was published by Orison Swett Marden as a means of promoting his "New Thought Philosophy," advocating positive thinking and self-determination. Anne is similar to May Iverson—a fifteen-year-old convent student and aspiring writer who shares her discoveries about life. Jordan was not a proponent of New Thought Philosophy per se, but she embraced the idea of positivity and working for success. In the latter vein, Jordan was still working whenever possible on her next collection of stories, *Many Kingdoms*, written for the adult market. Little could she know at this point that a project she had begun to envision, *The Whole Family*, would delay her own book for nearly two years. *The Whole Family* was to be a multiauthor novel about a family that gathers for a wedding, only to have numerous issues intervene—and a different author would write each chapter.

The delay in her own work was caused by the many conundrums of trying to pull together all the threads of a collaborative novel. Jordan's initial lineup of potential contributors included Howells, who had proposed the project and envisioned writing the first chapter and then letting the others follow as they wished, expanding the storyline based on the character they were assigned.[10] Jordan had anticipated the experience with "the most iridescent hopes," but from the beginning it became "a chastening experience."[11] If she thought negotiations with contributors to the *Bazar* sometimes tested her patience, she was about to confront new levels of frustration.

When Howells presented his proposal to her, he had a list of authors he thought would be right for the project. Jordan accepted some of them, but she had ideas of her own about who to include. Two names Jordan mentioned early on were Edith Wharton and Henry James. Howells insisted neither would be interested. He was right about Wharton, but James and Jordan had established a solid friendship by this time, and he agreed to contribute. With Howells and James on board, it was much easier to attract other first-rate authors.

It was necessary, however, for Howells to produce the first chapter so Jordan could send a copy of it to potential authors with a basic outline of the story. Howells was traveling in Europe but promised to have the chapter to her as soon as possible.

By June she was rounding up responses from the initial group of writers she hoped to include. Alice Brown agreed immediately on receipt of Jordan's invitation to write the chapter about the young bride-to-be.[12] However, Margaret Deland declined due to other commitments, and, as Jordan noted, "she threw a stimulating dash of cold water on the whole project" in her reply. "I am dazzled at the distinguished names that have entered your domestic circle," Deland proclaimed, "but it doesn't seem to me that you are, any of you, taking the rank that belongs to you in literature when you make yourselves into this pleasant sandwich."[13] It was an insight Jordan later wished she had listened to more carefully.

She felt heartened when others (Henry Van Dyke, Kate Douglas Wiggin Riggs, and Samuel Clemens) initially agreed to the project, pending receiving Howells's opening chapter. Soon others joined in: John Kendrick Bangs, Mary Stewart Cutting, and Mary E. Wilkins Freeman. In the midst of these negotiations, Jordan had to squelch Howells's repeated suggestions about changing the concept of the novel. At one point—to Jordan's horror—he suggested the authors should write their chapters autobiographically.[14] Back and forth their letters went, out went the invitations to participate, and still by mid-summer she did not have a final lineup of authors.

The time-consuming demands of negotiating with the contributors to *The Whole Family* came to feel like a full-time job. Finally, Howells's opening chapter had been sent out to the other authors, but, as Mary E. Wilkins Freeman was preparing the second chapter, Kate Douglas Wiggin Riggs pulled out of the project. She had read Howells's opening chapter and thought it offered "delectable hints about the mother-in-law & maiden aunt, & not throwing a crumb to me for the daughter!—and I am afraid to try it."[15] This was followed by the surprising content of Freeman's chapter, "The Old-Maid Aunt," which was to come second in the volume. Whereas the title reflected Howells's vision of the spinster aunt, Freeman envisioned a progressive, modern-day woman. She also realized Howells had not really set out much in the way of a plot.

Freeman wrote to Jordan that Howells's "conception of [the spinster aunt] was so hackneyed. . . . I did think some plot ought to be started—and I could see no other way."[16] That "way" would set off a battle of howls among some of the other contributors and applause from those who recognized that Freeman had changed the entire scope of the novel. It shook the very foundations of the enterprise. But Jordan was delighted with Freeman's chapter and resisted all calls from other authors to have it rewritten. To her delight, Henry Mills Alden, editor of *Harper's Magazine*, whose opinion carried great weight with the Harper and Brothers publishing operation, thoroughly agreed with Jordan's decision.[17] Jordan also ignored Howells's suggestion that Freeman's chapter not be sent to the other contributors. Out it went to everyone who was on board as a contributor at present.

Never before had her talents as a negotiator been put to such a test. As late as October 1906, Henry James was dithering about whether he would actually contribute to the collective novel. Jordan sent him the first drafts of chapters by Howells, Freeman, and Mary Heaton Vorse, who wrote "The Grandmother." Jordan insisted James come to a decision once he had read these submissions. He replied that he might start writing his own chapter, but he began what would be the first of his *many* ideas for altering the volume by suggesting Jordan redo the order of the chapters.[18]

Had Jordan allowed such changes at this point—with which she did not agree—it would have meant every author who had already submitted a draft would have to completely rewrite their entry. No matter how hard she tried to hold the line, many more disruptions would occur before the book could be published.

Frederick Duneka, Harper's general manager, read the chapters as they were produced, since Harper's would be publishing the book. In mid-December, when he saw Edith Wyatt's contribution, he immediately sent a note to Jordan: "This chapter of *The Whole Family* is simply awful—confused, dull, stupid, vapid, meaningless, halting, lame, holding up the action and movement of the story which has run along so splendidly thus far. . . . You have got a great book—vigorous, direct, swinging into a well-concealed dénouement—and it would be a calamity to stop it with this cruelly incompetent drivel. My advice is—don't publish it."[19]

As much as Jordan appreciated Duneka's input, she refused to cast Wyatt aside—perhaps the worst decision she made during the entire process. Her letter to Wyatt suggesting extensive revisions were required would have been difficult to receive, no matter how judicious, but Wyatt undertook the revisions without complaint.[20] For all that Jordan worked with Wyatt on revisions, Duneka had been right—it remained the weakest chapter in the collection. But everyone forged on, writing their sections.

So ended one of Jordan's most arduous years as an editor.

Over the holidays, Jordan devoted herself to her own writing and contributed two stories to journals. Both "The Perfect Lady" in the *Smart Set* (a critique of high society's treatment of women) and "The Case of Katrina" in *Century Magazine* (the story of an orphan who is deposited at a convent school and what happens in her subsequent life) appeared in February 1907. No matter how much of a reprieve her own writing offered, she could not long ignore the authors' needs for *The Whole Family*. Henry James notified her that he really would like to write the "Mother" chapter as well as his own.[21] James's capacious desire to take over the book had only just begun, and days later he would declare that, truly, he would prefer to write all the chapters himself.

Then Alice Brown decided that she did not like the man with whom her character was supposed to be in love and wondered whether he could be rewritten, which would mean other authors had to alter their chapters. Such letters continued to arrive in Jordan's mail almost daily. Not least stressing was James's submission; when Jordan suggested revisions around one character, he was not pleased, insisting she misunderstood the story. In the same letter, he suddenly shifted and said she could edit it as she pleased and then added two postscripts asking her to leave it as submitted. She edited and returned it to him, and he sent back a shouting letter that he had never said he would accept edits. Back and forth it went. Somehow, she kept her sanity.

In the interim, the *Bazar* was thriving, and Jordan believed it did so because she never rested on her laurels, preferring to find new contributors to enlighten her readers. One such contributor was a powerful voice in the women's rights movement, Mary Heaton Vorse—one of many upper-class feminists who embraced not only the suffrage movement but also women's economic independence, education, and birth control. She published fiction and essays in the *Bazar*, including "The Bear at Home," which addressed spousal abuse. Jordan had met Vorse years earlier at the Women's Press Club in New York, and she admired Vorse's activism, which had been a major part of why she invited Vorse to contribute a chapter to *The Whole Family*. They remained in touch for several decades, and Vorse would contribute to another multiple-author novel that Jordan edited several years later.

After months of requiring rewrites from Edith Wyatt, *The Whole Family* seemed to be coming together. *Seemed*. In August, Jordan received a scathing letter from Henry James about Alice Brown's contribution, which followed his. He insisted Brown's chapter reflected "nothing of my own imagined little *direction given*." He found almost nothing in the chapter had been accomplished to *his* satisfaction.[22] He went on for pages with critiques of other chapters. Jordan rejected some of his criticisms, but where she agreed, she undertook to make the necessary changes. It was October before James wrote to apologize for his tirade—as he put it, he had "overflowed into judgment" and was "very red in the face."[23] Thankfully, opera season started the next month, and Jordan could lose herself in music once again.

But not even the opera could relieve her frustration when Henry Van Dyke, who was to write the last chapter of the novel, contacted her just before Thanksgiving to say he had not even started his chapter, let alone read the preceding chapters that had been sent to him. He said he could not possibly begin working on the chapter until after the holidays and anticipated it would be the end of January before he could send it to her. Through much cajoling on Jordan's part, he managed to deliver the chapter to her on December 31.[24] At last she had drafts of all the chapters and set to work editing the novel as a whole.

In spite of her work demands, Jordan was increasing her political activism as well. Most of this activity focused on the suffrage question, but in February 1908 she was among twenty American women of letters who responded to an international call for support of Prussian Poles who were suffering under political persecution from Germany's violent ethnic-cleansing practices. Those who joined the call included Mary Hallock Foote, Charlotte Perkins Gilman, Sarah Orne Jewett, Edith M. Thomas, Kate Douglas Wiggin Riggs, and Mary Wilkins Freeman.[25] In the years between 1908 and World War I, Jordan became increasingly concerned about broader realms of civil rights, a position she pursued during both world wars.

Such events made the constant sniping among authors contributing to *The Whole Family* seem ridiculous, but negotiating such issues was her job. At last, however, the negotiations ended, and the manuscript went to press.

The novel's first chapter appeared in the *Bazar* in February, with no author assigned. Readers were given a list of all the contributors to the novel and asked to guess who had written this first chapter, as they would be for each subsequent chapter. Readers loved the idea, and letters poured into the *Bazar*. Quite a few guessed Howells, others suggested Mary Stuart Cutting or Henry Van Dyke, and a few readers were adamant that it was *not* Henry James.[26] Readers reveled in the guessing game throughout the serialization of the remaining chapters.

With *The Whole Family*'s publication underway, Jordan immediately turned her attention to her own writing, working on stories that would be part of the *Many Kingdoms* collection and other stand-alone pieces. Over the next several months she published stories in *Everybody's Magazine*, the *Bazar*, *Harper's Monthly*, *Scribner's*, and the *Smart Set*. Near the end of the year, Jordan also published "Mrs. Dixon's Culture Course" in the *Atlantic Monthly*. After its publication, she received several requests from playwrights to dramatize the story. Jordan considered the offers but began to think she could do that herself. She had only written one other play to date, the short one-act satire in the *Bazar*, but this did not deter her. The story would become the comedic core of Jordan's play, *The Lady from Oklahoma*. She spent the next year writing and revising the play. It was the beginning of a new avenue among her many writing paths, one that would lead her to Broadway.

The big event in the spring of 1908 was the book publication of *The Whole Family*. It had been running in the *Bazar*, chapter by chapter, even as some final negotiations took place. The idea of guessing who had written which chapter had created a significant buzz around the novel, as Jordan had hoped. Only when it was published in book form was the author-chapter link revealed. The buzz extended to reviewers as well, and the book received many positive reviews. But Jordan knew the toil and complications behind the scenes. Years later, she gave her final assessment of the project:

> *In the end the book was finished and published. It had cost a great deal of money, time, and nervous wear-and-tear . . . during its first years it sold well and earned a reasonable profit for Harper and Brothers. They were satisfied; but my own reaction was different. . . . However, as I have so freely revealed the impression of the others concerned, it is*

only fair that I should now confess my own. I do so, with accumulated zest.

The Whole Family *was a mess!*[27]

At last, summer came and Jordan headed for the wonderful Bayreuth Festival featuring Richard Wagner operas. To her delight, both Harriet and Martha joined her this summer. The festival was held in a specially designed theater constructed to accommodate the large orchestras needed to perform Wagner's work. The audience was made up of classical music lovers from around the world. It was a decidedly different experience from her convent school days when she rode in a curtained bus to hear performances of *Der Ring des Nibelungen* in Milwaukee.

After days of relishing performances of Wagner, the roommates traveled to Gertrude Atherton's home in Munich, where she hosted a luncheon for them, followed by a special treat. Atherton had purchased tickets for an opera—an uncut version of *Tristan and Isolde* that ran from four in the afternoon until midnight, with a six o'clock interval for dinner. It was the finest treat Jordan could imagine. She lay awake all night, going over the score and the scenes again and again,[28] just as she had when she was at the convent. She returned to New York in October, refreshed and ready to jump into her editorial duties and to celebrate the publication of her latest collection of short stories, *Many Kingdoms*.

The stories in this collection signaled a significant advance in Jordan's stories for adults. More complex in plot and psychological explorations, the selections in *Many Kingdoms* signaled Jordan's development into a more assured writer. The success of the collection overshadowed any residual discomfort she had with *The Whole Family*, and her turn to psychological facets in her characterizations foreshadowed the way in which her mystery writing would emphasize the psychology of each amateur detective.

Reviews of *Many Kingdoms* were heartwarming. The *Philadelphia Inquirer* declared, "Elizabeth Jordan is one of the premier short story writers of this country." In this collection, they noted, each story "is a little masterpiece."[29] The *New York Times* offered one of the most nuanced analyses: "The range of interest in these stories is very wide, varying through many sorts of character and kinds of experience. The author's method is modeled after that of the great French short stories, taking usually a single episode in a life, treating it with detail, and following out elaborately its effects upon the person in question. . . . Her characters are genuine human beings rather than mere puppets for the exploitation of the author's incidents, and her episodes are worked out into closely reasoned plots."[30]

Friends' responses were always heartwarming as well. By this time, several of Jordan's contributors to the *Bazar* were also her friends, and a surprising number of them felt so close to her that they created private nicknames for her to suggest that they were more intimate than a normal contributor or friend would be. For Margaret Deland, Jordan became "my nintimate friend," while Katrina Trask called her "my Ladye" or "the beautiful Elizabetha." Josephine Daskam Bacon and Jordan had become very close during these years, and Jordan became godmother to her daughter. Daskam Bacon was one of the few author-friends who seems to have known Jordan was a lesbian, and her nickname for Jordan was "George Anne," which she used often in the personal letters she sent Jordan. The nickname, royal in nature, defied gender norms.

Exciting for Jordan, too, was the way in which the suffrage movement regained vitality and urgency in these years, in multiple ways. The National Woman's Party organized protests and marches demanding the vote for women, while the National American Woman Suffrage Association dedicated its efforts to legislative lobbying. Jordan captured the excitement of the moment in the *Bazar* with prosuffrage articles by Ida Husted Harper, coauthor of the four-volume *History of Woman Suffrage*, who identified eminent women committed to suffrage (including Jordan) and updates on suffragists' activities.

Over the next three years, Jordan published dozens of prosuffrage articles in the *Bazar*. Ida Husted Harper wrote a number of these, as did the Rev. Anna Howard Shaw and Evelyn Sharp, who wrote about English suffragettes. Occasionally, antisuffragists were given an opportunity to respond, most of whom decried having the vote forced on them, but the majority of *Bazar* articles in these years ardently supported the cause.

At this time, Jordan also developed a new and lasting friendship through her work on the magazine. For several years, she had been publishing the poetry of Edith M. Thomas in the *Bazar*, but it was not until February 1909 that the two women finally met in person. A friendship emerged that lasted until Thomas's death in 1925. Thomas fascinated Jordan—she was a shy, seemingly lonely woman who created "beautiful and deathless" poetry "for the cultured few," and about whom Jordan felt she would like to have written a book.[31]

The fascination was mutual. Jordan took Thomas under her wing from the time of this initial meeting, and the importance of that day for Thomas was commemorated in a poem. Calling it a "Perfect Day" when she met Jordan, Thomas suggested her life had been "hard" and "frozen" until "suddenly, into the Day / Shot a golden fire-tipped ray / . . . when I met and knew my Friend."[32] The "unfreezing" of Thomas's life by coming to know Jordan suggests a passion, not unlike that of Kate Field and Rose O'Neill, that lasted throughout the years of their friendship.

Jordan was busier than ever as the year came to a close. Once again, she had decided to change the format of the *Bazar*, beginning with the 1909 Christmas issue. She developed an enlarged magazine, increasing the number of color plates and illustrations, especially in the fashion pages—making the magazine one of the most aesthetically appealing periodicals of its day—while maintaining the length of seventy pages, and creating an impressive magazine that caught the discerning eye.

This special issue also included an impressive array of contributors. Jordan had now been editing the journal for ten years, and her power to attract outstanding writers had continued to increase over the years. This issue included the first chapters of Gertrude Atherton's new novel, *The Woman in Love*; Mark Twain's "Marjorie Fleming, the Wonder Child"; a story by Alice Brown; a poem by Julia Ward Howe; and an article on

"New York Society at Work" by Ralph Pulitzer, son and heir to Joseph Pulitzer's publishing company. In addition, there was a study of "Mrs. Pankhurst—Leader of the English Suffragettes." No antisuffrage articles were included.

Once the issue was published, Jordan waited for the expected backlash that was the usual initial reaction to any change in the magazine. To her delight, she received "hundreds upon hundreds" of letters praising the *Bazar*'s new look.[33]

Chapter 15

The Progressive Era and the Playwright

JORDAN, AT FORTY-FOUR, COULD HAVE CHOSEN TO SETTLE INTO HER life, but she always had a new Plan. Her life was yet to take many new twists and turns, both personally and as a writer. One that came with the New Year as 1909 became 1910 was her desire to enter the field of playwriting.

The American theater had become one of the most popular forums for espousing the country's new Progressive Era values. Performance—in all its manifestations—became the vehicle for negotiating the radically changing culture of the 1910s,[1] and the "New Woman" was central to demands for cultural change. Over the years, Jordan had become close friends with the actors Maud and Otis Skinner. They encouraged Jordan's growing interest in playwriting. So, for two years she worked on converting her short story "Mrs. Dixon's Culture Course" into a four-act comedy. In January 1910, she copyrighted the play under the title *The Lady from Oklahoma*, though she would wait until the play came to Broadway to publish it. The play traced the evolution of a traditional Midwestern woman into an astute political maneuverer in the nation's capital.

Soon after the play was copyrighted, Jordan joined the Society of American Dramatists and Composers (later the Dramatists Guild). Then she began the long process of learning the ins and outs of having her play produced for the stage. It would be a year before its first out-of-town performances, but Jordan was invigorated by seeing theater life from the creator's perspective.

Unfortunately, her decision to designate *The Lady from Oklahoma* as a comedy undermined its broader themes. Only the second act, set in a beauty parlor, was comedic—indeed, it was a hilarious critique of the latest in hairstyles, electric baths, and every imaginable means through which women attempted to improve their looks. The play as a whole, however, fit the Progressive Era's interest in working-girl stories and upward mobility.[2] *The Lady from Oklahoma* centered on the lives of working women—a magazine editor (Ruth Herrick again appears as a reporter, and her transitions in life continue to echo Jordan's), a beautician, a typist, an elocutionist, and a political lobbyist.

Jordan sought every means possible to learn about staging a play. In March 1910, she was invited to join Kate Douglas Wiggin Riggs for a party of guests who were traveling to Bridgeport, Connecticut, to see a production of Wiggin Riggs's *Rebecca of Sunnybrook Farm* before it came to New York.[3] Seeing the production and discussing it with the members of the party gave Jordan a sense of the importance of out-of-town performances as a means of honing not only the acting but also a play's rhythms and nuances so each act had an impact on the audience. By April, Jordan's *Lady from Oklahoma* had found a producer. Mary E. Wilkins Freeman sent a note, offering Jordan her warmest congratulations: "I hope it will be a great success. I will be sure to go when it is presented, and take an umbrella and pound, and I will weep if you wish me to do so."[4]

Jordan's joy at these developments was dampened when, on April 21, Samuel Clemens died. His funeral was held two days later at the Brick Church on Fifth Avenue. It was a grand memorial in terms of the attendance, but the service itself was relatively simple—a Scripture reading, a short address, and a prayer. Jordan was one of four hundred individuals who had tickets to attend this part of the ceremony. After they walked past the casket, the church was opened and a throng of New Yorkers entered to pay tribute to their beloved Mark Twain.[5]

In the summer of 1910, Henry James returned to America for what would be the last time. He was suffering from eye problems and attending numerous appointments for tests. He spent a good deal of time during these months in Jordan's Gramercy Park apartment. She took time off from work to be with him when she could, dimmed the lighting in the rooms to shelter his eyes, and sat together with him in the "gloaming."[6] She could not know at this time that she herself would, in coming years, have to face the "gloaming" herself.

In early May, Jordan began making frequent trips to Atlantic City as the cast and producers of *The Lady from Oklahoma* prepared for their opening week out of town. She loved the seaside locale, and it would soon become a place she visited when she needed a quick getaway. The play opened in Atlantic City on May 15 at the Apollo Theatre. The *Baltimore American*, *New York Times*, and other newspapers noted that the play was well received.[7] According to an advertisement in *Harper's Bazar*, "Miss Jordan's comedy in four acts is said by a leading critic to be 'the most widely discussed play of the season.' Its most startling novelty is 'the act without a man' [the beauty parlor act]. It reads as well as it acts."[8]

With these early positive assessments of the play, the producers decided to try it out around the country, a process that lasted for almost two years. Throughout these days of preparation, Effie Shannon, who was to play the lead, kept up a steady stream of letters to Jordan regarding her concerns that the manager, Mr. Delamater, was not selecting the best cast members for the secondary parts in the play. Shannon's correspondence proved helpful, as she offered knowledgeable insight into the machinations of stage productions, but it also left Jordan with a steady stream of headaches.[9]

Jordan negotiated with the producers and Delamater until she was as satisfied as possible with how the Poughkeepsie and subsequent productions would appear. Throughout the play's two-year run across the country, Jordan fought to maintain its integrity against repeated changes to various acts. When suggestions seemed to strengthen the story and its reception by audiences, she agreed; many times, however, she argued adamantly against producers' ideas of "popularizing" the content, but most often it was a losing battle. When Delamater was replaced in August with William A. Brady, a former actor and soon to be one of the major stage producers in the country, things went much more smoothly.

In June, Jordan's short story "May Iverson Writes a Play" appeared in *Harper's Monthly*. As Jordan confessed, she put her own experiences into this story, the disheartening lessons about what happened to a play as it went from print to production. When May and her friend Kittie are allowed to attend rehearsals for the production of a play, May learns that lead actresses cut large sections of the play, turning a four-act play into a four-act monologue. As May remarks, "It was like seeing a purse stolen, or a baby slapped, or some other low act."[10]

Harry E. Andrews, managing editor of the *Los Angeles Times*, sent Jordan a letter in response to the publication of "May Iverson Writes a Play": "We—the reading ones and writing ones of the *Times*, the editors, publishers, literary critics, dramatic critics, musical critics, reporters and errand boys, all play-writers, of course—wish to thank you for your delicious, yes, bully story in the June *Harper's*. It ranks with the very best short stories of the French masters. That is not saying enough. It is better than anything any of us ever wrote. We could not let the joy of it pass without writing to you."[11] Writers of all stripes understood the pain of having their work edited in ways that damaged its intended meaning.

In December, the book publication of *The Lady from Oklahoma* appeared. The reviews were excellent. Most found the play delightful, the dialogue sparkling with wit, and its many characters amusing. But the *Chicago Tribune* recognized its more complex elements: The play's humor was successful, the reviewer wrote, but the subject was rooted in "a heartache as real as the world we live in. . . . On every trial this little comedy rings true, and in its gently humorous way bears a message to us all."[12] The reviewer captured exactly what Jordan had fought to retain during the play's out-of-town run across the country.

For now, Jordan was ready to move on from playwriting. As winter swept through the city, she was forming her latest Plan. At this time as well, Alma and George Harvey were celebrating their twenty-fifth wedding anniversary, and Jordan joined several of their friends in arranging to host a dinner for them at Delmonico's. She headed the reception committee, which meant she needed to be at the restaurant at least an hour before guests were to arrive—which would have been fine if that night had not brought on the worst blizzard New York City had seen in decades. She had not yet purchased a car, though almost everyone else who was coming owned one and could more comfortably navigate their way through the snow. Jordan still relied on cabs, a fact that resulted in one of her most treacherous nights of travel.

Dressed in gold slippers and a stunning cloth-of-gold evening gown made especially for the occasion, she donned a velvet evening wrap around her shoulders and ventured out, not realizing how lightweight the wrap and slippers would soon feel. She called for a cab, only to discover there were none to be had. After negotiating with the taxi company, she finally secured one, but it arrived forty minutes late. She jumped into the vehicle, trying not to think about how late she would be, only for the car to become stuck in a snow drift one block later. After fifteen minutes of the driver trying to pull them out, she abandoned the cab and began running, pounded with freezing snow as the blizzard strengthened. Several blocks later, she caught an electric car. Collapsing into the seat, she caught her breath, but almost instantly she felt the car jerk and stop before starting again. After several such efforts, the conductor told her and the only other passenger that they would have to exit the vehicle. It was going nowhere.

Out into the storm she went again. By then, "My fighting blood was up. I would get to Delmonico's if I died doing it." She lurched through the streets, seeing no other people or cars. Finally, she came upon an empty horse-drawn hansom cab and convinced the driver to take her to Delmonico's. It was almost ten o'clock when she arrived, a bedraggled sight that no one would have recognized as the highly fashionable editor of *Harper's Bazar*.[13] It would not be long before she purchased a car of her own.

Writing a play, for all of its headaches, increased Jordan's love of creative writing in general, and her interest in editing the *Bazar* was beginning to fade. She wanted more time for her own work. It would be nearly two years before she ended her tenure as editor, but the idea of change had been sparked.

The success of her next novel, *May Iverson Tackles Life*, published in May 1912, also whetted Jordan's appetite for more time to write. She was ready to move on from young adult literature, however, so she pronounced at the end of the book's foreword that this would be the last book she wrote about convent life. Thus, she took May and her friends, now sixteen, into the world of burgeoning womanhood—they became interested in "beauty culture," dreamed of whom they might marry, and confronted issues about body image, but broader cultural issues entered their debates as well, most notably women's suffrage. Since this book was to be the farewell to May Iverson, Jordan concluded the collection with a tribute to May's beloved Sister Irmingarde (based on Sister Ethelbert): "Troubles will always come, and we will bear them—because we'll have to," May says. "But I think we'll bear them better because we are Sister Irmingarde's girls."[14]

The reviews for *May Iverson Tackles Life* were some of Jordan's strongest yet. The *Boston Globe* declared that the stories "fairly bubble with the gayety of youth. The young girl will read every page with unalloyed delight, and the older person will find May Iverson's method of tackling Woman's Suffrage and other problems of modern life irresistibly amusing."[15] As the *New York Sun* observed, the stories were popular with girls, but they amused adults even more, which was true of all the May Iverson novels. Most notable was the review in Chicago's *Inter-Ocean*: "The creator of May Iverson ranks with the highest among modern humorists, and with true humorists of all time." The *Louisville Courier-Journal* captured the sense of readers and critics alike: "Nothing less than real genius could enable Miss Jordan to convey so delicately and subtly the psychological quality of a young girl's nature."[16]

Although Jordan had stated that *May Iverson Tackles Life* would be the last book centered on the beloved convent student, public demand was more than either Jordan or her publishers at Harper and Brothers expected. She would write one more May Iverson book to meet that demand, but she was forming another Plan for her future and still wished to move on from the schoolgirl character.

Soon the spring months had passed, and Jordan was ready for another trip to Europe. Traveling was her passion and offered untold adventures. One year she and Harriet met a couple on board their ship who were from New York, Katherine and William D. Barbour. They hit it off so well on the crossing that the four of them traveled together the entire summer, including to two bullfights. The first was in La Línea de la Concepción, and Jordan nervously watched, but since no horses were employed in the fights, she managed to get through the event. As an avid horse rider, she could not endure the fear that they might be gored. Later in Seville, however, the royal family was in attendance and horses were used. As she noted, "I left the scene of diversion with such haste that I may have stepped firmly on the feet of most of the grandees of Spain."[17] In spite of such moments, travel was always a refreshing reprieve for all the roommates.

When she returned to New York and the fall set in, Jordan was approached by a playwright who wanted to dramatize the May Iverson stories. Jordan refused. She had learned firsthand how radically a play could be rewritten—and, to her mind, trivialized—as it toured the country in tryouts. Even if she undertook to create the May Iverson stories into a play herself, there was no guarantee that the love and respect she had for convent life would not be altered into a version that would appall her.[18]

She turned her attention instead to the *Bazar*, but a distinct diminution of her interest became apparent at this time. The editorial comments section was reduced to a single page, and by the end of the year it was gone altogether. Jordan was clearly coming to the end of her years as editor.

It was an exciting era in which to think of new directions personally and collectively. This year the Heterodoxy Club was founded, which declared itself an organization for "unruly and individualistic females" and would be a central site of twentieth-century feminism and women's rights. Located in Greenwich Village, the group dedicated its meetings to rigorous debates and celebrated differences of opinion. Heterodoxy brought a wide range of speakers to its members—birth control advocate Margaret Sanger, anarchist and activist Emma Goldman, and Edith Ellis, a lesbian who maintained an open marriage with the sexologist Havelock Ellis.

Jordan attended Heterodoxy Club meetings whenever possible. Many friends were also members, and over the years she met a number of women there who would become good friends. Several also became colleagues in literary or suffrage projects, including journalist and activist Mary Heaton Vorse, playwright Susan Glaspell, radical activist and author Charlotte Perkins Gilman, and feminist poet and activist Alice Duer Miller.[19] The women of the club brought new ideas to Jordan's life and helped fuel her desire for change.

By January 1913, Jordan had her new Plan in place, and she began to transition out as editor of *Harper's Bazar*. At the same time, she was working closely with William Brady to bring her play to New York. As a prelude, the *Buffalo Inquirer* published an article about her playwriting practices. She admitted that the first and second acts had come easily to her, which gave her the incredible idea that playwriting was quite easy. As she began the third act, she was chastened and learned the challenges of creating a full-length play. But it was when she had finished the play that life became truly difficult:

> *Managers, stars and kind friends began to advise me. A famous critic told me I had a play that would thunder down the ages if I would rewrite the fourth act. A mighty star said glory awaited anyone who played the second, third and fourth acts, but he suggested rewriting the first act. A great manager said the fourth act was a polished gem, to which it would be a crime to apply the chamois of criticism; but he pointed out a vital weakness in the second act. Another star said the first act as it was would be the hit of the play, and that my only problem was how to make my other acts "top" anything begun at such a lofty elevation. He suggested a radical change in the third act. I made it. For a time I made every change anyone suggested. I thought they all knew more than I did. Deep in my heart I believed they couldn't know less.*[20]

By March, *The Lady from Oklahoma* was ready for its New York debut, but, to Jordan's dismay, her four-act play had become a three-act "drammer" (a drunken mess), and she let it be known publicly before the first production opened what she thought of the changes the "great production mill of theatrical enterprises" had made.[21]

The Lady from Oklahoma opened at the 48th Street Theater in New York on April 2, 1913.[22] It ran for thirteen days, receiving mixed reviews. As with most of its out-of-town experiences, the opening night was a smashing success and then ticket sales quickly diminished. The *New York Times*' mixed assessment was representative—they faulted the topic of the "brown sparrow" woman who turns into "a bird of brilliant plumage" as hardly new, and they criticized the direction as well as noting that Jessie Bonstelle, the new leading lady, overacted and was overshadowed by some of the secondary actors. Despite these shortcomings, they agreed the play "has the interest which comes from cleverness of observation and a sense of humor on the part of its author." The most enthusiastic review came from Acton Davies of the *Sun*, who declared the play "gave the audience some of the best laughs of the season."[23]

The sting of the experience lasted a very long time. Years later, in her autobiography, Jordan recalled the joy of the successful opening night in New York—one "would have received the impression that the play was one of the hits of its day." She gave a speech on opening night, "one of the things that my theatrical associates agreed that I could do." She rewrote scenes in between performances, but, in each instance, "After the tumult and shouting of those first nights [in Baltimore, Chicago, and New York] had died down public interest also died. In the end the beauty-parlor act was put on separately and ran eighteen months as a 'big time' feature of the Keith vaudeville circuit. I received a flat payment of sixty dollars a week during that run, which cheered me a little. . . . But I was fed up. No one was asking me to change my short stories or novels and write them over. Wearily and gratefully I returned to my own last."[24]

The one real and lasting benefit of the experience was the many theater people she met and befriended along the way—other playwrights as well as actors, theater managers, and producers. She had loved the theater since she was a young girl, and she would continue to have connections not only through friends and as an avid theatergoer but also, in a few years, as a theater critic herself.

Jordan's thirteen-year editorship of *Harper's Bazar* ended on May 1, 1913. From the public's perspective, this was Jordan's choice, but in letters to her friend Katrina Trask, Jordan revealed that the change in editorship was more complicated and explained why her interest had been waning: Harper and Brothers had been in negotiations to sell the magazine to William Randolph Hearst. In reality—and in spite of the significant increase in advertising she brought to the magazine—the *Bazar* had been losing money for some time.[25] Jordan's frustration about the reasons for the loss boiled over years later in her autobiography: "The *Bazar* could have carried all its manufacturing and editorial expenses and rental and shown a reasonable profit. It could not carry in addition, without going in the red, a full quarter of the great Harper overhead . . . when the *Bazar* reached the point where the more circulation it had the more money it lost, the situation seemed hopeless. Colonel Harvey sold it to William Randolph Hearst."[26]

Meanwhile, Harper and Brothers had another role in mind for Jordan, one that appealed to her because it put her entire focus on literature—the position of literary adviser for Harper's publishing arm. The position required her to find the best authors for book publication with the firm. It was work she would come to love and at which she would excel, holding the position until 1918.

She took no break between leaving the *Bazar* and starting at Harper's. She immediately contacted authors whom she wanted to bring on board. One of the first she approached was Eleanor H. Porter; she had tried earlier to connect Porter and Harper's for a book that Jordan thought had excellent potential—*Pollyanna*—but that book went to L. C. Page and Company. Porter responded this time that she was committed to Page for the sequel. Undismayed, Jordan would soon bring an impressive array of new authors to the company.

In the early summer of 1913, Jordan and Harriet Prescott crossed the Atlantic to Europe, heading for the seaport of Trieste in Italy. What seemed like her usual summer venture turned out to be unforgettable in several ways. Aboard the ship, the roommates met a couple who were so remarkable that Jordan would soon write a highly successful, comedic story about them: "The Crosby's Rest Cure." On this trip she also met the Marchioness Caroline Lagergren, whom she found "charming and magnetic" and with whom she corresponded for several years.[27]

The most notable experience of this trip, however, was renewing her acquaintance with fellow passenger Frances Hodgson Burnett. It quickly became a far more significant relationship than either woman could have expected. They had met briefly years earlier and exchanged business letters, but the intimacy of shipboard life led to each becoming the most enduring love of their lives. The ship took the southern route, which meant it was a longer, twelve-day journey that gave them hours on board to talk as they sat in deck chairs and, after dinner, when Jordan slipped into Frances's cabin under the pretext of smoking cigarettes.[28]

Snapshot of Frances Hodgson Burnett

THREE ROUSING CHEERS

The ship stopped at a number of places, including Palermo and Naples, and Frances joined Jordan and Harriet for many of the shore excursions. In these days, their friendship developed into an intimacy that would last until Burnett's death eleven years later. Jordan was forty-eight and Burnett sixty-six, but the age disparity made no difference. Nothing mattered but that they were together for the rest of their lives. What first drew Jordan to Frances was her "marvelous sense of humor," a trait they shared that would sustain them through any difficulties in the coming years.[29]

When they landed in Trieste, Jordan and Frances had to part. "Fluffy"—as Burnett was known in her family, a nickname she had encouraged Jordan to use—was in poor health and had scheduled a medical treatment in Trieste, while Elizabeth and Harriet went on as planned to Vienna and Budapest. They agreed to meet when both returned to New York, and they began writing to one another soon after they parted. After these days on board the ship with Burnett, everything about Jordan's subsequent travel seemed lit with beauty: "I remember especially the nights in Vienna, when we dined under the trees in the parks, listening to famous regimental bands and looking at hundreds of handsome officers."[30] The light that Frances brought to Jordan's life would burn throughout their time together.

When they returned to New York, Jordan's last May Iverson novel, *May Iverson's Career*, began serialization in the November issue of *Good Housekeeping*. This was a notable break with Harper's publishers, which had serialized the stories for her earlier Iverson collections. *Good Housekeeping* offered her a much higher price for the series; she accepted it not only for the financial benefits but also to post notice with Harper's that she was a sought-after author now. Harper's did not fail to receive the message. They quickly negotiated with good terms for her subsequent books for several years to come.

Chapter 16

Harper's Publishing

Taking over the position of literary adviser at Harper and Brothers was not a difficult transition in terms of the work itself. As editor of *Harper's Bazar*, Jordan had long been working with the book publishing segment of the firm to bring them novels serialized in the magazine, and she had often helped lure writers whom Harper's wanted to add to their authors' list even if they weren't associated with her magazine. This was a position in which she already had considerable experience and she excelled.

Jordan had been following the work of one author in particular whose short stories interested her—the young Sinclair Lewis. Jordan's friend Gertrude Atherton was back in New York City and, on the third Sunday of every month, hosted a gathering for authors and artists. Atherton recalled Jordan asking whether she might bring "a young author, in whom she was interested, to one of these Sundays. She had great faith in his talent and went so far as to predict that he would make a reputation for himself in American letters."[1] The young author was Lewis, and this gesture was typical of Jordan's mentorship of authors—making sure they were introduced to the famous and about-to-be-famous so they could quickly build their own community among writers.

Jordan intended to make the novel Lewis was currently writing her first big push as literary adviser. She worked closely with him, editing his sometimes-rambling manuscript and bringing to fruition the publication of *Our Mr. Wrenn* during her first year with Harper and Brothers

Sinclair Lewis
LIBRARY OF CONGRESS

Publishing. A strong, enduring friendship formed between editor and author, and Lewis recorded his admiration of Jordan on the flyleaf of the copy of the novel he presented to her: "To Elizabeth Jordan, who accepted the Ms. of *Our Mr. Wrenn*, suggested changes that were not just 'editorial suggestions' but inspiring and creative finishing touches, and always by her kindliness and good-fellowship and trained knowledge, by hours in the office and on the roof that overlooks all the city, enabled me to make a book of this. Sinclair Lewis." A note was added: "And with affectionate greetings from the girl to whom it is dedicated." The "girl" was Lewis's wife, Grace Hegger Lewis, an editor at *Vogue* magazine whom he had married shortly before the novel was published. The rooftop that Jordan and Lewis often used for their editing sessions was that of her Gramercy Park apartment building.[2] She became to Lewis and many other authors what Maxwell Perkins was to Ernest Hemingway and F. Scott Fitzgerald.

Jordan quickly earned a reputation as an excellent editor for novelists. The position required working with an extraordinary range of authors and their sometimes fragile egos—Josephine Daskam Bacon was funny and often used humor to elide the fact that she was not going to meet her deadlines; Gertrude Atherton was intense but productive; and Mary Austin was talented but volatile—nevertheless, Jordan managed to draw the best work from them and remain on friendly terms, in large part because she understood the creative process firsthand. Challenging as it could be, Jordan loved this new life, and she was deeply moved by the authors' appreciation of her editorial contributions.

At this time, Jordan's status as a writer and editor warranted membership in two exclusive women's residential clubs—the Colony Club and the Cosmopolitan Club.[3] In the spring of 1903, the New York Women's Colony Club had been founded by a group of wealthy socialites who summered together at Newport and wanted a fashionable place to stay when in New York City for a few days.[4] While the club was initially intended as a place only for people of their class, they soon invited women of prominence in the professions to join, including Jordan.

At the Colony Club, Jordan became closely associated with the suffragists and activists who were members. The club became known for the debates they sponsored about controversial issues confronting American society at this time, including the right of women to vote.[5] Jordan frequented the club, often holding meetings and luncheons in its luxurious facilities.

In part, the time for her own writing career and the socializing that was a central component of her professional life was due to the tough negotiations she had entered into with Harper's before agreeing to join the literary department. Tired of having to find time on weekends, evenings, and holidays for her own writing, she negotiated a contract that allowed her to work in the office Mondays through Wednesdays and to be able to focus on her own work Thursday through the weekend. She was making "many times as much as I received from Harper's for a working week of six days" at the *Bazar*,[6] and she made excellent use of her time.

In addition to Sinclair Lewis, one of the authors Jordan sought for Harper's was Frances Hodgson Burnett. She contracted to publish Burnett's next two novels—the children's tale *The Way to the House of Santa Claus* and a novelistic reflection of Burnett's beliefs about the afterlife, *The White People*. When Jordan first read the manuscript of the latter, she found it "beautiful and mysterious."[7] Burnett had a home in the village of Plandome on Long Island, where she lived with her widowed sister, Edith Jordan (no relation to Elizabeth), Burnett's youngest son Vivian, and Edith's two sons from her first marriage, Archer and Ernest Fahnestock. Soon Jordan was welcomed warmly into the family.

In these early years of their relationship, Burnett always referred to Jordan as "Beloved Elizabeth" or "Darling Elizabeth" and sent her passionate notes such as "my precious dear . . . I want you so. You will comfort me again with life. . . . All my love goes to you, Queen Elizabeth."[8] When Elizabeth spent the weekend, they followed a comfortable routine—Friday night was spent with the family and other houseguests, but what Jordan loved was that "Saturday morning was always sacred to literature. We breakfasted together in Fluffy's room, she in bed, I stretched out on a chaise-lounge beside the bed, very comfortable in pajamas and with a light robe over me." Then Frances would read her latest manuscript to Elizabeth, which often took until lunchtime. "We loved those hours equally well," Jordan said. "I was like a happy child listening to bed-time stories, and Fluffy was like an equally happy child weaving tales for an engrossed and appreciative playmate."[9] Jordan was proud that her beloved Frances read every book aloud to her as she wrote it. Theirs was both a personal affair and a literary one.[10]

In addition to bringing Lewis and Burnett to Harper's, Jordan convinced Gertrude Atherton she should write a history of California. Atherton had been planning to travel to Europe but had been delayed in New York. She had not been in the city for a week before "my old friend Elizabeth Jordan . . . approached me with a demand for a history of California in one volume. The great Panama-Pacific Exposition was to be held in San Francisco during the following year, and as all histories of the State were in large and bulky tomes, the Harpers were convinced that the thousands visiting the Exposition would welcome a bird's-eye view of California in a volume of convenient size."[11]

Atherton refused at first, wanting to leave for Europe, but Jordan was "pertinacious" and the idea began to appeal to Atherton, especially since the history, "as the canny Miss Jordan pointed out, was my opportunity to obtain a nation-wide public."[12] Atherton settled into an apartment near Columbia University so she could use its library. She set about writing her state history—and thereby managed to avoid being in Europe when war broke out.

At this time, Jordan was associated with another person who deeply impacted her life: Rev. Dr. Anna Howard Shaw, one of the first women ordained in the Methodist church, a physician, and a powerful leader among suffragists. At sixty-seven, Shaw was president of the National American Woman Suffrage Association (NAWSA) and came to New York in February 1914 for a suffrage meeting that Jordan and 1,500 other suffragists attended.

Jordan had long admired Shaw, who, like herself, combined progressive thinking with religious devotion. Jordan was part of a committee of the suffrage organization that had arranged a tea and dramatic fête in Shaw's honor, with actresses giving short performances.[13] On her way to the event, however, Shaw fell and suffered a compound fracture of her right leg. She had to be taken back to her rooms at the Hotel McAlpin. Friends and admirers came by day after day to offer assistance or simply to commiserate.[14] But Elizabeth Jordan saw another opportunity in the fateful accident.

For years, Jordan had been encouraging Shaw to write her autobiography, but Shaw professed she could not find the time with all her suffrage activities and her ministry. Jordan suggested that this moment of inactivity was the perfect time to jump into the project. At first, Shaw remained unsure, but then Sonja Levien, assistant editor of the *Metropolitan Magazine*, had the same idea as Jordan and approached Shaw, who referred her to Jordan. Together, they devised a plan—Shaw would relate her life story to Jordan, who would write it, and Levien would serialize the book in the *Metropolitan*. Shaw liked the idea, and Jordan agreed, with the stipulation that Harper and Brothers would publish it in book form after the serialization.[15] "That was," Jordan noted, "the beginning of one of the most interesting episodes of my life."[16] It was a collaborative effort far more enjoyable than had been her experience with *The Whole Family*.

She and Shaw quickly established a working routine: Jordan arrived at the hotel every morning at nine, accompanied by her secretary, Charlotte Lambrecht. From nine o'clock until lunchtime, Shaw related the story of her life while Lambrecht took it down in shorthand. Jordan's role at this stage was to draw out the details of Shaw's life; it took a while for Shaw to feel comfortable talking about herself, and she did so in bits and pieces, so Jordan's job was to organize Shaw's anecdotal memories into some kind of comprehensive narrative.

When Shaw had recovered and Jordan began writing the auto/biography, Shaw came to the Gramercy Park apartment when each chapter had been drafted. Their routine was to dine and then shut themselves in Jordan's study, where she read the chapter aloud to Shaw. Though it seemed too good to be true, Shaw asked for no revisions. She was enthusiastic about the final project, as was the editor of the *Metropolitan* when the chapters began to appear.[17] The book form was published the following January as *The Story of a Pioneer* "by Anna Howard Shaw, D.D., M.D., with the collaboration of Elizabeth Jordan." It remained the standard life of Shaw for nearly a century.

The reviews were excellent, none more so than that which appeared in the *New York Times*: "American literature has been enriched and the chronicles of human effort and aspiration adorned by many books written by Americans. . . . But not one of them has told a tale more remarkable than does Dr. Shaw."[18] Jordan received little recognition as the ghostwriter of the project, but she was delighted with the results. Shaw, however, knew the extent of Jordan's contributions. She sent Jordan an inscribed copy of their book: "I hope I may see you in New York sometime next month and tell you how much like a thief I feel getting so much credit for your book."[19] The enthusiasm Jordan felt in working with a suffragist she admired encouraged her to rethink literary collaboration.

The 1910s saw the film industry move from a novelty to a multimillion-dollar industry. The impact of film on popular culture was immense—shaping fashion, public opinion, cultural attitudes—and movies became a major competitor of live theater.[20] Jordan was about to jump into this new field in multiple ways.

In April 1914, she published "The Crosby's Rest Cure," a satire based on the couple she had met the previous summer. It struck a note of recognition for all ocean travelers and was immensely popular with that crowd. William Dean Howells penned a note of appreciation to Jordan, exclaiming the story was so aptly rendered—"cruelly, killingly true, and perfectly done. Do some more—you can't do too many more—like it!"[21]

Many of the people Jordan had met in the theater industry were now moving into film, and the story struck the comedy team of Lucile McVey Drew and Sidney Drew as a perfect vehicle for their talents. They worked with Jordan, who was credited on the project with writing the scenario, and two years later the film, under the same title as the story, was produced for Metro Pictures Corporation.[22]

Writing, acting, film—these aspects of modern life fascinated Jordan, and she often combined them with her abiding commitment to the suffrage movement. She was not in the financial class of the Newport and Manhattan millionaires who had joined the suffrage movement, the "gilded suffragists," but many of them were her associates in the cause. She had covered their activities in the pages of the *Bazar* and worked with them on the Empire State Campaign Committee and in the New York State Woman Suffrage Party. She belonged to the luxurious Colony Club founded by society suffragists, and her acquaintance with so many foreign dignitaries and duchesses and baronesses drew this group of suffragists to her as well.

Thus, she was invited to join in a new form of demonstrating interest in the suffrage movement. There had been many tea parties used as vehicles to promote suffrage—afternoon teas, dancing teas—and now Jordan joined in a new form: the motion picture tea. Many film actresses supported the suffrage movement, and they came together in New York in May 1914 to promote both suffrage and the film industry. The host was Norma Phillips, who had found success that year in *Our Mutual Girl*, unique one-reel episodes that ran in theaters each week.

With the use of a new Edison home moving-picture machine, the suffragists viewed D. W. Griffiths's *The Escape*, a rather odd choice for a tea since it had a horrific plot promoting eugenics (which Jordan did not support). At any rate, in addition to Jordan, suffrage-supporting guests included newspaper columnist Dorothy Dix; Belle da Costa Green, librarian to the late J. P. Morgan; playwright Helen Arthur; poet Zoe Atkins; arts patron Mabel Dodge (Luhan); and Henrietta Rodman, president of the Feminist Alliance. The *New York Times* covered the luncheon in detail, offering it as a model for "motion picture teas" that could be conducted by suffrage supporters around the country.[23]

In spite of these enjoyable events, everyone in the country was aware that war loomed near. Although friends cautioned Jordan against taking her annual summer trip to Europe, she insisted on continuing her travel tradition, and her roommate Harriet joined her on board the *Hellig Olaf* in July 1914. In these years, Jordan had developed a code to celebrate successes and offer a "buck up" means of support in hard times: "Three Rousing Cheers!" Originally, only she, Frances, and Maud and Otis Skinner used the term. Later her roommates, Alma and George Harvey, Arthur Brisbane, Frederick Duneka, and Mark Twain joined in using it.[24] She was going to need to "buck up" sooner than she imagined.

Jordan had tried to convince Frances to join her and Harriet on this trip, but Frances did not feel up to such travel and spent six weeks resting at her beloved Bermuda estate instead.[25] The day before Elizabeth and Harriet were to leave, Frances frantically tried to telephone Elizabeth to discourage her from going. News of impending war in Europe was everywhere. Unable to reach her by phone, Frances sent a note saying she was sure Jordan should cancel her plans and signing it "Yours in some anxiety."[26]

But Jordan ignored Frances's pleas, believing war would not emerge for some time yet, and she and Harriet set sail. They had a lovely summer planned, stopping first in Kristiansand, Norway, before traveling to Sweden to visit Caroline Lagergren, and then they would be off on their first visit to Russia. In most years, no one would have given a thought to the fact that they were sailing on a Norwegian liner, but in this unusual moment, it mattered a great deal. Although Norway would declare neutrality in the war, nearly half the country's merchant ships were destroyed in subsequent years.

Normally, because international travel had become routine for them, Jordan, Harriet, and Martha did little planning ahead of time—once Elizabeth and Martha decided overnight to leave the next morning and off they went—but because Russia was new to them, Elizabeth and Harriet had planned ahead and had a letter of credit for more money than they usually considered for such travel. Jordan also carried one hundred dollars in gold, at the insistence of her friend, journalist and banking expert Charles Conant, who thought it might be necessary if war broke out.[27]

And indeed it did. On July 28, while they were still at sea, war was declared in Europe. Although the United States would not join the battle for several years, it left the passengers of the *Hellig Olaf* in a precarious position.

All went well until they were about a day out from the Norway harbor. Their ship was stopped by the *Blondin*, a British torpedo-boat destroyer whose crew came on board to examine the ship's papers and to be sure it was not carrying supplies for Germany. "For an hour on Aug. 8," Jordan noted, dramatically, "I was virtually a prisoner of war on the wind-swept, foggy North Sea." Their ship was loaded with wheat, corn, and machinery—"a valuable cargo in war time." After the inspection, their ship was allowed to proceed and expected to sight land by midday, but fog set in. Then, through the thick mist, Jordan and the other passengers began to see "a sail. Then another and another emerged from the foggy horizon and we discovered that they were torpedo boats, eleven in number, and were heading directly toward us." Once the ship's captain informed the torpedo boats' commander who they were and where they were bound, they were allowed to proceed.[28]

The passengers did not know at the time what Jordan later learned—that

> *after allowing us to proceed on our way the commanding officer [of the torpedo boats] sent a wireless message to a flotilla patrolling the North Sea and suggested that he look over our ship's papers to be sure no mistake had been made in passing us upon signals. . . . Soon from the west emerged a torpedo destroyer steaming directly toward us. When a hundred yards off our starboard bow, we were ordered to stop the engine and heave to. Needless to say, the order was obeyed.*

After the ship's papers were again deemed acceptable, they were at last allowed to proceed. It was hardly a propitious beginning for their summer holiday.

When the ship put in at Kristiansand, the travelers found the city in a state of panic, fearing they would be at war any moment. It was impossible for Jordan and Harriet to return home immediately, as "all the fiords had been mined," Jordan learned. "The few trains still running were operating without lights. Russian and German war planes passed above Norway in flocks."[29]

They headed to their hotel as they tried to figure out how they could return to the States. When they reached the Grand Hotel, their American Express checks, bank notes, and letters of credit were all refused. Thanks to Charles Conant's foresight, they had gold, which was acceptable to the proprietor.

After years of travel and hosting international visitors in New York, Jordan had many acquaintances in Europe, but she scrambled to think who she might know in Norway. Then it struck her. Ten years earlier, she had received a letter from a Norwegian journalist, Anna Hvoeslef, who had said she would be visiting New York and hoped to meet Jordan, Gertrude Atherton, Frances Hodgson Burnett, and Fannie Hurst, among others. Jordan had arranged a tea with all the hoped-for guests, and Hvoeslef had been appreciative.

So Jordan contacted the newspaper office where Hvoeslef had worked a decade earlier and, to her great fortune, discovered she was still a journalist there. Hvoeslef came to Jordan's hotel and offered to help in every way she could. Jordan knew how fortunate they were to receive this assistance: "The little bun I had so lightly tossed toward Miss Hvoeslef ten years before now came back to me an entire bakery."[30]

Even with Anna Hvoeslef's help, Elizabeth and Harriet were forced to remain in Norway for more than a fortnight. They tried everything they could think of to find passage home, and influential friends in the States such as Conant and Mary Harrison McKee went to the State Department in an attempt to garner help for them as well. Hvoeslef continued her support, dining with them several times a week, revealing the news that was pouring in to her newspaper office but not always reported to the public, and trying to find some means for them to leave Norway.

When word arrived that the Germans had taken Brussels, fear shook the entire community of people trying to find a way out of Norway. Finally, five weeks after their arrival, the roommates managed to gain passage home on the *Frederick the Eighth*, a Norwegian-American line. Though some people in Norway discouraged them from leaving while war raged, they longed to return home. The ship was severely overcrowded, but they were thankful to be on board. When at last they arrived at the dock in New York, crowds of cheering people awaited the ship's passengers. And there, among them, Jordan spotted "my mother's face in the crowd, as she alternately waved her handkerchief and wiped her eyes."[31] They were home at last.

But on her return, Jordan discovered a country at odds with itself. Vigorous debates emerged among politicians and citizens about whether the United States should join the Allies. Many American businesses had already become involved, through bank loans and sending war supplies. At the same time, people were expected to carry on with their work as usual, but that was easier to expect than to do.

The Red Cross hosted one of the benefits for the war effort in which Jordan participated as one of the patrons. It was held at the Park Theatre in late October to raise funds for the Committee of Mercy, which sought to purchase food and clothing for women and children left destitute by the war.[32] In addition, Jordan wrote letters to personal friends asking for donations.[33] Harriet also hosted a luncheon to support people impacted by the war, which Jordan attended.[34] It was only the beginning of the roommates' efforts to support the victims of war and call for American involvement.

During these tumultuous months, Jordan continued to court authors for Harper's, including hosting luncheons for Margaret Deland and other literary figures as well as theater people such as Maud Skinner, always adding a splash of socialites into the mix. In November, for instance, she held a luncheon at the Plaza for an impressive list of guests: the wealthy hostess Josephine Jewell Dodge; Elizabeth Custer, widow of George Armstrong Custer; Mary Harrison McKee, daughter of the former president; authors Frances Hodgson Burnett and Gertrude Atherton; and several others.

Beyond allowing Jordan to show her appreciation for her wide array of friends and associates, these luncheons made her a significant influencer, since it was customary for guests to exchange cards at these gatherings and thus expand their own range of social contacts. Such events typically came with the reciprocity of other luncheons, dinners, or teas—all of which extended one's influence even further. For instance, after attending this luncheon, Atherton responded by hosting a tea on December 5 in honor of Jordan with a guest list of one hundred.[35] They saw each other at least weekly at this time, but both women understood that these public events were part of their lives as author and editor. The notices of these luncheons appeared in all the major New York newspapers and signaled that the host and honoree were people to be cultivated.

In November 1914, Jordan published her latest—and last—Iverson book, *May Iverson's Career*. Readers and critics alike had long declared they hoped May would never grow up, but Jordan was insistent on bringing May to fruition as a capable young woman, prepared to go out into the world. This volume signaled a true end to the series as May became an adult and launched her career as a journalist. If this novel did not always have the humor of the previous books in the series, it was a stunningly realistic look at women in the field of journalism.

The episodes in this book were more powerful than her earlier look at newspaper life in *Tales of the City Room*. Here were no romantic dramas or stories filled with pathos. In *May Iverson's Career*, Jordan presented an account of what a young convent girl actually faced in going to New York to begin her journalistic career. The characterization of May had always been heavily autobiographical, and the fact that Jordan drew on her own life in this collection was made even more evident by having May's life directly follow her own, including her conflict at graduation about becoming a nun, her father's suggestion that she try newspaper work first, and so on. May had to face a feature editor who was always rough in his language and perpetually angry, and she was assaulted while on assignment, and yet she found the courage to continue her work and become a respected reporter.[36] May was still very much an appealing character, but now she navigated adult worlds and grew into a capable, professional woman.

In spite of challenging the expectations readers had when they picked up a May Iverson book, the novel was a hit with readers and reviewers, though many, including the *New York Times* reviewer, lamented May having grown up. The *San Francisco Chronicle*'s reviewer found the stories to be so full of the "instinct of human nature that they cannot fail to hold the interest of any reader" and concluded that Jordan's writing was appealing because of its "freshness and verve."[37] Of particular note were comments from the reviewer at the *Continent* magazine, who declared that "many of the chapters have enough thrills to form part of a detective yarn," foreshadowing a turn Jordan's fiction would soon take.

Frances told Jordan that she loved the "delicious psychology" of the "In Gay Bohemia" chapter of *May Iverson's Career*. She closed her letter by letting Jordan know she would arrive at the Plaza Hotel in New York that week. A few days later, she sent a note to Jordan: "We must see each other. Is it possible for you to run away to 'dine & sleep' as they say in England."[38]

Elizabeth and Frances had created a unique partnership for themselves. This was no quaint "Boston marriage" of the nineteenth century; it was closer to the relationship of two other authors, Willa Cather and Edith Lewis, who crafted their personal and professional lives together.[39] But Elizabeth and Frances never lived together. When they met and fell in love, neither was willing to alter her well-established lifestyle, and that choice satisfied their needs for most of the years they were together. Only at the end of Frances's life did she long for Elizabeth to live with her.

It was a very modern, loving relationship that offered each woman a great deal of independence. They forged a lifestyle that worked for them. Frances had a houseful of family members in Plandome, and she liked having them gathered around her. She did not mind visiting New York City, but she did not want to live there. Elizabeth had her roommates and her mother living with her in the city, and throughout her life she refused to jeopardize that family life in any way. Elizabeth frequently visited Frances and her family in Plandome for weekends, they met in hotels when Frances came to New York, and Frances would soon rent an apartment in the city, which would allow them to meet more frequently.

In addition, Frances had been spending summers in Bermuda since 1910, and Elizabeth began joining her there for several weeks in the summer—but she would not give up her European travel, which Frances's health no longer allowed her to do. In addition, Jordan would soon begin spending part of her summers at Martha Cutler's family home in Florence, Massachusetts. Burnett and Jordan were happy in their independent love affair.

In the interim, they kept in intimate contact by phoning one another frequently and sending notes every few days. Frances's note of December 1, 1914, from Plandome was typical:

> *I wish you were here this afternoon, my dear. It is a trifle melancholy but most beautiful because I've set in the midst of a cloud of mist—& from far away comes the periodic booming blast of the fog horns over the rock on the Sound. . . . I do want to come & have that delightful play day with you on Saturday but my Limousine will not return from its beauty parlor until Monday. And when I come I want you*

> *to drive home with me after our last debauch. Shall we wait until the Saturday after next—far away as that appears to me!*[40]

It was a lifestyle that perfectly fit two busy professional women who loved one another but also loved the lives they had crafted for themselves.

The following year, as their love deepened, Jordan suggested they have a name exclusively for one another that would be private to them. Jordan was used to people using all kinds of affectionate names for her, and Frances's family had nicknamed her "Fluffy," so Jordan settled on "Querida," and Frances loved the idea.[41] In her autobiography, Jordan defines the word as meaning "dearest," but she had been taught Spanish by her grandmother, and she well knew the multiple meanings of the word—dear, sweetheart, lover, inamorata—and Jordan clearly desired the multitudinous quality of the endearment. They signed all their letters with this term for the rest of their lives together.

Chapter 17

A Second Composite Novel

JANUARY 1915 BROUGHT A RENEWED EXCITEMENT AROUND THE PROSpects for women to gain the right to vote. The previous year, women in eleven Western states and territories had gained voting rights for state and local elections, which invigorated the movement. The publication in January of Jordan's collaborative auto/biography of Anna Howard Shaw came at the perfect moment, encouraging other women to fight for equality and marking an important contribution to the cause by Shaw and Jordan.

At the same time, Jordan was continuing to support Sinclair Lewis's career. She worked closely with him as he penned his second novel, *The Trail of the Hawk*, which would be published later in the year. His first novel had required considerable editing by Jordan, but he learned his craft quickly and the second novel was much more carefully developed. In addition to the many writers whose careers she advanced while at the *World* and *Harper's Bazar*, as a literary editor she aided not only Lewis's career but also those of Zona Gale, Eleanor H. Porter, Dorothy Canfield Fisher, and numerous others.

Jordan's own writing career was flourishing as well. In addition to the publication of the most recent May Iverson novel, she continued to publish short stories in a variety of literary magazines and newspapers; this past year saw her work in *Harper's Magazine*, *Ladies' Home Journal*, *Pearson's*, *Harper's Bazar*, *McBride's*, *Good Housekeeping*, and *Every Week*. Most of these were standalone stories, but a few were planned as part of her next collection of short stories, *Lovers' Knots*.

The year had started well and everything seemed to be on track for the Plan she always had for advancing her career, but then she received a telephone call from her longtime friend Charles Conant. He informed her that he had just disembarked from his steamer, having returned to the States from Cuba to consult his physician, and he wished to see her. She was giving a dinner party at the Colony Club that evening in honor of the Baroness de Seidlitz of St. Petersburg. The baroness, lady-in-waiting to the czarina, was in New York and had a letter of introduction to Jordan from Maurice Francis Egan, American minister to Denmark, and Jordan could not cancel the engagement at such a late hour. Instead, she invited Conant to join the party at the Colony Club, assuring him they could talk afterward.

A little after eleven, when the party broke up, she and Charles found secluded seats in the club lounge and she immediately asked him about his health. To her shock, he told her that he had stomach cancer and his physician had informed him he had only six months to live. She insisted he should see specialists, but he had already done so, all with the same result. After an hour of talking together, he walked her home and they parted at the door.

As soon as she was inside her apartment, she felt she had not said all that was in her heart at the moment, so she sat down and wrote a long letter to Conant. He replied the following day, "It is worth being ill to get that letter from you this morning!" But their parting at the door was the last time Jordan would see Conant. He decided to return to Cuba, in spite of his diagnosis, and died there on July 15.[1]

Jordan would be fifty years old this year, and her subsequent decades would be marked by the loss of many of her dear friends. The death of Conant was hard enough, but few would be as sorrowful as the unexpected passing of her beloved friend Jack à Becket. It had started out as a lovely day. She spent the morning with Josephine Daskam Bacon and her daughter Deborah, Jordan's goddaughter. To celebrate Deborah's birthday, they spent hours at the Bronx Zoo and then lunched at Delmonico's, concluding the meal with ice cream and a birthday cake.

It was nearly two o'clock when Jordan returned to her office, only to find a number of urgent messages awaiting her and indicating she must go to the hotel where Jack was staying. When she arrived, a number of his friends were already present, preparing to take him to the undertaker. He had died before she arrived, but no one could bear to send him away. As Jordan related,

> *As my apartment was the nearest approach to a home that Jack had ever known, I had him sent there and went back, stunned and dazed, to get ready for him. . . . When my friend had been placed in the coffin the men left. There was nothing for me to do now but to light the candles at his head and feet. . . . I was alone—I had insisted that my family should leave me alone—and I was in a nightmare. All this simply could not be happening.*

She arranged for a Requiem Mass for Jack at St. Francis Xavier's Church and for his burial in a Catholic cemetery on Long Island. She was heartbroken. Harriet and Martha did all they could to help her when she returned home,[2] but the playboy she had dearly loved was gone.

Work and her faith were, as always, her salvation from despair. She had a special project underway that helped her through her loss. *Puck* was a highly successful humor magazine, and suffragists had found that humor, especially satire, could be a very effective means of conveying their ideas. The magazine agreed to support a special issue on women's suffrage. It was sponsored by a number of suffrage groups, including the Empire State Campaign Committee and the New York State Woman Suffrage Association. Jordan agreed to serve on the editorial board for the special issue along with some of the leading lights of New York suffrage: Carrie Chapman Catt, Anne O'Hagan Shinn, Vira Boarman Whitehouse, Margaret Ayer Cobb, and Alice Duer Miller.

Several male suffrage supporters served on a Board of Honorary Editors for the special issue. Among these supporters was Jordan's longtime friend Arthur Brisbane, editor of several Hearst newspapers; Norman Hapgood, editor of *Harper's Weekly*; and Frank Munsey, publisher of *Munsey's Magazine*. With such advocates, the issue received wide notice before publication.

Each board member contacted friends in the movement, seeking their contributions, and they gathered a wide array of suffragists for the cause that read like a roster of Jordan's friends: Gertrude Atherton; the author and playwright Ethel Watts Mumford; the *New York World* journalist Nixola Greeley-Smith; illustrator Rose O'Neill; and author Mary Austin. The Men's League of the National Woman Suffrage Association was also one of the sponsors, and a comparable group of men who were Jordan's friends also contributed, including Charles Hanson Towne of the *Smart Set*, author Hamlin Garland, newspaper columnist George Ade, and music critic James Huneker.

This was just one of many ways in which Jordan supported suffrage in these months, and a new and exciting venture in relation to the cause would soon arise.

On May 7, 1915, the *Lusitania* was torpedoed by a German U-boat, killing over a thousand passengers, including 128 Americans. Among them was a friend of Jordan's, the powerful theater producer Charles Frohman. She and Maud Skinner attended his funeral together. The deaths of so many on board brought the horrors of war home, even to isolated Americans: "New York life was a nightmare," Jordan noted. "One could hardly endure the tension of it."[3]

Impact from the war was inescapable, and in the summer, Jordan began to look for some place to escape, since travel to Europe would be impossible this year. She finally decided to return to a camp in Maine she had visited several years earlier. Her mother joined her, and they spent six weeks in the countryside, which helped ease the tension of the summer heat and the war—until she went out for a pleasant afternoon of boating in August with three other friends. All seemed well until suddenly their boat capsized and Jordan felt herself go down deep into the water. Nearby boaters rushed to their rescue and saved them all from drowning.[4] Newspapers published accounts of Jordan's narrow escape the following day.

Frances was motoring in the Berkshires when she heard Jordan had nearly drowned. Frantic with worry, she sent a letter to Elizabeth:

> *Edith has just had a letter from Archie in which he tells her that you have just escaped death from drowning! God be thanked that the word is "escaped"! My dear, my dear! One cannot even look the other way. Archie says that your poor mother was watching you from the bank. If she has suffered no bad results from the shock then surely you can comfort yourself with the thought that her heart is not as weak as the doctor has thought. Because you are the perfection of health & strength you have probably recovered without results at all. I am believing that because I will not believe anything else. . . . I want to see you very much—to make sure you're safe. I will come as soon as possible after you reach Gramercy Park.*[5]

Jordan received a letter from Sinclair Lewis after the accident as well: "Dear Elizabeth, I've just learned how narrow an escape from drowning you had and I hasten to send you Grace's and my—what is it one extends to a person yanked out of the jaws of death, congratulations or condolences? I fancy you must know how much it would mean to us both in a personal way and as regards my association with Harper's, had you gone. The narrowness of your escape accentuates that."[6]

Lewis's *The Trail of the Hawk* had just been published, and he promised to have a signed copy waiting for her on her return to New York. The inscription he penned on the title page read, "To Elizabeth Jordan, friend and boss, discoverer and maker of *Hawk* as she was of *Our Mr. Wrenn*, with more gratitude than can be expressed on this one small page."[7] While Lewis felt her input had been significant, Jordan insisted years later that she had offered very little to this novel. "No revision was necessary [this] time," she asserted several years later. "On every page of it a young genius had laid bare his heart and soul. Of all the books Sinclair Lewis has written, I still like that one best."[8]

The reference to Harper's in his letter, however, reflected Lewis's yearning for freedom to negotiate with other publishers. Jordan knew that as his fame grew, they would be unable to retain him as a member of the Harper family. Being able to negotiate among publishers would bring him much greater payments for his novels, but, as he told Alfred Harcourt not long after the boating incident, he loathed the idea of leaving Jordan as his editor.[9] Sinclair published two more books with Harper's, and at present Jordan was content in her position as literary adviser and not ready to leave.

Whatever happened in their personal lives, war issues loomed with the greatest intensity for Americans, and its presence was particularly felt in late October when Edith Cavell was executed. A British nurse who helped Allied soldiers escape from Belgium during Germany's occupation, Cavell was captured, charged with treason, and executed, creating an international outcry at the injustice.

The *New York Tribune* devoted three-quarters of a page to responses. Judges, physicians, psychologists, and authors were quoted in the article. Jordan's response placed Cavell's death in the broader contexts of the war when she identified Germany's "three appalling outrages" which also constituted three political blunders: "the invasion of Belgium, the destruction of the Lusitania, and the execution of Edith Cavell." Germany's attempts to justify these indefensible acts, Jordan asserted,

> *has shown to a horrified world the vulnerable spot in her mighty armor—the quality which, great as she is, must lead to her ultimate defeat. No nation which performs and defends such actions can long survive; no such nation can triumph over the civilized peoples of the earth. For Germany is undermining her own social structure as well as the world's; she is tearing away from beneath her the splendid foundation of civilization and high ideals which her own people built. That the many high-minded and heroic Germans should suffer for the blindness and blunders of the few is the real tragedy of the Fatherland.*[10]

Cavell's death haunted Americans, and Jordan would return to the subject in a few years.

In the midst of such international crises, all the demands of Jordan's work life went on. She nudged, cajoled, and encouraged authors to sign their contracts and finish their manuscripts, and she edited them with care for each author's distinct style and intent. Mary Austin continued to take months to decide whether to commit to a book, and even Jordan's beloved Frances Hodgson Burnett became frustrated with the pressures Harper's—and, thereby, Jordan—placed on authors to produce their work in their idea of a timely fashion.

Frances wrote Jordan in frustration in November about being pushed to sign a contract with Harper's for her next book. She complained that "to sign a document on command with a vague unborn thing was superfluous & could not be a comfort & a support to any one." She went further: "I told you almost with tears—my Elizabeth, when you talked to me in your softly nefarious & beguiling manner in the Limousine." Frances stopped, saying she was cross and had tried to telephone and would try again. Then she changed the subject and said she hoped Elizabeth would come for the weekend and that she would come into New York on Saturday to pick her up if she was able to get away, signing off, "Always with love, Querida."[11]

It was Jordan's job to sign authors for their upcoming books as soon as possible so they did not go with another publisher before completing the manuscript. As much as authors sometimes resisted, she had a talent for finishing the deal, and Frances signed the contract the same day that she penned the letter of protest.

In December 1915, Jordan received the honorary "Regent of the League" award from the National American Woman Suffrage Association. The honor was granted for "her valued support and service to the cause of the enfranchisement of women in the United States of America during the campaign of nineteen hundred and fifteen."[12] Such recognition was particularly important this year when the suffragists had finally been able to compel New York State legislators to place on the state's ballot a constitutional amendment to enfranchise women. While the bill did not pass, it gave the movement momentum to push forward in upcoming sessions.

Suffrage was not the only area in which the country saw progress developing rapidly. At mid-decade, New York and the nation were experiencing radical changes on multiple fronts. The Provincetown Players moved from Cape Cod to Greenwich Village, giving Jordan and her friends another theater to attend; Margaret Sanger opened her first birth-control clinic in America; and new and provocative artists such as Georgia O'Keeffe and Man Ray were gaining significant attention.

But other changes were less welcome, particularly the distress suffragists felt when a split developed within the movement regarding whether the United States should join the war. Jane Addams, Carrie Chapman Catt, Zona Gale, and others opposed US involvement and promoted the peace movement. On the other side, Jordan and a good number of suffragists felt the country should have become involved long ago.

Fearing the split would undermine the cause, Jordan and her associates sought a way to demonstrate suffragists' collaboration. They settled on the idea of developing a composite suffrage novel. In her introduction to the book, Jordan said the idea grew out of a New York State Woman Suffrage Association (NYSWSA) committee meeting in the spring of 1916; in fact, it began much earlier. The idea emerged after the defeat of the 1915 New York State suffrage referendum. In response, the novel was suggested as a collaboration among suffragists that would reach a wide audience. Vira Boarman Whitehouse, chair of the NYSWSA's Publicity Council, wrote Jordan about the project in February 1916, "I cannot tell you how delighted I am that you are going to take it in hand and see it through. I almost feel as if the cause is won and I know this great stunt will have a very large share in winning it!"[13]

Whitehouse was an important ally for Jordan. She was one of the gilded suffragists, owner of the Whitehouse Leather Company, a member of the Heterodoxy Club, and a proponent of birth control. The project would not by any means be an easy one, in no small part because of the impact of the war on publishing, but it would prove to be far more enjoyable than *The Whole Family* had been. The Publicity Council decided on

The Sturdy Oak as a title, a play on the concept of men as the "sturdy oak" and women the "clinging vine" in personal and societal relationships,[14] and thanks to Jordan's expertise in publishing, the novel would indeed reach a large audience in spite of many complications along the way.

Jordan began contacting people she thought would be amenable to such a project. The organizers wanted to include male supporters of suffrage as well, feeling that they could be persuasive to their sex. Five of the ultimate fourteen contributors would be men. By March, Jordan had commitments for *The Sturdy Oak* from Frances Hodgson Burnett, Gertrude Atherton, Mary Austin (who contributed the theme of the novel), Alice Duer Miller, and Mary Heaton Vorse. The most radical contributor to *The Sturdy Oak* was Vorse, a journalist who established her reputation by reporting on labor protests, primarily by women and immigrants in the textile industry. When she turned to novel writing, she drew on these experiences for subject matter. The political content of *The Sturdy Oak* that moved beyond suffrage to the dangers of powerful political machines made her a particularly valuable contributor.

With this group of suffragists on board for the project, Jordan was assured of a large and diverse readership. She had expected to contribute a chapter herself, but the project, with its multiple venues, became so time-consuming that she decided eventually to focus on editing and handling the negotiations for publication in periodicals and in book form as her contribution.

In April 1916, Frances was en route to Bermuda when she sent a note asking Jordan to join her. Bermuda was a popular vacation spot for wealthy Americans, but Burnett chose it primarily because of her health. Whenever possible, Jordan joined Frances there for a few weeks in the summer, but with all that she was involved in at present, there was no way she could get away so early in the year. Frances was sixty-seven years old, still actively writing but in increasingly poor health. She was moving toward the end of her career, while Jordan was in her heyday. It was in the coming years that Frances would begin to wish that Jordan would give up her life in New York and live with her, but Jordan would not do that. Her family and her work life were centered in the city. Jordan and Frances's love for one another never wavered, but their lifestyle desires would cause increasing stress as they negotiated when and where to be together.

When Jordan said she could not leave New York yet, Frances replied with disappointment: "This is more than flesh & blood can bear my own dear Elizabeth—But I had a secret feeling that Bermuda in April was too lovely to be true. We should have *loved* it so. You don't *know* how dear it would have been!"[15] Her next letter to Elizabeth was written as Frances's ship approached Bermuda: "It is very lonesome my dear that you are not with us. The repose & beauty of the place would be perfect for you. We have had a wonderful winter together & you have suggested to me the possibility of a better one next year. . . . I only wrote this scrap to repeat—and re-repeat that you *ought* to be with us."[16]

In the meantime, Jordan had sufficient contributors in place for *The Sturdy Oak* that by the end of April she could send notices to newspapers about the project. The *Chicago Tribune* declared it the "Most Novel Thing in Book Form," and suffrage journals such as the *Woman Citizen* widely publicized the forthcoming book.[17] It was imperative that the serial and the book appear in time to influence another suffrage referendum planned for November 1917. This task would take an enormous effort on Jordan's part, and she could not have imagined when she agreed to undertake the project how much her life was going to change in the next year and a half.

After the announcements appeared, Henry Maule, an editor for Doubleday Page & Company, contacted Vira Whitehouse and asked whether they had contracted the novel; if not, he wished to have a first reading because it seemed like something his company would like to undertake. Jordan made a decision at this point that proved injudicious. Instead of accepting Maule's offer, she replied to Whitehouse that it would be better if the novel was published by Harper and Brothers. Whitehouse demurred: "The matter of publishing the book as everything else in connection with it, is entirely in your hands."[18]

Of course, Jordan looked to her own publishing firm first, but, to her dismay, they declined the project. Eventually, she secured another publisher, but it left the publication of the book in a tenuous situation for months.[19] Many magazines and newspapers were facing difficult financial times in the period leading up to the country's engagement in World War I; *Harper's Weekly* was subsumed by the *Independent* this year, so it is possible that the publisher simply could not afford to undertake the project, but it was a disappointment to Jordan to be turned down by her own firm, especially for a project of such importance to her.

As with *The Whole Family*, the plan was that each author would receive the preceding chapters before writing their own. Unlike *The Whole Family*, however, these contributors did not complain about the direction the other authors had taken. They offered suggestions about ways in which the plot might develop, but, as Kathleen Norris noted, "what my predecessors said was an *enormous* help to me." In turn, Jordan was happy with the novel's development, telling Norris she found her chapter to be a "coarker!"[20]

In the midst of the unending publication negotiations surrounding *The Sturdy Oak*, Jordan was bombarded by letters from Frances, who was still unhappy that Jordan had not joined her in Bermuda. Frances pleaded with her to come in May, which was no less impossible for Jordan. Letter after letter from Frances, all signed "Querida," insisted, "You so obviously *ought* to be here. . . . O! Why are you not here? . . . Let us live here forever, Elizabeth. . . . Really Elizabeth I shall drag you to Bermuda with [arms?] of steel if you will not come without resistance." Or a few days later, "Elizabeth dear! Are you coming?" And again, "Why are you not here this brilliant and entrancing morning, my dearest?"[21]

But Jordan had just undertaken several other suffrage projects at this crucial moment in the movement and could not leave for a vacation, as painful as it was to disappoint Frances. Everyone in the cause felt the urgency of making a major push for suffrage in the coming year. While participating in all these activities, Jordan was trying to finish proofs for the publication of her next short story collection, *Lovers' Knots*, and she was still editing novels for publication by Harper and Brothers.

By early June, Jordan was exhausted and decided that she must take a break and have some time with Frances in Bermuda. She spent glorious days in the healing warmth of the island where Frances's summer home was located, returning to New York three weeks later. She worked diligently for the next six weeks before deciding to join Harriet and Martha for a few weeks at Martha's family home, Spreadwings, in Florence, Massachusetts, as an alternative to her usual European vacation. The house had been built in the late 1860s in the Romantic Italianate style and was notable for its two-story screened porch and a cupola on its north side;[22] the porch was added in 1920, so on hot summer nights they could sleep in the screened-in area.

It was the beginning of a ritual that the roommates, Jordan's mother, and Martha's family would make an annual event; Spreadwings became a second home for the New York group. Before long, Jordan would establish a studio in its carriage house, which gave her a place to write away from the activities of the busy household. Among the family's help at this time was Leda Carpentier, a cook, who would soon be more influential in their lives than anyone could have imagined.

Spreadwings
BETSY DEVINE COLLECTION

Jordan had to return to New York at the beginning of September to prepare for a week-long trip to Atlantic City to attend the NAWSA. This emergency gathering of suffragists had been called in response to the Democratic and Republican conventions in June. The suffragists needed to determine the course of action for the coming year, but there was a split among those who wanted to focus on the federal amendment and those who wanted to emphasize state legislation. Carrie Chapman Catt, president, termed the moment "a crisis" for the movement and demanded even greater commitment to the cause.[23]

That sense of urgency pushed the NYSWSA Publicity Council to seek as early publication of *The Sturdy Oak* as possible. By mid-September, however, Jordan still had only six of the *Sturdy Oak* chapters in hand, putting the project well behind where they had hoped to be at this point. She had expected to have chapters from Mary Austin, Zona Gale, and Ernest Thompson Seton, but all had written to say they could not meet their deadlines. Many had taken off for summer vacations, and Gertrude Atherton, who had just returned from Europe, indicated she could not produce anything until fall.

For once Jordan's cajoling had not worked, and she had to report to the committee that the novel would not be ready for publication before late the following spring. Even that date applied only to newspaper serialization; the book version would be pushed to early autumn—nudging very close to the November date for the next suffrage referendum to the New York legislature.

Jordan's next collection of short stories, *Lovers' Knots*, was published in October 1916 and perfectly defined by its subtitle: *The Whimsical Twists and Tangles of a Dozen Youthful Love Affairs*. After the serious nature of *May Iverson's Career* and the Dr. Anna Howard Shaw auto/biography, Jordan returned to humorous stories for which she had received such high accolades in the past. As *Good Housekeeping* noted, she was equally well known for her ability to write unusual love stories, and *Lovers' Knots* brought both talents to the forefront.

But writing "different" stories could lead to mixed reviews. The *New York Times* harshly termed the stories "marshmallow fiction." Other reviewers offered more balanced assessments: "The stories have much originality and ingenuity of conception and the manner of telling is always pleasing and so skillful as to make even the most absurd situations seem plausible." The *Sun*, however, was aligned with the majority, finding the collection entertaining and "contrived ingeniously."[24]

Frances was ill over the holidays, delaying their plans to spend the time together. But she delighted in the gift Jordan sent—a gold knife, which Frances found "far beyond my means & above my station. It is so beautiful that I shall keep it before my eyes on my table forevermore." She in turn sent Jordan an antique silver coin, which she said would assure her "that no evil spell can work between us. . . . Shall we ever meet again. It is so long since last Friday when I first went to bed. Querida."[25] They would indeed be together again soon, but in the last decade of her life, Frances suffered a number of ailments that limited her movements. Nothing, however, could limit their love for one another, which would last until Frances's death—and beyond.

Chapter 18

Golden Apples

The year 1917 brought many changes for the country, not least the emergence of automobiles as part of an increasing number of households. Frances already had made great use of limousine services as a means of visiting Elizabeth in the city, and the growing predominance of the automobile was recognized when the last horse-drawn street car was removed from New York City streets this year. At the same time, moving pictures became even more popular and gave rise to the concept of "stars" such as Mary Pickford and Buster Keaton.[1]

Jordan began her year by preparing a letter that agent Julia Tutwiler could use to approach approximately one hundred newspaper editors in an effort to solicit agreements for the serialization of *The Sturdy Oak*. Jordan reminded the editors that the authors involved in the project were receiving, on average, $1,000–$1,500 for a single short story, so the papers would be gaining a great financial advantage by serializing the novel.[2] The suffragists were now seriously on their way toward publication.

While working on *The Sturdy Oak*, Jordan came to know Fannie Hurst well. A contributor to the collaboration, Hurst was a popular novelist in this era, but in the 1930s she would come into her greatest recognition—and controversy—when she published the race-inflected novel *Imitation of Life*. At this time, Hurst was known for her political activism, which included supporting equal rights for white women and all African Americans. Jordan immediately began introducing Hurst to famous writers in the city.[3] It was only the beginning of her efforts to promote Hurst's career.

The high hopes for *The Sturdy Oak* were seriously impacted by the war, however. Soon word came from newspaper, magazine, and book publishers that they were facing a shortage of paper, which significantly restricted their selections of materials to publish. Additionally, when Tutwiler contacted G. Verner Rogers at the *New York Tribune*, whose syndicate was known to be one of the best in the country, she received disturbing news. As Jordan reported to Whitehouse, "the entire bottom has dropped out of the syndicate business; material for which thousands of dollars would be paid a year ago now goes begging."[4]

Negotiations would go on for months, and it was becoming clear by May that they might still publish the serial before they submitted their resolution to the legislature in November, but it seemed increasingly unlikely that the novel could appear in book form before that date. Jordan worked closely with Tutwiler in an attempt to place the serial with the *Saturday Evening Post* and all of the Hearst publications, to no avail. A few weeks later, however, she was able to inform Whitehouse that serialization had been sold to *Collier's* magazine for $3,000, with the book rights and second serial rights retained for the NYSWSA.

Collier's agreed to begin publication in September so the novel would run throughout the suffragists' campaign period, and the magazine agreed to release it in time for book publication on November 15. Attempting to find a book publisher was still ongoing, however.[5] Jordan's disappointment that Harper and Brothers had not agreed to publish *The Sturdy Oak* had to be visceral. She had worked for them for seventeen years, bringing many important writers to their company, and she had published all but one of her own books with them.

In spite of the New York Tribune Syndicate's initial rejection of the novel for second serial publication in newspapers, Tutwiler and Jordan convinced them to reconsider, and this time they agreed—and the syndicate waived the usual fees in order to assist the NYSWSA. The newspaper serial would appear about one year after the book publication. Negotiations would continue for several months, including Jordan's decision to add two more chapters to the novel to strengthen the content. With a final chapter count of fourteen, the novel was on its way to publication.

For all that she immersed herself in her work, Jordan could not ignore the larger issues bearing down on the world at this time. One way in which she participated in war issues was through the American Defense Society's Authors Committee. Fellow members included George Ade, Hamlin Garland, Mary Roberts Rinehart, Otis Skinner, Owen Wister, Gertrude Atherton, Alice Brown, Brander Matthews, and many other notable authors of the day. In the first days of April, the Authors Committee sent a resolution to President Woodrow Wilson demanding that the president and Congress immediately declare war against Germany and that provisions for universal military service be enacted.[6]

At last, it happened. On April 2, 1917, the United States declared that they were entering the war to support the Allies and defeat Germany. Even though the war did not take place on American soil, the impact was significant. After the initial shock and—for Jordan and others—relief, there was nothing to do but forge ahead with the daily routines of their lives while everyone wondered what was about to happen.

In the interim, Jordan continued to seek outstanding novels for Harper and Brothers. In May, she pursued a memoir by Edith Œ. Somerville, *Irish Memories*, but even then the war intruded. As they corresponded, Somerville noted, "I live on the sea, within a few miles of the Fastnet Light, the first 'land-fall' for vessels from America, & we feel very much in the war. Only last week I heard—but here I remember the Censor, & think I had better refrain."[7] They were only beginning to learn the new language they must now speak—or not speak.

By June, Jordan could report to the Publicity Council that the composite novel had found a book publisher: Henry Holt & Company. This was excellent news, as Holt was among the most successful and respected publishers in the country. Roland Holt, vice president of the company, assured Jordan he was himself in favor of women's suffrage.[8] The company offered a good price, and at last the magazine serial, the book publication, and subsequent newspaper serialization were in place. The timing was perfect because Jordan was just beginning an important new writing venture of her own. Her writing process was to do multiple revisions of a story before it was well enough developed to read to friends: "Slowly your story develops," she explained. "Slowly you write it, and rewrite it, and tre-write it."[9] Yet "slowly" was not going to be possible after she was contacted later that month by Arthur Brisbane, her longtime friend and former associate at the *World*.

Brisbane had recently purchased the *Washington Times* newspaper, which was part of the Hearst Syndicate. He convinced Jordan to become a columnist for his newspaper. In an astute negotiation, Brisbane had her publish in Hearst's *New York Journal* before appearing in the *Times*. The *Journal* piece was "Love and Duty Problems Brought Up by the War," published on the editorial page on June 25, 1917.

That Jordan would write for either a Hearst or a Brisbane paper at this point was notable, since she had long supported America's entrance into World War I, and the two newspaper owners' prior resistance to American involvement—and their initial support of Germany—had been so extreme as to have warranted both men being tagged as traitors.[10] Once America joined the war, however, Hearst and Brisbane became thorough supporters of the Allies, which may have eased Jordan's consideration of becoming a part of their organizations.

Once her initial article appeared in the *Journal*, Brisbane sought other items from Jordan for his own paper, beginning with a three-piece essay on the rise of Fannie Hurst as America's foremost short story writer, viewed by many as the new O. Henry. The Hurst essays crossed Jordan's various interests and obligations: she admired Hurst; the essays gave her a foothold in Brisbane's paper; and they offered considerable publicity for Harper and Brothers, for whom she had contracted Hurst's *Every Soul Hath Its Song*.

In spite of their age difference—Jordan was more than twenty years Hurst's senior—they met frequently in these years, especially to attend new plays that were opening in town, having become good friends over the course of working on *The Sturdy Oak* and preparing *Every Soul* for publication. Hurst's humor appealed to Jordan, and their friendship would last for the rest of Jordan's life.

The articles about Hurst were quickly followed by another war-related article in the *Washington Times* on "Facing Death Afar and Near." With the success of these essays, Brisbane offered Jordan a regular column on the editorial page of the *Times*, with the agreement that some of the pieces would also appear in Hearst's *Journal* and the *Los Angeles Herald*. Her essays for the *Times* appeared under the column heading "Elizabeth Jordan Writes On," with subtitles indicating the particular subject. This approach replicated the title of a popular column in Hearst papers: "Mabel Dodge's Article On." Thereafter, Jordan's column quickly became available to readers every few days, sporadically at first, and then usually three or four columns a week.

Having her own newspaper column appearing in three major papers offered Jordan an opportunity to have her work read by an audience that numbered in the hundreds of thousands. Brisbane offered Jordan a free hand as to the topics she wished to write about, and the diversity of subject matter she covered combined serious cultural critiques and light-hearted home remedy articles. This combination was in the tradition of women's syndicated columns at the time, including a column Ida Tarbell wrote about life in Paris during the war, which also included lighter topics. Such variation was an astute decision by columnists, as it increased the range of readers who came regularly to their writings. This was exactly what Jordan needed so she would have a strong base of followers when she began to work independently, which remained her ultimate Plan.

Over the next two years, Jordan's columns addressed a wide range of topics, from being alone in the city to developing one's business life; from babies to war economies and numerous other war subjects; from war brides to the war duty of husbands. In a very short time, the paper was flooded with letters from readers, not only commenting on her subject matter but also asking her to advise them on how to handle any number of situations. At the end of her August 13, 1917, column in the *Times*, she noted that her mail was increasing rapidly but she would answer every letter—most likely an impossible task, but it was a method Jordan had always used at the *World* and the *Bazar*, and one she tried to replicate here.

The success of this column and the wide range of magazines that sought her work assured Jordan that this was the right time to enact the next stage of her latest Plan. On November 3, 1917, she sent her letter of resignation from Harper and Brothers to her close friend and general manager Frederick Duneka. The formality of a letter was required for proper business practices but also because Duneka was confined to his home by an illness that would soon end his life. However, the letter she addressed to Duneka was touchingly personal:

> *If you listen closely on December first you will hear the sweep of pinions as I take my flight from Franklin Square. In other words, my dear friend, I am handing you my resignation from the staff of Harper and Brothers, to take effect on that day.*
>
> *Let me add that I am leaving with the utmost good feeling toward every one there. In many ways I am, of course, sorry to go. But with you and Colonel Harvey [he had departed for a diplomatic career] both away, the place no longer seems the same. . . .*
>
> *I enclose a report of my work as literary adviser for the past three years. I also enclose the outline of a letter I plan to send to our list of authors, for any changes you may suggest. Observe how tenderly I write.*
>
> *Good-bye, Dear F.A.D., and God bless you. I shall never forget what a good friend you have always been to me.*[11]

The list included fifty books that she had brought to Harper's in the last three years. The authors included Kate Douglas Wiggin; Sinclair Lewis (four books); religious writers such as Rev. S. S. McComb and Rev. Elwood Worcester, Episcopal priests in Boston; Ella Wheeler Wilcox; three of Jordan's own books; two works by Frances Hodgson Burnett; and one each by Mary Austin, Gertrude Atherton, and Fannie Hurst. She had an additional six books accepted for publication. It was an impressive contribution to American literature in the 1910s.

Duneka's response was a heartfelt recognition of what a loss this was for Harper's and himself:

> *Dear Friend:*
>
> *I am desolated at the thought of your leaving Harper and Brothers. But, of course, there is nothing else possible, when Fate comes tempting you with large golden apples. What a success is yours!*
>
> *The firm will miss you, and I shall miss you personally, more than I can say. We have worked together half a lifetime—indeed all your adult lifetime—and in those long years I have come to respect your untiring industry, your "manly" virtues, and your fidelity to the work at hand, pleasant or unpleasant.*
>
> *It is certain that you will be a distinguished success in your new undertaking, but I add the wish that all good luck and happiness may go with you. As they say so beautifully in the Spanish farewell, "Go with God."*
>
> *I am always,*
>
> *Sincerely your friend*[12]

"Large golden apples" indeed, for Jordan had revealed to Duneka that, in addition to her column in the *Washington Times*, she had accepted the position of editorial director of Goldwyn Pictures Corporation.[13] The position required her to find novels that would be readily adaptable to film and negotiate with the authors on behalf of Goldwyn Pictures. Jordan's longtime friend from her days at the *World*, Bayard Veiller, had been instrumental in helping her land this position. Veiller had married one of the leading actresses of the day, Margaret Wycherly. In recent years, the Veillers had introduced Jordan to several major players in the film industry—most notably Edgar Selwyn, actor, playwright, and Broadway producer, and his famous wife, actress Margaret Mayo, who owned several theaters in New York, Chicago, and Cleveland. "We all unwearyingly talked shop" whenever they met, Jordan noted, and she had learned much about both stage and film from these friends.[14]

The previous year, the Selwyns had formed a moving picture organization, the Goldwyn Company, with Samuel Goldfish, who would later buy them out and change his name to Goldwyn. The previous October, Margaret had phoned Jordan and asked her to consider going into the motion picture business. At first Jordan declined; she enjoyed films but felt she did not have enough knowledge of the field and she knew many authors who had been in and quickly out of the film industry. Yet Selwyn was adamant and repeatedly pushed Jordan to join their company. To put her off, Jordan finally made the outlandish response that she would do it only for $25,000 a year (around $600,000 today) and with "reserve time" for her own writing commitments.

To Jordan's astonishment, Selwyn asked when she could begin. Still, Jordan hesitated, so Selwyn set up a meeting for Jordan with Samuel Goldfish, and he convinced her, confirming the annual salary of $25,000 and with the promise that she would be required to work only Monday through Wednesday at their Fort Lee, New Jersey, studio, which was across the Hudson from Manhattan. The rest of the week would be her own time.[15] With the agreement in place, she gave her notice to Duneka and began to wrap up loose ends at Harper's. Notifying Duneka that she would leave at the end of November allowed her to take the month of December off before beginning her new position.

Just as she gave notice to Harper's, *The Sturdy Oak* was published in book form. The final roster of authors was an impressive group, all committed to the suffrage cause but diverse, independent thinkers. The title page read *The Sturdy Oak: A Composite Novel of American Politics*, and the contributors confirmed that assertion: Samuel Merwin, author and playwright; Harry Leon Wilson, author and playwright; Fannie Hurst, author and social justice activist; Dorothy Canfield, author and social activist who worked for the war effort in France; Kathleen Norris, author, journalist, and a pacifist; Henry Kitchell Webster, one of the most popular writers of the day; Anne O'Hagan, author, journalist, and a committed Democrat; Mary Heaton Vorse, journalist, labor activist, and a Socialist; Alice Duer Miller, influential feminist poet, playwright, and political activist; Ethel Watts Mumford, author, artist, and playwright; Marjorie Benton Cooke, playwright, monologist, and a pacifist; William Allen White, newspaper editor, author, and a leader of the Progressive movement; Mary Austin, author and political activist; and Leroy Scott, novelist, screenplay writer, and a Socialist.

Through the novel's family dynamics, political machinations, and a narrative full of twists, the authors led readers to understand how much better both family and public life would be when women had the vote. A lengthy review in the *New York Times* detailed the goal of the novel, noting that all proceeds would go to the suffrage cause, and then added, "And yet, be it clearly understood in the first place, 'The Sturdy Oak' is an exceedingly interesting story, and very amusing to boot."[16] The reviewer found the plot coherent, in spite of being written by fourteen authors, and very much to Jordan's credit.

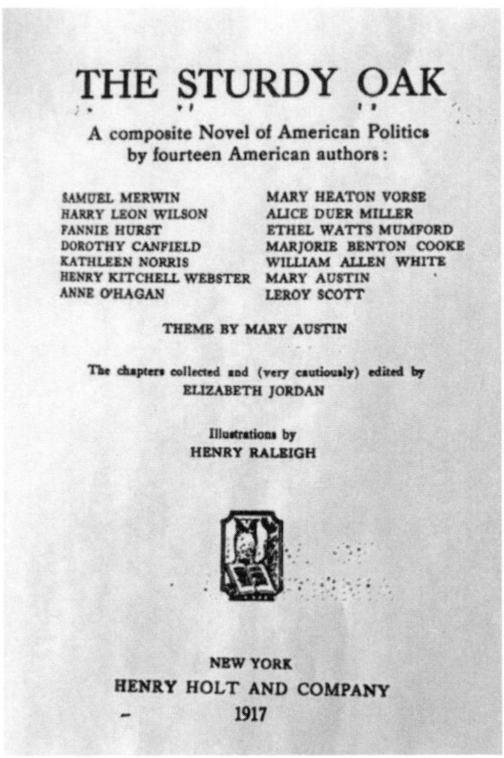

THE STURDY OAK

A composite Novel of American Politics
by fourteen American authors:

SAMUEL MERWIN
HARRY LEON WILSON
FANNIE HURST
DOROTHY CANFIELD
KATHLEEN NORRIS
HENRY KITCHELL WEBSTER
ANNE O'HAGAN
MARY HEATON VORSE
ALICE DUER MILLER
ETHEL WATTS MUMFORD
MARJORIE BENTON COOKE
WILLIAM ALLEN WHITE
MARY AUSTIN
LEROY SCOTT

THEME BY MARY AUSTIN

The chapters collected and (very cautiously) edited by
ELIZABETH JORDAN

Illustrations by
HENRY RALEIGH

NEW YORK
HENRY HOLT AND COMPANY
1917

Title page, *The Sturdy Oak*

With the publication of *The Sturdy Oak* behind her, Jordan could relax for a few weeks before she began her work with Goldwyn Pictures. Newspapers around the country published notices and indicated surprise that she was leaving Harper's. It had been an extraordinary seventeen years' collaboration.

Chapter 19
Goldwyn Pictures

It was fortunate that Jordan had December to recover before starting as editorial director at Goldwyn Pictures in January 1918, because she was about to enter a hornet's nest. No one had told her that for the past few months an eruption had been fomenting at the studio, and it spilled out just before she arrived. The Selwyns and Goldwyn were at odds, and they faced considerable financial losses, due in part to America entering the war, which put everyone off luxury spending such as going to the movies. But at this point Jordan thought only of the prospects of her new position.

Jordan needed only to take a ferry ride across the Hudson from the 125th Street pier to arrive at Fort Lee, the motion picture capital of the world. When she entered the Fort Lee studio with its glass dome, she was surprised to discover it was in desperate need of repairs, and the region was having one of its coldest winters in years. She and her secretary had to wear heavy ulster coats and rubber boots in the office because the pipes kept breaking, leaving the cement floor wet and cold. She was dismayed, too, to learn that her employers had never heard of the many classic and modern authors she recommended and that they largely ignored her recommendations of any classic literature.

As she had done when she faced a similar in-house dispute on beginning her position with the *New York World*, Jordan jumped into her work and tried to make the best of the situation without entering the dispute herself. She was being paid very well, she still had time to focus on her own writing commitments, and she had, in the midst of everything, begun writing her first novel for adults, which was about to go into print, so she pushed on, despite the tensions in the workplace.

The New Year began with a delightful letter from Sinclair Lewis, congratulating her on her new position and letting her know he was now working on a play. Never one to miss an opportunity, Jordan immediately replied, asking him to consider one of his novels for Goldwyn Pictures. He could make no commitment at present but assured her that if he ever changed his mind, he would contact her.[1]

The other person she immediately approached was Eleanor H. Porter, the author of *Pollyanna*, to inquire whether she had sold the motion picture rights to all her books. This time she received a more positive response. "I am glad that you remember me," Porter wrote. "I have followed your career with deep interest and pleasure." Porter indicated she had two novels that should work well as films, and Jordan replied immediately that she would contact Porter's publisher.[2] She already had her foot in the door.

She published an announcement in a wide range of magazines about the kinds of works she sought: "We wish writers to remember that all our stars are women and are young; that we use no war plays, or religious plays, or political plays; and that we use only full five-reel plays. We want good farce comedies with real situations for Mabel Norman, good love stories with dramatic comedies for Mae Marsh, and brilliant comedies for Madge Kennedy." She closed by asking that manuscripts be sent to her home address, which was listed.[3]

At the same time that Jordan was working at the film studio, she published her column in the *Washington Times* three times a week. It touched on war issues, personal health and responsibilities, family relations, and public engagement. In addition, she published short fiction in the *Woman's Home Companion*, *Chicago Tribune*, and *Young's Magazine*. She also began a seventeen-year association with the *Extension Magazine*, a Catholic periodical for which she published short stories two to four times a year.

Further, she turned her attention back to novel writing. Jordan's first novel for adults, *Wings of Youth*, appeared in March 1918, published by

Harper and Brothers after being serialized in *Today's Housewife*, which had a circulation of more than one million readers. Like many of Jordan's forthcoming novels and mysteries, *Wings of Youth* was set among the wealthy circles of society, both a world that she knew well and one that she did not hesitate to dissect. The story follows an idle-rich brother and sister who make a pact to leave their luxurious country home and try to make their own living in New York City for one year, independent of one another and without the benefit of their wealth. The novel traces the tragedies and successes they meet and how they come to new understandings about themselves through these experiences.

Reviews were good, with most commentators remarking on the plot as "quite original," but Jordan did not receive the excellent reviews she had been used to with her previous books.[4] At this moment, she made an important decision—to leave the Harper and Brothers publishing house, which would mean having to find a new publisher for subsequent novels. The change meant she could negotiate with other publishing firms to garner the best price for her novels. It is likely that Harper's failure to publish *The Sturdy Oak* also impacted her decision. But she quickly found a home for her subsequent books with the powerhouse Century Company.

At the Goldwyn studio, Jordan encouraged the owners to consider classic literature and serious modern novels in addition to the love stories and dramatic comedies that they sought to produce. At present they seemed to have little interest in such books, but she jumped in to help with their goal of producing twelve films before the first of September. They did include one movie based on a modern classic, *Thais*, starring Mary Gardner and based on the novel by Anatole France. Gardner was an opera star, which undoubtedly also pleased Jordan. But the studio focused on films like *Polly of the Circus* for Mae Marsh and *The Scrub Lady* with the inimitable comedian Marie Dressler.[5] The year after Jordan left the company, Goldwyn began an "Eminent Authors" promotion in which they touted films based on prominent authors' works; Jordan certainly deserved some of the credit for this new branding, as it was a point she had argued throughout her tenure with the studio.

But Goldwyn Pictures was facing difficult times. Films were new ventures, and the producers had assumed that Broadway comedies would translate to film. They invested in several such pictures starring Margaret Mayo. But in spite of the quality of the productions, they incurred significant losses. As Jordan noted, "These failures . . . shook the confidence of the new partners themselves [the Selwyns and Goldfish] and in one another." Combined with the panic in the business world because of the war, it was little surprise that tensions led to a split between the partners.[6]

After Jordan had been with the company for only six months, Goldwyn announced plans to move the studio to California. Nothing could induce Jordan to leave New York and her family in Gramercy Park, so she submitted her resignation, effective July 1.

This was the first time in Jordan's life that one of her grand Plans for her future had failed. Despite being assured that she had ample skills to undertake the position of editorial director, she realized how unprepared she had been for "the mysterious goings-on in the picture studios."[7] She now had a remarkable new position to consider: that of an independent writer. For the first time in her adult life, she would no longer have a large corporation like Pulitzer's newspaper or Harper's publishing or Goldwyn's films to serve as the source of her income.

It had to be a bit frightening to no longer have these secure nets beneath her, especially since she had a luxurious lifestyle to maintain for herself and her mother, but it was also tremendously exciting, and there was nothing Jordan loved more than a challenge. She maintained her newspaper columns and published fiction in the *Saturday Evening Post*, which had a readership well into the millions in these years.[8] The *Post* would significantly advance her national reputation, which was important for the next step she wished to take in her career.

By early July 1918, when she left the Goldwyn Corporation, she had lined up a new avenue for her writing. It might have been the shortest time she had ever had to develop one of her Plans, but she gritted her teeth and moved forward.

Her work for the *Washington Times* would continue for a few months, but she knew that Brisbane's pattern was to take over newspapers, build them up, and then sell them to Hearst, so she turned most of her attention to a new position she had contracted—as a columnist for the prestigious *Philadelphia Inquirer*. What had formerly been "the woman's page" of many newspapers, featuring home-related articles, had been modernized in some publications, including the *Inquirer*. The page in which Jordan's column appeared was now titled "Woman's Varied Interests." Her column appeared every three days, and it would endure until 1931.

Jordan had learned a great deal about publishing through her work with Harper's and her experiences with her own fiction. She undoubtedly also had been tutored by her friend Mary Terhune, who (writing under the name "Marion Harland") had built a notable publishing empire by becoming a syndicated woman's-page writer. When Terhune began her columns years earlier, some critics sniffed that such writing was not literature, but Terhune understood exactly what she was doing, as her response revealed: "But it's influence."[9]

Jordan already had influence in the fields of journalism and literature, but there was nothing like the influence of newspaper columns that were read by citizens across the country. Such influence also aided the sales of the novels she now planned to publish each year. Additionally, in her contract with the *Inquirer*, Jordan retained copyright for her columns, so when they were syndicated or reprinted in other forms, she garnered additional profits. Having edited the woman's page of the *World*, she understood the intricacies of such publications better than most. She would always maintain women's domestic lives as the main thrust of the columns, but soon she expanded that focus to war issues as they impacted the home and other far-reaching topics, just as she had for Brisbane's paper.

Shortly after her column appeared, Jordan began to receive letters from readers, and she reshaped some of her columns as responses to these queries, thus entering the already extremely popular newspaper genre of the advice column. The first modern advice column had been penned in 1898 by Marie Manning under the name "Beatrice Fairfax"; in those days, such columnists primarily focused on etiquette and on the heartbroken, but by Jordan's era, advice columns were part of the new human-interest journalism. Jordan's occasional columns that responded to readers' letters and offered advice were designed to aid readers in coping with their rapidly changing lives in the metropolis.[10]

The selections that offered advice were a small part of Jordan's column, however. Most of her commentaries used dialogue as a means of personalizing cultural and domestic themes. This was a technique she had learned years earlier in her "True Stories" articles for the *World* as a means of personalizing a broad topic. In the Philadelphia columns, two speakers would debate cultural issues and lead readers to conclusions about appropriate behaviors and methodologies to succeed in modern American life.

Late in the summer, Jordan left the sweltering city for Spreadwings with Harriet, Martha, and her mother. With no position that required her to be in an office, Jordan began to spend every June to early November at Spreadwings, with occasional short trips into New York City and more regular trips to Plandome to be with Frances. When she returned to traveling to Europe each year, she would spend her time abroad and then join her family at Spreadwings. Harriet had the usual summer vacation, but her job required her to be in the city most of the year. Martha, by contrast, had received a considerable inheritance that allowed her to maintain a Manhattan studio for her work and to choose when and where she did that work, so she often stayed in Florence for months as well while she continued to publish articles about interior design.[11]

In October, Jordan officially ended her association with Arthur Brisbane and the *Washington Times* when he sold the newspaper to William Randolph Hearst. She could now focus on her thrice-weekly columns for the *Philadelphia Inquirer*, short stories that she sold to magazines and newspapers, and especially her new Plan to publish a novel every year.

Jordan, her mother, and Martha Cutler were still at Spreadwings on November 7, 1918, when news came that an armistice had ended World War I. They were so excited that they motored a hundred miles to Boston to celebrate with friends. Along the way they passed through many towns, and, no matter how small, people were in the streets, crying and cheering and waving flags.[12]

Another major change in Jordan's life occurred in December when her sister Alice and her husband Edward Beyer moved to New York City. The Gramercy Park apartment could not accommodate two more people, so Alice and Edward found accommodations in a boarding house while Edward tried to find work.[13] It was not ideal, with the cost of living in the city, and this is likely when Jordan began supplementing the Beyer family's finances. On the upside, after many years apart, Alice was able to be close to her sister and mother again.

Throughout the past, tumultuous year, Jordan had made every attempt to see Frances as often as possible, but it had been difficult at times because of both of their schedules. In February, Frances had written a letter addressed to "Elizabeth my lost beloved" in which she lamented, "I feel as if we are parted forever," but she realized she was as much the cause as was Jordan. "This has been a War winter for me," she explained, detailing all the family and household issues that had kept her in Plandome. Though they did manage to dine together in New York later that month, the weeks seemed to slip away with only rare moments of seeing one another or Jordan making a quick run over to Plandome for a weekend. By June, Frances was spending more time in the city due to legal issues that required her presence. That took hours of every day, but they managed to see one another in the evenings and on weekends.[14]

In October, when Frances returned home alone after being in Bermuda, she and Jordan hoped to have a good amount of time to spend together. But Frances's sister Edith returned sooner than expected because it was feared she had been exposed to the "Spanish flu," the great influenza epidemic of 1918 that took nearly 750,000 American lives. It turned out that Edith had only a bad cold, but their reaction attested to how frightening the epidemic was. Though it was safer for Jordan to be at Spreadwings as well, Frances's frustration burst forth. "Darling Elizabeth," she wrote at the end of one letter, "I want to see you, but God forbid that you should shorten your holiday. Perhaps you will be here in time to spend *one* weekend with me before the [summer] house is shut up. My love to you all my dear. Yours always, Querida."[15]

Fate seemed to thwart them at every turn. They managed to grab a day or two together here and there, but they were unable to spend Christmas together because Frances had a bad cold and needed to remain home and numerous other family emergencies arose, not the least of which was that, although Frances owned a car, her chauffeur had debunked. Frances and Jordan exchanged gifts by mail. At the end of one letter, Frances again lamented, "How I want to see my Elizabeth. Perhaps, Oh I wonder *if* we could get to Bermuda!"[16] It had been a hard year, but their love endured, and they would indeed see Bermuda together again.

In the city for the winter, Jordan sent frequent notes to Frances when she could not get to Plandome and telephoned her often. Meanwhile, Jordan worked on her columns, short stories, and another novel. When she looked back at the war years, she felt she had only been "able to be of a little use to my country during the first World War."[17] She had served on the American Defense Society's Authors' Committee and the Committee of Mercy as well as trying to help readers of her newspaper column negotiate the challenges of postwar America. But in reality, she had little time to look back on these tumultuous years. Her path lay forward.

Chapter 20

Mystery Writing

It was one thing for Jordan to find her career taking different turns than expected. It was quite another to have a child come into her life. In early 1919, newspaper stories began to appear asserting that Jordan and "a friend"—never identified—had adopted a young French girl. Like so much of celebrity journalism, there was a hint of truth in otherwise inaccurate reporting; ironically, this was a myth that Jordan herself helped perpetuate. As late as 1943, she stated in a biographical essay that "a friend and I adopted (when she was eighteen months old) and brought up a little French girl and sent her through Smith College."[1] She, her roommates Harriet and Martha, and her mother did indeed "adopt" a child, in the sense of taking her to heart and making her part of the family, and Jordan did assist in the girl's education, but the truth was less glamorous and more complicated.

The biggest heart in relation to the young French girl and to all of Jordan's New York family was that of Martha Cutler's mother, Louisa Adelaide Plimpton Cutler. Years earlier, Louisa had taken in Jordan, Harriet Prescott, and Margaretta Jordan as part of her family because they lived with and were loved by Martha. If someone needed a family or a place to live, Louisa Cutler stepped forward. It was she whom this "adopted" child, Clothilde, referred to as "Mummy"[2] or "Grand-mëre."[3] Certainly the three roommates played significant roles in the child's life, but they did not adopt or raise her in the traditional sense.

Clothilde Elizabeth Reo was born in Burlington, Vermont, on August 9, 1917. Her mother was Marie Emelie Eliza Carpentier (1887–1958) and her father Jean François Reo (c. 1888–?). Shortly after Clothilde was born, Marie and Jean divorced, and he remarried the following year. Marie was unable to care for Clothilde, but Marie's sister, Leda Carpentier, had been a cook in Louisa Cutler's household since at least 1910,[4] which is most likely how Cutler learned about the child's situation. Clothilde was eighteen months old when she came to live at Spreadwings. She would be an integral part of that household for the rest of their lives.

Despite the excitement and joy Clothilde brought to everyone in these early months of her life, Jordan had to turn her attention to writing. A self-employed woman could not be distracted for too long. In 1919, she continued her column for the *Philadelphia Inquirer* and wrote

Clothilde Reo
BETSY DEVINE COLLECTION

for a notable number of magazines. She wisely pursued control over her publications; in addition to copywriting her *Inquirer* columns, she sought second serial rights to her stand-alone fiction. When *McClure's* granted her those rights for "On Terms to Suit the Lady," for example, she then sold the story for reprinting to the *Chicago Tribune*.[5]

Just as she was settling into the new year, Jordan was devasted to learn of Frederick Duneka's death. Even though he had long been bedridden by spinal problems, he had often sent her short notes to keep in touch. A few years earlier, when she published a humorous story in the *Saturday Evening Post*, Duneka wrote, "When it comes to *Saturday Evening Post* stories about people's hats, Mark Twain has nothing on Little Elizabeth."[6] Even though Jordan knew Duneka's death was imminent, the loss was devastating. They had been friends since she had arrived at the *World* three decades earlier. Though only in her early fifties, it seemed as if every year, another dear friend left her, and this year would be no different.

If public interest in Jordan had been strong when she was a journalist and magazine editor, it increased multifold when she became a columnist. Periodicals of every stripe published biographical pieces about her throughout the year, including the 1918–1919 *Who's Who*; her birth year was erroneously listed as 1867, though the "error" was suspicious.[7] To be included in *Who's Who*, an individual had to fill out a lengthy form that included their birthdate. This was the beginning of Jordan intentionally shaving two years off her age. The date of 1867 was picked up by other periodicals, and she used the new date herself in later publications.

This spring, Frances began to think about having Jordan stay with her at Plandome more often. She suggested that, instead of the short weekend visits, Jordan stay with her from the middle of the week through the weekend and that she bring her work with her. "I have for years," she said, "been seeing times when you could be here writing in one room & I in another in the mornings & talking or motoring in the afternoons. . . . I shall not give up the dream." She realized it was an impossibility at present, but she added, "It *can* be sometime—somewhere. I wonder if it will be in Bermuda. How we should love it!" She closed promising to see Jordan in New York a few days later, whatever it took, "either triumphant in my own limousine—or crawling on my hands & knees."[8]

While Frances, now sixty-nine, wanted the two of them to seclude themselves away, Jordan, at fifty-four, needed to be in the center of a vibrant, ever-active life. As much as she loved Frances, she chose independence. The reality was that Frances was the source of many of their cancelled plans to be together as her health grew worse. When Frances was better, Jordan visited her or Frances's chauffeur drove her to the city to see "Queen Elizabeth."[9] Jordan made every effort to see Frances as often as possible, as she longed for them to be together just as much as Frances did. In addition to her time in the city or at Spreadwings and, with the end of the war, the return to her beloved European travel, Jordan would never give up spending part of every summer with Frances in Bermuda.

This summer also marked a major transition in Jordan's writing as she turned to the genre of mysteries, a field in which she would excel and for which she would become recognized as one of the major mystery writers in America throughout the 1920s and 1930s. She had actually begun writing mysteries while still in school at St. Mary's; they included, as she had May Iverson explain at one point, "grim, mysterious blood-curdling happenings."[10] But she had abandoned the genre as she matured and became a reporter. Between 1919 and 1943, however, she would publish fifteen notable mysteries that helped reshape the history of mystery writing in America.

In many of her early mysteries, she placed the twenty-something men and women (almost always orphans) into difficult situations in which they must become amateur detectives. Even more important, they must uncover something about their own innate character and their abilities—their own mysteries—in order to move forward in their lives. In the Jazz Age, young Americans were frequently depicted as destroying themselves through pursuits of freedom at any cost, but Jordan presented that generation as capable of finding their way through the challenges of modern life and forging new paths to self-awareness and success.

She did not develop a recurring amateur detective who would appear in several books, as Agatha Christie would soon do with Monsieur Poirot. Each of Jordan's mysteries were standalones in which she used classic techniques of the genre—the locked room, the country estate, the mysterious stranger, based on fact, the closed circle, and others—and all of her mysteries relied on psychological storylines to lure her readers.

Jordan's mysteries did have murders that needed to be solved, but she also loved the tension that arose from a *potential* murder. If the amateur detective could not determine who posed the threat, someone would die. In some ways, Jordan came naturally to the mystery genre with her experience covering the Lizzie Borden case and other murder trials as well as the true crime and psychological studies that were part of her reporting when she was a journalist. This new path began in August 1919 when she published *The Girl in the Mirror*.

Just as Agatha Christie's first mystery the following year would draw on personal experience—working at a hospital dispensary—Jordan's drew on her love of the theater with characters linked to that world. One of the first things she had done when she arrived in New York City was take a letter of introduction from a hometown friend to A. M. Palmer, manager of the famous Wallack's Theatre, "because I was immensely interested in plays and players. He immediately put me on his free list and sent me tickets for first-night performances of all the plays presented at Wallack's."[11]

Jordan claimed *The Girl in the Mirror* emerged out of her own experience,[12] which was probably true but also a smart marketing tool. Readers loved personal anecdotes about the authors they read, and the sense that a mystery was based on an author's actual experience proved even more alluring.

Jordan understood that the theater world was pregnant with the possibilities for suspense. She revived Laurie Devon, the brother from *The Wings of Youth*, who in that novel had fallen in with the New York theater crowd and wrote a play that was a big hit on Broadway. In this mystery, he is enjoying his success so much that he can't settle down to work again.

One morning Laurie sees reflected in his mirror a young woman from the apartment across the alley; she seems in despair and he races to her apartment, but she refuses to explain. As Laurie tries to discover the mystery of the woman's fear and the strange people with whom she associates, he is drawn into dangerous activities. From there, Jordan created a taut mystery with lots of action and a surprising twist at the end.

Reviews were varied, however, with *Life* magazine offering only a two-line assessment, which discounted the mystery as "written to sell, and for no other purpose," and the *New York Sun* insisted it read "like a moving picture scenario that had gone wrong and had been made into a novel." Others, however, praised the story's twists and turns and its "startling dramatic conclusion," as *Outlook* termed it, and the *New York Times* called it an "ingenious and entertaining" mystery.[13] The book sold well, and it would soon become a motion picture.

The Girl in the Mirror and the additional fourteen mysteries Jordan would write over the next twenty-four years placed her in the forefront of Golden Age mystery writers in America. She now belonged to a long tradition of American mystery writers, going back at least to Edgar Allan Poe. In Jordan's own time, Mary Roberts Rinehart had gained a reputation as a mystery writer who published her inaugural work in the genre, *The Circular Staircase*, in 1908, and Agatha Christie would soon publish her first mystery, *The Mysterious Affair at Styles* (1920).

For all that Jordan had worried about reestablishing herself after the fiasco of her tenure with Goldwyn Pictures, she was happy with the successful sales of her first two novels and of another new venture that began in September 1919. She had published several short stories with the *Chicago Tribune* over the years, but this month the Tribune Newspapers Syndicate decided to create a new and elite idea for its Sunday edition, and it was syndicated widely to other newspapers. The "Blue Ribbon Fiction" series was under the aegis of the fiction editor of the *Sunday Tribune*. Advertisements in the *Tribune* announced that they were spending $75,000 on fiction for the series. The first Blue Ribbon issue appeared on

September 21 and became a standing feature of the Sunday newspaper for the next fifty years.[14]

The series' goal was to publish original fiction by America's best short-story writers; in addition to Jordan, its authors included F. Scott Fitzgerald, Booth Tarkington, Zona Gale, and others. Their pay was exceptional for Jordan's era as well, up to $2,500 per story.[15] Notices began to appear in several newspapers about this "Fiction Scoop" by the *Tribune*. The Blue Ribbon stories were syndicated throughout the country, once again enhancing Jordan's literary reputation; she would continue as a regular contributor to the series for more than twenty years.

As thoroughly busy as Jordan was in these months, she did not fail to continue her support for women's suffrage. On May 21, 1919, the US House of Representatives passed the Nineteenth Amendment to the Constitution, which afforded women the right to vote. The Senate quickly followed suit, passing the bill on June 4. Jubilation burst forth among suffragists who had worked from generation to generation for more than seventy years to accomplish this remarkable goal of true citizenship.

On a personal front, Jordan also celebrated the news that Frances would be spending the winter in Manhattan. However, despite their hope to go to the theater and dine together, Frances's health did not allow it. They were together for her seventieth birthday in November, even though she had to receive her guests from her bed. By December, Frances had suffered such serious attacks of "nervous prostration" that she was taken to the Fishkill Landing Sanitarium. This was not her first stay at a clinic for extended bed rest, but it was an unwelcome development, especially since they could not offer any real relief from her ailments.[16] None of this stopped Frances from sending her usual frequent notes to Jordan or Jordan from sending treats, books, and gifts to Frances and visiting as often as possible.[17] These health issues would haunt Frances through the final years of her life.

As Jordan and Frances negotiated the changes in their lives, the country was undergoing a radical change as well. A postwar recession brought forth in some Americans an anti-immigrant resentment as soldiers returned home in search of work. By the end of the year, one in five US workers had gone on strike. The labor leader Elizabeth Gurley Flynn called the decade after 1917 a "hideous nightmare."[18] The next decade would see the establishment of Prohibition, the Jazz Age, and "flapper girls"—all of which Jordan would address in her fiction and her newspaper columns.

Chapter 21
The Roaring Twenties

AT THE END OF 1919, THE NEW EDITOR OF THE *LADIES' HOME JOURNAL*, Barton W. Currie, met with Jordan at her Gramercy Park apartment. Currie offered her an unbelievable opportunity: to publish short stories and special articles over the next year with annual payments reaching $18,000 (nearly $300,000 today). She was writing three columns a week for the *Inquirer*; generating short stories for the *Tribune*'s Blue Ribbon series as well as for *Extension*, *Chicago Tribune*, *Woman's Home Companion*, and *Collier's Weekly*; and pushing herself to produce another mystery, but she could not turn down such a generous offer.[1] With so many commitments already in hand, she negotiated for her first story to appear in April 1920, giving her time to slot this new venture into her work schedule.

Jordan managed to take a quick break in mid-June, but she did not head to Bermuda to see Frances because it would require too long to travel. Instead, she went to the new playground of the wealthy: Atlantic City. Jordan had been to the city when her play was in production and for suffrage meetings, so she knew the area well. She spent a week there. The Chamber of Commerce ran advertisements in these years describing the city as both "The Playground of America" and "The City of Robust Health."[2] Jordan would make Atlantic City a quick spring getaway for several years to come.

Primarily, though, she was spending her time on her next mystery. Its working title was *Red House*. News that the film version of *The Girl in the Mirror* was soon due out made Jordan very popular, and publishers wanted to capture her next mystery for their magazines. It was John M. Siddall, editor of *American Magazine*, who won the day. The magazine had been established in 1906 by muckraking journalists Lincoln Steffens, Ida Tarbell, and Ray Stannard Baker. By 1920, it focused less on muckraking and more on human interest stories and fiction, which suited Jordan's strengths.

She did not know Siddall personally when she began publishing in the *American*, but she had heard good things about him as an editor, "and I greatly liked the man himself when I met him." He was a no-nonsense negotiator. When she finished the manuscript, she sent it to him on a Friday, and by Monday morning he telephoned and asked to meet with her. She went into his office to discuss terms. He was upfront about the fact that the magazine had commitments for publications through that year, so they could not publish her mystery until the following year. He offered to publish it in six installments for $7,000. But Jordan had made a commitment to herself—part of her Plan for this period in her life—to publish a novel every year, and she wanted compensation if she delayed her book to fit their schedule. She asked for $10,000 for the serial rights, to which Siddall agreed. He then asked her to change the title from *Red House* to *The Blue Circle*, and she agreed.

Jordan published several essays over the winter in the *Ladies' Home Journal* about preparing women for their new roles in presidential elections. "Women in the Presidential Campaign" offered an excellent overview of the process of women gaining the vote, while "New Women Leaders in Politics" compared the dire warnings of antisuffragists with the reality of women having the vote. She offered other articles encouraging women to vote in every election to better their community and explained how best to prepare themselves for this rite of citizenship.[3]

For all the joy this year had brought, it did not end on a happy note. Frances had to spend part of the fall in a sanitarium, which aided her enough that she was able to go to Bermuda on an overnight steamer in early December with her sister Edith.[4] On arrival, she wrote several letters to Jordan with the usual sentiments they felt when apart: "Oh, my dear. *How* I want to see you!" She teased Jordan about her productivity, asking, "Have you written two new books & a thousand articles?"

But Frances's health was deteriorating: "I am not well—I am not," she wrote to Jordan. "I walk in a dream though the doctor says the blood pressure is not very high. I eat only toast & milk & an occasional egg."[5] Within a short time, doctors would order her to bed for rest, and her bedridden state would last for several months.[6] Jordan kept close tabs on Frances, but it was impossible for her to travel to Bermuda—because of a secret of her own that she was keeping.

As heavily committed as Jordan was with contracted publishing agreements for the *Philadelphia Inquirer*, the *Ladies' Home Journal*, and the *Chicago Tribune*'s Blue Ribbon series, she would undertake new adventures in publishing in 1921 as well. She wrote seventy columns for the *Inquirer* during the year. She also expanded from standalone short stories for the *Journal* to include half a dozen essays and a novella, as well as standalone stories and a novella for the *Woman's Home Companion*. She would have her second mystery published in November, and at the end of the year she would contract to write a second newspaper column that would rival the *Inquirer* for its yearly output. Instead of slowing down her pace as she neared fifty-five, Jordan pressed her foot to the pedal.

But the beginning of the year brought a heartbreaking event for all the residents of 36 Gramercy Park and Spreadwings: Louisa Cutler died on January 27, 1921, leaving Martha as the sole surviving member of her immediate family. Louisa had been the force that bonded everyone at Spreadwings, and her absence was deeply felt. Her death left a troubling gap as well—she had been Clothilde's primary caretaker. Clothilde's aunt, Leda Carpentier, was still with the family as their cook,[7] but it was decided that Jordan's sister and brother-in-law should become permanent residents of Spreadwings. Alice and Edward Beyer's move to Florence worked for everyone involved. They had found New York an impossible place in which to thrive, and in Florence they helped as caretakers of the house and of Clothilde.

Unfortunately, Alice was never an easy person to have around, and most of the household found her "annoying."[8] Clothilde recalled years later that she loved the Aunts, but she "couldn't stand Aunt Allie and Uncle Ed."[9] Regardless, this was the family arrangement for years to come.

Jordan threw herself into work, as she often did as a means of coping with loss. Her popularity with readers and critics soared in these years, and the *Boston Post* took advantage of this fact by serializing in its Sunday magazine two of her previously published novels, *The Wings of Youth* and *The Girl in the Mirror*. This, of course, also advanced Jordan's income, since she had retained second serial rights for herself. Through it all, she worried about Frances, sending frequent letters and small gifts. She was somewhat relieved when Frances was finally able to return to Plandome, but Jordan could tell that, in spite of Frances's efforts to put on a cheerful face when Jordan joined her, she was not well. By late May, Frances had returned to Bermuda's warm, healing environment.

In May 1921, Jordan contracted with the *Los Angeles Herald* to publish her column from the *Philadelphia Inquirer* in their paper as well, starting on May 2, 1921, but with the title "Elizabeth Jordan's Column," with the day's topic as a subtitle. It appeared on "The People and Their Daily Troubles" page.

Despite her productivity, health issues loomed. In the spring, Frances had confessed to Jordan that she was not sure that "telling lies about ones [*sic*] health is the best thing in the world," but she did not want "to make every one wretched."[10] It was a philosophy Jordan understood well, since she had been keeping a secret about her own health—she had been diagnosed with cancer. On July 18, 1921, she was admitted to the Presbyterian Hospital for surgery.

Martha Cutler kept Frances updated about what was happening during the surgery and telegrammed her afterward to say it had gone well. Frances sent a note of thanks, telling Martha that she had prayed for "my darling beloved Elizabeth" at the hour of the surgery and stayed in prayer for two hours. "I was with her every moment," she declared. She lamented that she was not well enough herself to be in New York with Jordan but commanded Martha, "Give my love & love & love to the dearest one & tell her that I *never* leave her—& though she does not see me in her room I am there."[11]

Frances was able to return to New York in early August, not knowing that she had just made her last visit to her beloved Bermuda.[12] Within a month she was admitted to Dr. Fowles's Sanitarium on Park Avenue. Although she and Jordan exchanged letters as soon as both were able, they would not see one another for months as each recovered.

When Jordan was released from the hospital, she spent three months in Miami on her doctor's recommendation, with Martha helping care for her until she was strong enough to return to New York. Being in Miami for recovery did not mean Jordan would forgo writing. She produced new columns for the *Philadelphia Inquirer* and the *Los Angeles Herald*, but, given the current situation, she could not keep up with the *Ladies' Home Journal*'s demand per her contract with them, so she sadly informed them that she would no longer be able to write for the magazine at the agreed-on pace. It was a significant loss of income, but it was her only choice under the circumstances.

By the end of October, Jordan was well enough to leave Miami. Rather than go directly to New York, she and Martha headed for Atlantic City, where everyone who was anyone was attending the city's annual golf tournament. Harriet joined them as well.[13] Jordan asked Frances to join them, too, but she was not well enough.[14]

The roommates returned to New York after two weeks, and Jordan attempted to pick up the pattern of her normal work routines. She visited Frances often at the sanitarium. When she entered the room on Christmas Eve, Frances spotted her. "She uttered the crow of a happy child," Jordan wrote with delight, "and bounced ecstatically up and down in bed, exactly as the child might have done."[15] Being in a sanitarium was certainly not the way either wanted to spend Christmas, but they were together. It was as good an end to a difficult year as they could have hoped.

Chapter 22

America's Theater Critic

The early 1920s brought considerable changes in women's lives. They now had the right to vote, and the Jazz Age offered new avenues for their employment and enjoyment outside the home. There was a backlash, of course, and part of the country railed against the loss of traditional values and customs, while another (typically younger) segment embraced the "modern" in every sense. Willa Cather best captured this phenomenon when she asserted that "the world broke in two in 1922 or thereabouts."[1]

One of the most culturally debated figures of this era was the so-called "flapper girl," on whom so much of the weight of changing cultural values inordinately rested. These young women, seeking to move beyond the mores of their mothers, rolled their stockings, wore short skirts that exposed bare knees, bobbed their hair, and abandoned corsets and bras. Jordan wrote frequently about this figure in her newspaper columns and in her mysteries.

Part of what Jordan addressed in nearly a dozen newspaper columns devoted to the flapper was the transition that came with the Jazz Age—a sense of progress, but one that came with a new sense that the American Dream was no longer based on morality; rather, it was based on money. A 1920 film called *The Flapper* presented this type of young woman as defying social norms and capable of thinking for herself but also as easily led astray by decadent men into criminal activities. In addition, a pulp magazine, *Flapper Experiences*, played up the shocking lives that flappers supposedly led.

With such dire examples offered to the public, Jordan began addressing the issue in her *Philadelphia Inquirer* columns. Like many of her generation, Jordan's concern about flapper girls was that some of them did not have the experience or training to avoid being led into dangerous situations when they thought they were only out to have fun and shake off the rules of moderation embraced by their parents. She would soon exemplify this perspective in her novel *Black Butterflies*.

In the interim, Jordan's next mystery, *The Blue Circle*, was published in 1922. She granted copyright of the novel to her beloved roommates, Martha Cutler and Harriet Prescott, so all profits from the book would go to them in thanks for their assistance through her surgery and recovery.

The Blue Circle appeared in the same year as *The Waste Land* and *Jacob's Room*; T. S. Eliot and Virginia Woolf were high modernists who received praise for their innovative ways of approaching the war in literature. Agatha Christie's first mystery, *The Mysterious Affair at Styles* (1919), introduced Hercule Poirot as a refugee from the war, and Jordan had her own unique way of addressing war issues in *The Blue Circle*. While this mystery had the classic setting of the country estate, its theme was unique and provocative. John Renshaw comes to the estate of the wealthy David Campbell with a proposition: "I—have come here to ask you to buy me!"[2] He explains that he recently had a terrible shock that has left him with "a fear of the responsibility for my own life and self-support, a fear that amounts to a nightmare."[3] Campbell takes Renshaw on as his secretary.

Then strange things begin to happen at the estate. Is Renshaw losing his mind? Or is somebody attempting to destroy everyone in the household? A two-fold mystery develops: What is happening at the estate, and why would a man sell himself to another? As in so many of Jordan's mysteries, the protagonist's own psychology is an underlying mystery that has to be uncovered in addition to the overriding danger that forms the main plot.

The reviews were stunning. The *Buffalo Courier* termed it "an original, breathlessly exciting and cleverly-told mystery," while the *Century Magazine*'s reviewer asserted that Jordan's depiction of John Renshaw constituted "a portrait of many ex-soldiers with war psychoses whom she has known." While the reviewer for the *Philadelphia Inquirer* insisted that, with only a few exceptions, "women do not make superlative creators of mystery stories," he found Jordan to be a rare exception—"a quite fresh and flexible talent adorning the faded surfaces of the mystery story . . . [and] she can fabricate a whirlwind finish with the best of them."[4]

After the thrill of such accolades for *The Blue Circle*, Jordan and her mother left New York for Spreadwings.[5] Martha was in Florence as well, Harriet joined them as often as her work schedule allowed, and the roommates had the joy of spending time with Clothilde, who was now five years old. The roommates had been granted the title of "Aunts," which they took to heart.

It was at this time that the family had a debate about Clothilde's schooling. Jordan argued that a Catholic education was the best preparation a young girl could have, while some of the others wanted her to attend public school. There were multiple religions among the family members—Jordan, Leda, and Clothilde were Catholic; Alice and Edward were Christian Science; Harriet was Presbyterian; and Martha professed no religious alliance.[6] It was finally decided that Clothilde would attend public school, but by the fourth grade the Catholic contingency would win out and Clothilde would be enrolled in parochial school.[7]

Jordan motored to Spreadwings now. Having a car of her own gave her a renewed sense of independence, and a chauffeur made traveling that much easier. For now, she ignored the fact that driving in these days was lawless—automobile accidents were almost impossible to avoid with roads as yet unprepared for this new form of travel and certainly not marked clearly as to who should stop at country crossroads—but she enjoyed this new adventure in travel and the freedom it offered her.

At last Frances was feeling better. She was able to return to Plandome, and by June she was working in her garden again, which always lifted her spirits. At this time, Frances had a new plan, one that would give her and Jordan much more time together—renting an apartment in Manhattan. She fantasized about what it would be like: "There ought to be *two* sofas in my room & I am wondering if there will be space enough." She attempted to create an alluring image for Elizabeth: "If I can make my room at the Madison Square livable the next step would be to create two or three madly extravagant loose gowns & lie flat upon my back on my Chinese brocade couch & pathetically & subtly beguile fascinating persons of great conversational gifts into coming to talk to me. If I can get in another couch you could put on your Chinese Mandarin coat. . . . Oh—*do* let us get well! With love always Querida."[8]

As Frances aged and her health declined, she clearly would have liked to have Jordan living with her. She never demanded such a change, but she created scenarios like this one that suggested what a happy life they would have if they were together all the time. Jordan still frequently spent weekends at Plandome and when she was away sent love and gifts, but she was unwilling to give up the life she had built for herself in New York with her roommates. The city was in her blood; it was who she was, and she would not give up her independence, even for Frances.

Jordan was thrilled at the end of the year when she was approached by the publishers of New York's leading Catholic periodical, *America: A Catholic Review of the Week*. The editor in chief, Richard H. Tierney, S.J., knew of Jordan's love of and frequent attendance at the theater and invited her to become the magazine's drama critic, writing a monthly column. Combining two of her most beloved activities—writing and attending the theater—made for an ideal opportunity.

Her first column in *America*, "The Season's Plays," appeared on December 9, 1922, and examined a variety of dramas currently on Broadway. She highly recommended John Barrymore in *Hamlet*; while she liked the social lessons that John Galsworthy always offered, she thought his play *Loyalties*, which pitted a wealthy Jew against a group of English gentlemen, would have been better if the Jew had been presented as "more appealing." She also covered comedies, two plays by Somerset Maugham, which she concluded represented "careful workmanship" but unpleasant themes. She included an assessment of the play of the season that everyone felt they must see—*The World We Live In*, in which insects represented human life and the "futility of mere human effort." She noted that some of this drama's ideas were intensely interesting, but through too much of the performance the audience yawned behind their programs.[9]

In this initial foray, Jordan established techniques that she would carry through her years of reviewing for the periodical: praise where it was warranted, but a critical eye to gaps in narrative, overblown themes, or unfulfilled promises. Jordan would continue as *America*'s drama critic for the next twenty-three years, reviewing plays by George Bernard Shaw, Eugene O'Neill, Lillian Hellman, and many other playwrights as well as performances by actors ranging from Ethel Barrymore to Paul Robeson.

In 1923 alone, Jordan published eighty-three columns in the *Philadelphia Inquirer* (most also appearing in the *Los Angeles Herald*) and eight multipage theater reviews for *America*, serialized her next mystery while she began writing another novel, contributed to the *Chicago Tribune*'s Blue Ribbon series, produced two stories for *Extension Magazine*, and published six standalone stories in major magazines.

By the spring, Frances's health had improved to such an extent that she was frequently able to visit Jordan in Manhattan, and Jordan spent many weekends with her at Plandome.[10] These times together might not have been quite the fantasy of living together that Frances had imagined, but it was close enough. They both blocked out hours for writing while they were together, and it was a congenial lifestyle.

At this time, Jordan invited Mary King to visit Spreadwings when she came to the East Coast in the summer of 1923. King had been Jordan's editor with the *Chicago Tribune*'s Blue Ribbon fiction series for nearly five years, and they had come to like and admire one another. Though King was thirty years younger than Jordan, they had much in common—both were Catholic, both had succeeded in breaking the ceiling for women in journalism (King was editor of the prestigious *Sunday Tribune*), and both had built independent lives. King had a joyous time with the extended family, and Harriet came down from New York to meet her as well.

King wrote Jordan shortly after leaving: "Those were heavenly days I had with you. I am grateful to you not only for your charming hospitality but for introducing me to this lovely, lovely country. . . . It made me very happy to be a part of your interesting household. I've had only tantalizing glimpses before of Miss Cutler and Miss Prescott and it is a privilege really to know them. Your mother and sister too were so awfully sweet to me."[11] Theirs was a friendship that would last until Jordan's death.

They were soon involved in a new venture together. Jordan's next mystery, *The Lady of Pentlands*, was a new publishing experiment in serialization by Mary King's *Chicago Tribune*—a "daily serial" presented in forty-nine installments, beginning on September 17, 1923. The book form of the novel appeared the following spring.

This was Jordan's third mystery, and it was a gem. A tribute to her dear friend Henry James's *The Turn of the Screw*, *The Lady of Pentlands* presented a masterful blending of mystery, gothic, and horror. Rich characterizations and many narrative twists and turns made it a story that readers could not put down. The mystery opens when Valerie Knight's father dies and she discovers that their constant world travel has left them penniless, though her father always insisted on staying in the best hotels and dining in the best restaurants. Thus, when widower Bruce Gordon offers Valerie a business arrangement to marry him and care for his country estate, Pentlands, with no attachments and enough funds to secure her future, she agrees. Gordon's twins, Bruce and Genevieve, are six years old; Bruce is a mannerly little boy, but Genevieve, as the servants believe, is possessed by the devil. Valerie investigates the horrible events at the estate, trying to discover why such horrid things are happening and why Genevieve is such a haunted child. Is she evil? Or is there another force working against the child? The tension Jordan created throughout the story held readers to the end.

In spite of her productivity, at fifty-eight Jordan was beginning to have occasional health problems that she could not forgo addressing. She could not at present imagine how medical issues would soon impact her life.

Chapter 23

Rebuilding from Loss

Mary King had so enjoyed her initial visit with Jordan that she planned another visit to New York City in the spring of 1924. Jordan hosted a luncheon for her, and, as King wrote to Jordan afterward, "I am ever so grateful to you for your wonderful hospitality. I shall always remember that charming luncheon and the evenings I have spent in your home have done much more than fill lonely hours or take the place of ordinary ones. They have given me rich and happy memories."[1]

After Jordan's early summer trip to Europe, she and her mother headed for Spreadwings. The day after her arrival, she, her mother, and her sister set off on a motoring jaunt to enjoy the summer weather. As always, they had their usual chauffeur at the wheel. They traveled as far as Hadley when, at a crossroads, a truck carrying four men skidded into cross traffic, having failed to yield, and smashed into Jordan's car.

Polish laborers working in a nearby field heard the crash and came to help; they stayed with the injured in the long interval before ambulances arrived. Jordan's head "had been cut open, both eyes were full of blood, and I was convinced that my left eye was lying somewhere in the road." Then she heard one of the spectators who had gathered around the accident proclaim, "The old lady's unconscious."[2] It was then that panic set in.

Margaretta Jordan, now eighty-two, had suffered a broken rib and was in shock; Alice had contusions and a bruised rib; and Elizabeth had cuts on her temple and near her left eye. It was feared at first that she might lose sight in that eye, but she eventually recovered. Two of the men in the truck were badly injured, one having suffered a fractured skull; Jordan later reported that they would "never fully recover."[3]

Harriet Prescott came to Spreadwings to help care for Jordan and her family as often as she could, but, as happened most often, it was Martha Cutler to whom the care of the recovering injured fell. Though Cutler had a somewhat flexible schedule, she had gained considerable fame as an interior designer by this time. But she set aside her professional demands and stepped forward, doing all she could to help Jordan and her family recover over the next month.

Jordan had little time to lose in spite of needing to recover. In addition to her columns, her next mystery, *Red Riding Hood*, was about to begin serialization in the *Chicago Tribune* and *Washington Post*. The daily serializing of *The Lady of Pentlands* had been so successful that the two newspapers sought to start immediately with this next mystery, which would be published in book form the following year. The *New York Daily News* had also noticed the success of her daily serial, and they contracted with her to publish *Red Riding Hood* as well, under the title "Alias Hope Emerson."

Just as Jordan was beginning to improve, Frances's health took a serious turn for the worse. When Jordan had recovered enough from the accident to travel, she made the trek to Plandome to see her beloved and thereafter wrote from Spreadwings to "my precious Querida" with the encouragement for recovery that she always offered Frances: "This attack will soon pass, as the others have done, and that very soon you will be feeling yourself again. No one knows better than I do . . . how wretchedly ill one can be, how discouraged one can get—and how well and happy one can also be when it is all over. So cheer up, my beloved, and make the brave fight you always do make."[4]

But Frances did not recover. Jordan visited her again before returning to Manhattan and wrote her daily after she settled back into Gramercy Park. What Jordan could not know was that there would be no period of recovery for Frances this time. The letters—mere notes, in reality—that she received from Frances in return were filled with words of love: "Darling Lover, I am a weak [] thing today & cannot write only I want to tell you how I love you & love your letter & thank you for it. How good it would be to see me, my Elizabeth. Querida."[5]

Days later, Frances sent her final note to Jordan: "Darling best beloved—I love you. You are my valentine. Your Querida."[6] Frances died on October 29, 1924. Jordan's sense of loss was cavernous. The funeral was held on November 2 at the Plandome house. Jordan, editors, authors, and family friends attended.[7] Then Jordan returned to Spreadwings, where she spent a month in mourning before she could manage to return to Manhattan.

Jordan had always been close to Frances's son Vivian, and in mid-December he wrote to tell her he had decided to write a biography of his mother. He added, "I want to tell you how much I appreciate all you have been to my mother. I know that her love for you was deep and real, and that the intellectual companionship you gave her was a very important factor in her life and work. Your letters to her in her last days were a great tribute of love, and they meant a great deal to her. And you know that for all of this I have a gratitude that can not be properly expressed in a letter."[8] As Vivian worked on the manuscript, Jordan sent him items that might be of interest, and he came to her apartment to read selected chapters to her. "The reading," she said, with undoubted understatement, "was a poignant experience to us both."[9]

Though Jordan would live another twenty-three years, there would be no other long-term relationship in her life. She had found her love in Frances.

After Frances's death, Jordan slowly began to reenter her life and tried to find joy in the publication of her latest mystery, *Faith Desmond's Last Stand*. The story's tension was excellent, as were its strong characterizations; it was a significant contribution to the closed-circle subgenre of mysteries, set on a ship headed for France. In this era of anti-Catholicism, Jordan explicitly identified her main characters—Faith and the doctor who becomes her lover—as Catholic, which may be why it was her first and only book published with the Catholic publishing company

Extension Press, and not with her usual publisher, Century Company. Since the resurgence of the Ku Klux Klan in recent years, Catholics had come under extreme attacks. The Klan believed the rise of Catholicism in America to be as threatening as the notable progress among African Americans. Jordan would not squelch her depictions of Catholics in fiction, though it apparently required the shift to a Catholic press in this instance.

One other surprising element of *Faith Desmond's Last Stand* was that the woman criminal who belongs to a gang of thieves was named Marie Carpentier—the name of Clothilde Reo's birth mother. Perhaps nothing so readily described Jordan's dislike for the woman, even so many years after she had faded from their lives, as to cast her as a criminal.

While *Faith Desmond* was appearing in book form, Jordan had *Red Riding Hood* running as a serial, *The Blue Circle* was again in syndication in newspapers, and her columns in the *Inquirer* and *America* reached a massive national audience. It was impossible not to know who Elizabeth Jordan was. A biographical piece was included with the first chapter of the resyndicated *Blue Circle*, stating that any story with Jordan's name on it offered "assurance that it's a tale worth reading." The paper added, "Never was there a woman who had more irons in the fire . . . she's a member of the Mayor's Committee of Women, which had been established in 1917 to address national defense; Big Sisters' Association, National Institute of Social Sciences, Authors' League of America, American Commission of Mercy, Society of American Dramatists . . . American P.E.N., vice president Notre Dame Alumni Association, regent National Woman's Suffrage association, etc., etc."[10]

Only a writer of extraordinary discipline and commitment could have had such a diverse and productive life. And productivity was what Jordan needed in the aftermath of Frances's death.

In 1925, Jordan added two new periodicals to her long list of places of publication: *Liberty Magazine* and *Holland's Magazine*. The latter was a women's magazine with a commitment to social change ranging from farming practices to wildlife protection acts. *Liberty*, an illustrated weekly, was published by the Chicago Tribune Company. In a short time, it became a leading magazine in America, second only to the *Saturday Evening Post*. Mary King would soon move to New York City to become editor of the magazine's women's section, though she would continue to be the fiction editor for the *Chicago Tribune* as well. Having this friend nearby in these years of recovery was just what Jordan needed.

Notably, Jordan's *Philadelphia Inquirer* columns this year were reduced in size, about two-thirds their previous length. While she wrote on many of the usual topics—familial relations, poverty, accomplished women—these shorter columns gave her a bit of additional time for her books and short stories.

In March, Jordan published her latest mystery, *Red Riding Hood*, in book form. It was another mysterious stranger, psychological mystery like *The Blue Circle*, this time with a young woman going to a country estate to escape danger, offering a modern take on the classic story. "Hope Emerson" takes a position as the wealthy Mrs. Schuyler's assistant as a means of trying to hide from a sexual predator who has damaged the young woman's life in ways others cannot understand because they see only his pretense of kindness and generosity. Part of the mystery surrounds who Hope Emerson really is—she tells Mrs. Schuyler she cannot give her real name, so Mrs. Schuyler insists on naming her for the expectation of future hope and draws from the literary world to find the surname of Emerson.

The *Boston Globe* and *Washington Post* both commented on the strength of Jordan's characterizations, and the *New York Times Book Review* agreed, noting that Jordan captured the "little ways" of characters that distinguished them in readers' minds and made them want to know more about the characters as well as the mystery. The *Times* concluded that "Miss Jordan tells her story with a deftness of phrasing and a deal of understanding and insight."[11]

Cover of *Red Riding Hood*

Jordan barely had time to celebrate the book's success before entering the Manhattan Ear and Eye Hospital in March 1925. Difficulties with her eyesight had plagued her for some time.[12] Nothing could be more frightening for a writer and for a critic who must see stage plays in order to prepare her critiques. She was treated and dismissed, but it would not be long before her problems recurred.

In April, Jordan hosted a group of Frances's friends in her Gramercy Park apartment. They came together to plan a memorial for Frances. In attendance were the writer Marguerite Merington, Frances's lifelong friend Gertrude Hall Brownell, her publisher Frederick Stokes, and actor Eleanor Robson Belmont, who had starred in one of Frances's plays. The famous actor Mary Pickford had also agreed to participate in the project, but she did not attend the planning meetings.[13] Goodwill prevailed at this first meeting. Although they did not know each other well, they all had loved and admired Frances and believed that connection would carry them through working toward their goal.

As a project built on love, it should have been a heartfelt, congenial effort, but it would turn into nothing but frustration for Jordan. As chair of the committee, she approached the planning as she would any other project—dig in and get the work done. Almost from the beginning, however, she clashed with Merington, who seemed to want as much socializing as planning. While they agreed on the basics of what needed to be done, their ideas for accomplishing it diverged. Jordan immediately began the process of a selecting an architect, while Merington wanted to fundraise by contacting celebrities to join them, and Brownell wanted to move slowly, considering each proposal carefully before moving forward.[14] It immediately became a fraught association. The project slugged along, and the final dedication would not occur until 1937.

Just as Jordan seemed to be finding some balance in her life after Frances's death, she received word that her longtime friend, the poet Edith M. Thomas, had died. The loss, coming so soon after that of Frances, seemed doubly difficult. Lengthy tributes to Thomas appeared in several newspapers, and Jordan added her own in her *Philadelphia Inquirer* column. She identified Thomas as "one of America's greatest poets" and felt it was tragic that someone of her genius lived "for seventy years almost without recognition" and died "poor and alone."[15] Even years later, when Jordan wrote her autobiography, she remembered her friend and wrote, "As to Edith Thomas, I should like to write a book about her."[16] Unfortunately, she never did.

One of Jordan's articles in the *Saturday Evening Post* this year, "On Being a Spinster," grew out of an experience Jordan had faced when a woman on a train asked whether she was married. When she said no, the woman replied, "Never mind. You're a woman, anyway." In the article, Jordan argued that the public must let go of the old view of the spinster as a woman who lived with a relative, totally dependent on them, and earned her way by caring for the house and children. That woman saved the family an immense amount of money, Jordan noted, "but more importantly, such a creature must be recognized as a thing of the past." The unmarried woman of today typically had a far more varied life and experiences than the married woman. Nor was she without romantic love. Jordan concluded, "Surely, at this period of feminist history, we are justified in admitting not alone the great economic strides made by woman, but her right to remain unmarried, if she chooses."[17]

Speaking out in favor of women who did not follow the traditional path of marriage was a subtle but significant step toward confronting the archaic attitudes about homosexuality that still prevailed in America. It would be several years, however, before Jordan briefly but explicitly invoked lesbian love in one of her mysteries.

The following month, Jordan's latest mystery, *Miss Blake's Husband*, was published in book form. It marked a different kind of mystery for Jordan, with a shift from country-estate locales to the great metropolis. This time, multiple mysteries must be solved involving questions about family secrets, illegitimacy, the ways in which a father's sins are left to his daughter to rectify, and what one's identity truly is if all one has known is lost. Though reviews were mixed, it sold well.

To this point in her novel and mystery writing, Jordan had used links between her books to emphasize themes that were important to her, each time offering a twist. A male figure in *Wings of Youth* becomes the protagonist of *The Girl in the Mirror*, with both novels emphasizing the dangers of idleness and of "adventures" that can turn perilous—themes that would recur in *Black Butterflies* as well. In another link, with *The Blue Circle* Jordan had presented the idea of contractual bondage with a male character, but in *The Lady of Pentlands* and *Black Butterflies* the female leads enter contractual bondage via loveless marriages intended for business purposes only. Thus the mysteries became critiques of marriage for financial benefit, so common among the upper classes, and an acknowledgment that for women without economic means, marriage became a business transaction, not a love affair.

After the mixed reviews for *Miss Blake's Husband*, Jordan returned to traditional novel writing for a period. *Black Butterflies* (1927) was a cautionary tale about the dangers of making the idea of "freedom" a cultish force in one's life to the detriment of love and happiness; it was Jordan's "lost generation" novel. The Black Butterflies are a club of young people who make being unconventional the goal of their lives, to disastrous effect.

Reviews of *Black Butterflies* were powerful. Some were shocked at the vividness and realism of her depictions of evil characters and their retribution, but all declared that the story held the reader's interest to the end. One reviewer effused that there was "a wealth of cleverness" in the novel and concluded, "This is the most powerful story Miss Jordan, graceful and brilliant writer, has done yet."[18] The popularity of *Black Butterflies* also led to a film version that appeared the following year. The third of her books to be made into a film, it would not be the last.

In April 1928, Jordan followed the success of *Black Butterflies* with a new mystery, *Miss Nobody from Nowhere*, the story of a young woman who is hospitalized after a horrific train wreck and suffers from amnesia. Knowing nothing about who she is, the woman assumes the name "Eve." While trying to find her way in New York, she is unwittingly drawn into the city's dangerous cabaret world. It is her own identity that is the mystery to be solved. Jordan wrote often about finding strength to solve the mysteries hindering one's life, but this psychological story extended the idea a step further: Can the self be recovered after a trauma so severe it results in amnesia?

It was no coincidence that Jordan chose this moment to write about the subject of memory loss. One of the most controversial episodes in the history of mystery writing had occurred shortly before Jordan began writing *Miss Nobody*. On December 3, 1926, the now-famous Agatha Christie was immersed in stress after the death of her mother and learning her husband was having an affair. In a state of distress, she left home late one evening and did not return. The following day, her abandoned car was found. Christie appeared to have been in an accident, and, especially concerning, several personal items were found left behind in the car.[19]

One of the most expansive manhunts in British history played out over the subsequent days, and American newspapers made it front-page news as well. The world wanted to know what had happened to Agatha Christie. When she was located, safe and seemingly in good health, many people found it hard to believe her claims that she had suffered from amnesia. They argued that she was lying, that it was a publicity stunt. Others, however, believed Christie, that she had "lost her way of life and her sense of self,"[20] and Jordan was among them.

Jordan developed a plot in *Miss Nobody* in which the amateur detective must put her own life back together as she becomes a cabaret dancer in order to support herself. But one night a man asks her to join him at his table. Eve realizes she has known him—and feared him—but she doesn't know why. She must determine the danger this man represents, who she really is, and what happened that caused her amnesia. The multilayered mystery presents the loss of memory as a sometimes-unavoidable response to life's tragedies.

The mystery was well received. As the *New York Herald-Tribune* reviewer remarked, in reading this story, "you have given yourself up to a writer who thoroughly well knows how to handle her subject to its definite and quite plausible conclusion."[21]

This year Jordan also began publishing short stories in the Catholic periodical *Messenger of the Sacred Heart*. These stories of faith captured the side of Jordan that did not appear in her publications for mainstream magazines. In her first story for the magazine, she describes the main character's comfort in church: "In it she always felt like a wanderer at home."[22]

This image of the church as home spoke volumes about the comfort Jordan found in her faith. It was integral to who she was and how she lived her life. Between 1928 and 1941, Jordan would publish fifty-five stories in the *Messenger of the Sacred Heart*. In these stories, Jordan's abiding optimism about facing life and doing one's best was the recurrent theme.

On an equally happy note, in March 1928 Vivian Burnett published the biography of his mother, *The Romantick Lady*. Vivian sent a specially bound, "solid gold, diamond-encrusted volume" to Jordan with "three rousing cheers." On the title page, he wrote, "To Elizabeth Jordan, With the sincere gratitude and affection of one who well knows how much her inspiring friendship contributed to the latter years of *The Romantick Lady*."[23]

The year 1929 began as a wonderfully productive one for Jordan. She felt strong; though she still missed Frances terribly, she had let go of some of the grief in favor of valued memories. She continued her contributions to the *Philadelphia Inquirer* and *America* columns and published numerous short stories and essays. Most notable, however, was the publication of a powerful mystery, *The Devil and the Deep Sea*. It was a return to the by-now classic country-estate mystery in which family members had gathered and suspicions lurk that the deceased wealthy matriarch may have been poisoned. Jordan's story offered several important critiques of modern society, from drug abuse among the wealthy to her first explicit mention of lesbian love.

Depicting the use of cocaine or heroin by the upper classes would become common in mysteries of the 1930s, and Jordan's book was an important, early addition to that theme. What particularly shocked readers was Jordan's depiction of a fashionable mother who intentionally drew her daughter into opium dens with her.

The issue of lesbian love came full circle in this mystery. Jordan had hinted at lesbianism in her writings since her earliest works. *Tales of the Cloister* began with two nuns who deeply loved one another, though whether in friendship or more is left for the reader to determine. In the May Iverson books, sexuality emerged as well. May Iverson had her first true crush at age seventeen. While her friends were dreaming of who they would marry, she turned her affections toward Sister George.

In *The Devil and the Deep Sea*, a nurse, Hope Webb, reveals to the amateur detective, Nicholas Long, that she had loved her patient, Catherine Chandler. When he waves the comment aside with "I'm glad you were fond of her," Hope insists he hear her: "I wasn't fond of her. I tell you I loved her."[24] It is a short episode in the story, but its meaning is insistently forthright. In Jordan's later mystery, *The Life of the Party*, a spinster is clearly in love with the woman friend she brings home, but the book offers no similarly explicit statement about their relationship as there is in *The Devil and the Deep Sea*.

No reviews commented on the love of Hope Webb for Catherine Chandler (nor, surprisingly, about the wealthy women's use of drugs), but a *Sunday Evening Star* reviewer noted that "this novel presents a strange corner of that familiar domain of disquietude"; such a mixed group as appear at Chandler's estate, however, presented no problem for Jordan to handle "with a gusto and an edged wit, with an ingenuity and a clear flair for the unexpected." After detailing the complexity of the story, he added, "An agile writer, an adept romancer, is required to carry through along this novel line. Here she is. You have found that out from about ten novels already sent out by Elizabeth Jordan."[25]

This mystery was extremely popular, primarily because it was a page-turner but also because it offered readers an insider's view of the foibles of the wealthy. By January of the following year, *The Devil and the Deep Sea* had been translated into seven languages.[26]

Just as Jordan was celebrating the success of her latest mystery, the stock market crashed on October 29, 1929—one of the most infamous economic downfalls of the century. The scene in New York was absolute panic. People gathered by the hundreds in front of banks, hoping to salvage their savings, and some became desperate as they learned they were left with nothing. Jordan knew she was fortunate because she did not lose all her money, but the shock of what she did lose in a flash was overwhelming. Between the roommates, they were able to keep their Manhattan apartment, but the crash destroyed decades of Jordan's accumulated wealth. Slowly, through hard work over time, she would reestablish her economic standing, but it was a devastating blow and a hard road to return to economic stability.[27]

As if the market collapse did not engender enough difficulties, Jordan began to suffer eye problems again, this time far more seriously. After tests, it was determined that she had cataracts, a devastating blow. In this era, cataract surgery was often a dangerous procedure. Jordan's spirits plummeted; she envisioned "blindness—helplessness, uselessness—being a burden to others." After receiving the diagnosis, she went back to her apartment and looked out the window, wondering, "How long would I see beauty? How long would I see *anything*?" She told only Harriet and Martha, not wanting to burden her mother or friends. Her oculist recommended she wait five years to see whether the problem would progress so slowly that surgery might not be necessary.[28]

Jordan resolved not to worry if she had to wait so long for surgery, but other pressures emerged. The financial depression deepened, and people stopped buying books and magazines; it became increasingly difficult for authors to find publishers. Jordan tried to remind herself that even as her income dropped significantly, she still had a reserve and was not in as desperate a situation as many of her literary friends.[29] It was small solace, but all that she had to content herself with at present.

Chapter 24
New Directions

As Jordan worked to rebuild her financial security, she could not help but realize how fortunate she had actually been. New York, like the rest of the country, faced massive numbers of unemployed. Entire families entered homeless shelters. Still, in New York there emerged a small group of people who continued their lavish lifestyles. Manhattan was home to the "café society" whose comings and goings were covered daily in the newspapers and whose attendance at various restaurants and clubs could make such establishments instantly famous. There was little criticism of this group, however, largely because people at present still assumed the economic crunch would be short lived.[1]

Changes came for Jordan's family during this time. Margaretta Jordan decided to make Spreadwings her permanent home. At nearly eighty-seven, she preferred the quiet and comfort of life in Florence.[2] Jordan, Harriet, and Martha visited often, still spending several months in the summer and fall, and Margaretta now had the lively, intelligent Clothilde to share her life. At thirteen, Clothilde fulfilled every hope the family had for her.

The impact of the economic crisis for publishing came home to Jordan when the *Philadelphia Inquirer* cut her column this year from three times a week to twice monthly. While the reviews for *America* were also erratically published immediately after the crash, they were reestablished regularly in 1930, though not as weeklies. The magazine changed to a monthly, which meant Jordan's columns were a fourth of what they had been.

She also saw a reduction in the number of short stories that magazines were publishing. As a well-established author, she continued to have a small number of stories accepted—one in the *Chicago Tribune*, two in *Extension Magazine*, and one in the *Los Angeles Times* in 1930—unlike many of her lesser-known colleagues in the profession who struggled to survive. She also published two essays in the *New Yorker* this year, and the second serialization of *Miss Nobody from Nowhere* continued in the *Boston Globe* as well, adding to her income.

By the time Jordan published her ninth mystery, the genre had exploded in popularity among writers and readers. Offering a new twist to her repertoire, Jordan based her next mystery on a real murder case. *The Night Club Mystery*, set in the glamourous but increasingly mob-ridden world of Manhattan nightclubs, drew on the case of a murder in a Broadway speakeasy owned by the gangster Legs Diamond and his partner Charlie Entratta. One staff member who witnessed the event cooperated with police, but other staff members were killed so they could not corroborate the witness's story.

In Jordan's mystery, three innocent bystanders, two men and a woman, become witnesses to a mob murder when they hang out at a nightclub known for its mob activities, thinking it will be an adventure, and end up having to testify at the trial. The police accuse one of the male witnesses of being the murderer, and the story moves through twists and turns surrounding the identity of the true murderer, secrets among the three friends, and a tense final trial scene.

The story's timeliness helped its success as well. The restaurants and nightclubs haunted by the café society of fashionable New York had been overrun by criminal forces, and newspapers frequently covered this scene. Prohibition had ushered in massive opportunities for organized crime to grow into large syndicates. The East Coast was dominated by Al Capone and the seven hundred men who did his bidding and ran his thousands of speakeasies,[3] and the Italian thug of *The Night Club Mystery* resembles Capone in his arrogance and ability for cruelty.

Reviews were enthusiastic. The *News-Journal* declared that this mystery "has definitely placed [Jordan] in the front rank of mystery writers whose work is to be distinguished from the machine-made thriller." The *Atlanta Constitution* declared it her best mystery: "In all of her stories she has shown a genius for creating realistic characters . . . and stirs the reader's interest in solving one mystery only to fall into another. But in this book, there are no rest periods, no stopovers, you are willing to go the limit to keep up with the crowd. . . . It is a mystery story with an unusual combination, so well written that a thrill is not lost or wasted in the top speed which continues until the last chapter."[4]

Like most Americans, Jordan and her roommates assumed the Depression would be short lived, so they went ahead with planning their annual trip to Europe. They left in mid-April and spent three months in Spain and Italy.[5] By the time they returned to New York in mid-July, however, reality was setting in that the Depression would not be a fleeting instance. A good number of people were living on the streets in shelters made from wooden boxes or pieces of scrap metal. When the once booming automobile industry collapsed, no one could doubt that this was not a passing phenomenon. For the next few years, works of fiction and film would increasingly reflect the bleakness of life.[6]

For Jordan, the changes in publishing were stark. Throughout 1931 she published only four columns in the *Philadelphia Inquirer*—down from fifty to eighty columns annually in better times. Her review columns for *America* remained at one per month, but her standalone stories dropped to only one for the entire year. Her annual book of fiction also shifted to a traditional novel rather than a mystery. Readers lamented that she had "abandoned" mysteries, but this new novel delved into crime as much as a mystery might.

The Four-flusher was a powerful contribution to her catalog of novels. The derogatory term "four-flusher" was common at this time, coming from poker and having been used in magazines and elsewhere to imply a braggart who has little to back up his or her sense of superiority. Jordan's society crime novel explored the upper-class façade of success and the ruthless means a society woman would employ to maintain that façade.

The *Burlington Free Press* reviewer could not say enough about this "brilliant character study such as a reader is rarely privileged to find," and he found the story to be as full of suspense as any mystery.[7] Not all reviewers liked the plot that well, which shocked Jordan. She was renowned for her skills in characterization, but she was used to being praised for the complexity and interest of her storylines as well. Her next novel would also receive mixed reviews. The shock of such tepid evaluations of her work would shake her sense of her writing and push her into new avenues.

If all of this was not grim enough, Margaretta Jordan's health began to decline rapidly. There was no trip to Europe in 1931. Jordan spent much of the summer at Spreadwings, where she and Alice cared for their mother. One thing Margaretta loved was for her older daughter to read aloud to her, so Jordan gathered a number of books, including *The Good Earth*, and spent many hours reading to her mother. She also played the piano for her, which remained one of the great joys of Margaretta's life. As her health worsened, however, she slipped into long periods of near unconsciousness. Jordan and Alice tended to her day and night at first, but soon exhaustion set in, and Jordan hired two nurses to be with her mother during the long nights.[8]

Margaretta Garver Jordan, eighty-eight years old, died on July 27, 1931, with her daughters at her bedside. The passing of her mother left a gaping hole in Jordan's life that could never be filled.

Chapter 25
Writing against the Odds

As the Depression deepened, Jordan sought to maintain as much normalcy in her life as possible. She continued in every facet of her writing—producing columns, a novel, short stories—and she tried to participate in social activities as circumstances allowed. Still, she faced imminent changes. First, her column for the *Philadelphia Inquirer* was at an end. After eighteen years, she published her last column on April 8, 1932.

Jordan still had her monthly reviews for *America*, but this commitment actually brought about another difficulty. Her doctor's prediction that her eyesight problems might progress slowly proved wrong. She could no longer see the productions unless she sat in the first or second row of the theater. Her fears about her sight were undoubtedly exacerbated by memories of what drastic changes Joseph Pulitzer had endured in his life when he lost his eyesight and had to curtail much of his work.

Jordan found no reprieve from her difficult year, however, when she published her next novel in March 1932. The title character of *Play-Boy* was likely based on Jordan's beloved friend, Jack à Becket, whom she had often referred to as a playboy. David Kilmer is a charming character and a totally frustrating one, as he makes error after error in judgment. Gambling that leads to murder had become a common theme in mysteries of this era,[1] but Jordan chose a nonmystery novel this time because she wanted to focus her lens on the painful impact the gambler had on those he loved—specifically, his wife, who must not only cover his losses but also face threats to her own career due to his actions.

Most reviewers did not think it was Jordan's best novel, and the *Detroit Free Press* reviewer captured the way in which the gender reversal of the story made some readers uncomfortable: "She reverses the old plot of the young business man and the spendthrift young wife."[2] Further, readers were not as interested in tragic stories. With the painful realities of the Depression, the country became fascinated with forms of escapism.

Her next book received better reviews. A return to mysteries, *Young Mr. X* appeared in January 1933 and was set in two New York locales: the publishing world and the city's underworld of gangsters. *Young Mr. X* examined the psychological complexities of Perry Norris, a Jekyll-and-Hyde character. Penelope Lowell is the amateur detective trying to unravel Norris's mysterious actions. She becomes suspicious of him when he takes her to a nefarious speakeasy where a mob boss harasses a young woman. When no one helps the woman, Penelope steps in and is drawn further into the dangerous world of crime and abuse.

Reviewers praised the novel but struggled with how to classify its genre, largely because the genre of mysteries themselves were changing in these years, with the emergence of the "hard-boiled" version with graphic murders and hardened detectives. The *Chicago Tribune* described Jordan as "a famous writer of mystery tales" but cautioned that this story was not exactly a mystery, though there was a riddle to be solved that is worked out in effective ways at the end.

The *Boston Globe*, however, insisted it was a mystery, and a "satisfying" one at that. The *New York Herald Tribune* agreed that the work blended traits of a mystery and a traditional novel but concluded all that mattered was "You're not likely to guess what's wrong with Perry until the final pages."[3] This was Jordan's tenth mystery, and it was exhilarating to still receive appreciative reviews, especially after the tepid responses to *The Play-Boy*.

Though Jordan had had to curtail the quantity of works she published due to her waning eyesight, she was not one to sit back and moan. At sixty-eight, she decided that she should learn touch typing. She enrolled in a Northampton business school over the summer. "This was preparedness," she observed, "and time proved its wisdom. I still worked steadily. I still wrote a novel a year. . . . I even carried on reviewing [for *America*], sitting in the front rows of the orchestra and using powerful opera glasses."[4]

Proud as she was of her accomplishments under such debilitating circumstances, the truth was that vision in her right eye was nearly gone and the left eye was not significantly better. Still, her doctors advised her to wait as long as she could before having the surgery. Throughout this year, she "lived in a heavy fog," during which "even the faces of my intimate friends were lost and their figures moved dimly around me." To continue her work, she had to hire two secretaries to assist her. The saddest acknowledgment of her limitations, however, was that she had to give up most of her social life, "to the puzzlement of my friends . . . I changed my care-free stride to a cautious step," and she could not bear to have friends and acquaintances observe this change.[5] Always a dynamic woman, the center of any gathering, she would not be pitied.

The greatest gesture of friendship came once again from Martha Cutler. As Jordan recalled, Martha "dropped most of her own activities that year and was my shadow, guarding me everywhere I went, but the strain on her was great." After nearly falling on the stairs at an opera, Jordan restricted herself to home most of the time, working at her desk during the day and entertaining a few intimate friends in the evenings or having Martha or Harriet read to her "until their tongues must have ached."[6]

To supplement her income at this time, Jordan reprinted several of her earlier works in various newspapers. Having retained the copyright, these efforts paid off well. But as it became more difficult physically to travel around town, she reduced her reviews in *America* in the early months of 1934 to just three columns.

Jordan put most of her energy into writing her annual novels. *Page Mr. Pomeroy*, a closed-circle mystery, appeared in March. Mysteries of isolation were becoming as classic as their country-estate counterparts. If *Miss Nobody from Nowhere* had explored the isolation of amnesia, *Page Mr. Pomeroy* focused on the more common physical isolation, as the title character, an up-and-coming young businessman, is drugged and taken to an island with no means of escape. He is held by a Russian family, some of whom want him dead. Pomeroy must determine why he has been kidnapped, as well as what is behind the strange happenings on the island (including a murder), and find a way to escape.

Several reviewers commented on the tight pacing of the mystery: "a fast riddle in a picturesque setting." The *New Yorker* was particularly enthusiastic: "Fantastic stuff about the kidnapping of a young New York financier. The story is swift enough, however, to please people who go in for excitement rather than deduction."[7] The appreciation of this mystery convinced Jordan to continue in the genre.

By spring, Jordan had had enough when it came to her eyes. She informed her oculist that she wanted the eye surgery as soon as possible, assuming she could recover over the summer. However, the doctor said she should prepare for surgery over the summer and have it in the fall. "It was a blow," she admitted, "but I accepted it." She did, however, finally inform friends of the difficulties with her eyesight and that she would soon have surgery.[8]

In the intervening months, she began seeing double—"something of a nightmare"—but her doctor assured her it was a normal progression of the ailment. Finally, in October, she underwent the first of two planned surgeries. She had the second surgery early the next year and two smaller operations later in 1935 "to complete the good work of restoring vision." Recovery was time consuming, but she did regain most of her eyesight, only requiring glasses for distance. "Vision again!" she wrote in her autobiography, which she would start writing shortly after her recovery. "No one can imagine what this is who has not seen vision going." She ended her lamentations with her time-honored accolade: "Three rousing cheers!"[9]

Jordan returned to attending the theater and sharing her reviews with *America*'s readers and to publishing short stories for syndication in the *Chicago Tribune*. One of these stories, "Daddy and Miss Spencer," would be developed into her next novel. As challenging as her failing eyesight had been, she was still in the game.

Chapter 26

Three Rousing Cheers!

Pushing through the difficulties of the past year, Jordan published a delightful novel in April 1935 that appealed to readers and critics alike: *Daddy and I: A Chronicle of Small-Town Life and Youth, as Seen through the Eyes of an Ultra-Modern Young Lady of Fifteen*. The book was dedicated "To Clothilde / with awe and devotion." Very much in the vein of May Iverson, teenage June Drew wants to become a writer, but the main storyline is June's attempt to find a wife for her widowed father.

The appeal of the novel was so wide, it was purchased for a radio performance the following year and made into a successful film in 1937 under the title *Make Way for a Lady*. The novel also increased the number of requests Jordan received from readers for photographs and autographs, and she responded to each individually. One of the more interesting requests for a photograph came with questions that Jordan answered with honesty and her usual humor. "Who were the three best women writers of the past?" her correspondent asked. "George Eliot, George Sand, and our own Harriet Beecher Stowe—judging them by their appeal and influence," Jordan replied. As to present writers, "Yes, Gertrude Atherton is certainly a leader. Eugene O'Neil's [*sic*] work is powerful, but his mental outlook is usually so black that his work is depressing. I am no admirer of chronic pessimism. I think it has more to do with indigestion than with art."[1]

In September 1935, Jordan and her roommates were delighted when their beloved "niece," Clothilde Reo, entered Smith College. Clothilde became a member of the LUBA Club—Let Us Be Acquainted—which had been founded in 1920 to foster a sense of community for commuter students. The whole family rejoiced in Clothilde's accomplishment.

Another high note in Jordan's life occurred the following year with the success of her next mystery. *Life of the Party* was a masterpiece not only for its subtly diabolical characters and surprise ending but equally so for its exploration of what it means to be a detective. Jordan returned to the country-estate setting for this mystery. Caspar Kneeland is a millionaire who has allowed several guests to stay for the summer; they all were formerly wealthy but have become down-and-out in Depression-era America. Rex Hale, the son of Kneeland's best friend, is also visiting. Kneeland soon asks Hale to investigate strange happenings at his estate, Halcyon Camp—a cat and a dog have been poisoned and subjected to vivisection, several of the guests seem to thrive on observing and enacting the suffering of other guests, and his son Bert and niece Joan are both transforming from happy, active young people to nervous wrecks.

It becomes Hale's job to determine the cause of these events before a criminal disaster strikes. Kneeland insists Hale must learn to act as if he were a part of the "secret service." Jordan wanted readers to understand that he was not "one of those super detectives you read about in mystery stories," but rather a person who used observation, common sense, and, most of all, his brains.[2] Hale assures Kneeland he will not go around "with narrowed eyes and a mysterious expression" on his face.[3]

As in *The Devil and the Deep Sea*, Jordan exposed in this mystery the ease with which the upper classes abused drugs. Ruth Forbes is a heroin addict, and Hosanna, who is in love with Ruth, helps supply her with the drug, even though she knows Ruth will never return her love. Though a less explicit depiction of lesbian love than appeared in *The Devil and the Deep Sea*, there is no question about Hosanna's feelings.

Indeed, Hale understands that the real element of detection is discerning human nature, which often requires "watchful waiting."[4] Further, he does not have all the answers for how to discover the truth; by learning from fingerprint specialists and renowned psychiatrists, Hale unravels the layers of human cruelty enacted at the seemingly idyllic Halcyon Camp. This was a major shift in Jordan's mystery writing, joining the emphasis in these years on science-of-detection mysteries.[5]

Perhaps the most extensive project Jordan undertook this year, as she reached the age of seventy-one, was to begin drafting her autobiography. She referred to it, appropriately, as her "Book of Memories." She gathered materials and memories, both of her life and especially of the many people she had known over her lifetime.

At the same time, Jordan submitted her next mystery, *The Trap*, to Mary King for possible serialization in the *Chicago Tribune*. She sent the manuscript to King on a Saturday, and the following Wednesday King telephoned her with an acceptance. "If I were making a list of the most efficient and best executive women I have ever known," Jordan declared, Frances Willard would be at the top and King a close second.[6]

In July, *The Trap* was published in book form. It was a return to the blending of a ghost story with a mystery that Jordan had employed with *The Lady of Pentlands* years earlier. Horrifying figures, skeletons, and secret passages make for a thrilling story of an ancestral house haunted for decades—until the new young owner, Alida French, investigates the strange occurrences and threats that haunt the house.

The reviews were mixed. The *New York Times* tepidly concluded that the story "makes for pleasant reading," but the *Herald Tribune* insisted she had produced another interesting story: "Elizabeth Jordan writes a special kind of mystery, innocent of a professional detective and corpses. 'The Trap' is another bargain for those who do not wish to be too severely shocked, yet crave bafflement and whatever thrills may be" and "Miss Jordan is not one to shirk the scares. Complete with gay chatter, love suspects and plenty of surprises."[7] In this era, a reviewer's perspective clearly depended on whether he or she appreciated traditional mysteries or preferred the new, hard-boiled versions of the genre.

Then devastating news arrived: Frances Hodgson Burnett's son Vivian had been sailing on Long Island Sound on July 25, 1937, when he spotted a capsized boat and attempted to rescue the passengers. He managed to get all four on board his boat, only to collapse and die from a heart attack.[8] Vivian was Jordan's last real connection to Frances, and she mourned his loss.

In March 1938, Jordan published her autobiography, *Three Rousing Cheers*, which she dedicated "To the Memory of My Father and Mother." The book was a delightful collection of reminiscences about her youth, her years at the *New York World* and with Harper's, and especially a strong focus on the many people she knew throughout her life. The span of her life covered an extraordinary period in American cultural history, from her birth at the end of the Civil War until the publication of *Three Rousing Cheers*. The book was a great success and went into several editions in the coming years.

Perhaps one of the most interesting aspects of the book was the way in which she negotiated the presentation of her relationship with Frances Hodgson Burnett. Jordan had spent a lifetime keeping her sexuality behind a veil, but in her autobiography, she devoted a chapter to Frances and offered many overt declarations that she loved this woman and was partnered with her for many years, referring to "my beloved Frances Hodgson Burnett" and remarking that "she and I had been very close for many years" and in another instance referring to the period "when we had become almost inseparable."[9] She also included letters in which Frances called her "Darling" and "Beloved" and remarked "I want you so" or "I have a passionate desire to see you."[10] Frances had been central to her life, and she would not deny her love for her longtime partner.

There were complications to this account of her life, however. She rarely used dates, and her most common term for the era about which she was writing became "about this time." As she admitted at one point, "I may not be giving these chronicles in the order of their happening, but it must have been somewhere near this time."[11] Apparently, much of the recollections were from memory, because even the vague dating is frequently inaccurate. For example, she referred to the Lizzie Borden trial as taking place in August; it was in June. She claimed to be thirty when she started with the *Bazar*, while she was actually thirty-five, and so on.[12]

In spite of these minor issues, Jordan's charisma and sense of humor were apparent throughout the memoir, and it was a marvelous record of her many friendships with famous authors and international celebrities. Still, Jordan drew a different kind of veil over herself in her life's story. A reader feels they know her on some levels, and yet they are always straining to see behind the veil. One senses that she was smart, funny, deeply committed to her work, warm and loving with friends. Yet a significant part of Elizabeth Jordan remained cloistered, a mystery.

The reminiscences received rave reviews, without exception. The *New York Times* placed the strength of the book on the fact that Jordan "had always a zest and talent for friendship, the inborn 'sense of people,' which vivifies all her recollections here," and concluded the autobiography was not like some of the recent works in the field that were "freighted with problems of social or economic import"; Jordan's record of a life "is lively, clever, natural and richly human. Miss Jordan has a very bright mirror to hold up to her contemporaries and their scene; and it both reflects and sparkles."[13]

In celebration of the publication, friends hosted a cocktail party for her at the New York Newspaper Women's Club, and others sent letters, telegrams, short notes, and long congratulations. For Sinclair Lewis, writing before he finished the book, it brought back memories of when they worked closely together editing his books.[14] Margaret Deland found the book "alive on every page, and truly valuable analysis of the kind of mind that writes books."[15] Charles Hanson Towne of the *Smart Set* was dramatically enthusiastic: "Your autobiography is superb! Not in years have I read so lively a record, one more filled with fine American energy and purpose. And how beautifully it is written, how it marches along on velvet feet! I am proud to have known you, and glad to get these glimpses into your busy life. . . . It certainly should receive a Pulitzer award."[16]

Chapter 27

Passages

WITH THE SUCCESS OF HER AUTOBIOGRAPHY AND CONTINUED SYNDICATION of *The Life of the Party* three years after its publication, Jordan felt a renewed enthusiasm for her writing. She did not push herself in the way she had before her eyesight failed, but she wrote two stories for the *Chicago Tribune* in 1939, continued her *America* reviews, and published her annual novel.

Though there was a murder in Jordan's next book, *After the Verdict* was not a mystery. Here, her voice was much like that of her days of investigative reporting for the *World*. Drawing on so many modern instances of innocent people being charged with a scandalous crime and never fully exonerated due to "not proven" verdicts, Jordan traced the impact of such a verdict and subsequent media attention on a young woman's reputation and life.

She obviously touched a point of concern among the public with this storyline. The reviews were particularly strong. The *Washington Post*'s reviewer noted that "the demand for this kind of novel is extraordinarily well supplied" and concluded, "Miss Jordan seems to me to have done a better job than anyone had the right to expect." The *New York Times* assured readers it was a novel they would read with "unflagging interest."[1]

The most exciting events of this period, however, focused on family. First was Clothilde Reo's graduation from Smith College with a bachelor of arts in education. The following year she would begin her apprenticeship as a teacher. The Aunts reveled in Clothilde's success as she moved into adulthood, and they celebrated in December 1939 when Harriet retired from Columbia University Library. Harriet had loved being supervisor of the Cataloguing Department; as she wrote to the university's president on retirement, "Surely no worker anywhere has been more happily placed than I have been at Columbia."[2] Amazingly, it was a statement all three roommates could make about their own professional lives.

Jordan, at seventy-five, had no inclination to retire, and 1940 was a boom year in opportunities for publication due to the greater interest in reading among citizens, creating book publishing as a mass industry in these years.[3]

Jordan was able to negotiate again with the *Ladies' Home Journal* to serialize her next mystery, *First Port of Call*, which was published in book form later in the year. Mary King also sought stories from Jordan for both the *Daily News* and the *Chicago Tribune*; Jordan would publish nearly a dozen stories in these newspapers in the next five years. They became her primary places of publication, in addition to her novels.

Just as Jordan's writing was spinning out more and more ideas, she broke her arm and once again had to rely on Martha, Harriet, or her secretary to type personal and business letters for her. Fortunately, everything was already in place for the publication of *First Port of Call*, which appeared in April 1940, with a dedication to Mary King "with much admiration and affection."[4]

Jordan liked to use forms of fast-paced transportation in her mysteries—trains, automobiles, boats, airplanes—as settings to enhance narrative tension by bringing together a group of strangers in moments of crisis when it is impossible to know who to trust. Jordan's *First Port of Call* drew on the newness of commercial aviation. A well-to-do group of people are on board a plane that goes down in the ocean. After surviving on life rafts, they end up on a strange island where they are taken in by people who refuse to answer their questions. Then true horror begins as their hosts force each survivor to face the brutal truth of the horrific acts and choices they have made in their lives—and they must do so in front of the entire group, humiliating each person with the exposure of their past deeds. The protagonist, Maxine Perry, must uncover not only where they are but also why they are being subjected to such horrors.

Reviewers across the board were drawn to the novel. The *Chicago Tribune* was typical in concluding that it was a "strange and fascinating tale Miss Jordan tells—with implications of immortality."[5] Otis Skinner wrote her immediately after reading *First Port of Call*: "It is a marvellous tale that you've told! I followed your odyssey over that purgatorial isle quite breathless. . . . It is a perfect piece of writing, carrying the burden of your message with a rare imagination and philosophy and a deep insight into human character and motive."[6]

As successful as this mystery was, nothing could relieve the overshadowing gloom as the new war in Europe expanded. As in World War I, Jordan believed the United States should become actively involved in order to protect the nation and its allies—and religious freedom. In March, she joined leading Catholic priests and other renowned members of the faith in signing an appeal for aid to Britain, noting that "Hitlerism, like communism, seeks to subvert Christianity by setting up a warped vision of racial superiority and of the omnipotent State in the place of God. In Hitlerism, as in communism, the dignity and the rights of the human person are annihilated in brutal subjection to a collectivist State."[7] It was one of many war petitions she supported in these years.

Jordan's socializing also significantly declined in these years, but she managed to host a luncheon in honor of Mary King at her home early in the year. The gathering brought together several people of influence in society circles, including Belle Wyatt Roosevelt, daughter-in-law of Theodore Roosevelt; Jeannie Robinson Smith, widow of the lawyer and industrialist Charles Robinson Smith; and Candace Hewitt Willard, daughter of Jordan's friend, the inventor Edward Ringwood Hewitt. Also in attendance was Fannie Hurst. It had been some time since she and Jordan had seen one another, and Hurst replied to the invitation, "As always, I am delighted when the opportunity for a glimpse of you comes along."[8] A single such event was a long way from the weekly luncheons

Jordan had hosted in earlier years, but she was slowing down, and it was not a world in which socializing seemed as attractive as it once had.

In the spring she published a new novel, *Faraway Island*. In wartime, well-to-do Americans no longer vacationed in Europe, so in Jordan's story a dozen of them, largely unknown to one another, decide to go to Central America instead. Renting a yacht, they cruise through remote islands, but a horrible storm damages the yacht and they end up stranded on an island. The novel pursues the psychological impact of desperation for people who were used to being cared for and pampered; while the hardships are many and not everyone rises to the challenges, most of them develop into far more capable individuals than they could have imagined.

Reviewers seemed at a loss regarding how to address such an unusual novel from Jordan and insisted it had nothing to do with the war, missing the point not only of the reason the castaways chose this adventure but also that war demanded extraordinary efforts even from the wealthy. The *New York Times* was blunt: the story "bears no relation to life, but makes an entertaining fantasy." The reviewer for the *Oakland Tribune* admired the suspense that held up to the end, "integrating the more agreeable aspects of Robinson Crusoe, Swiss Family Robinson and Treasure Island" while doing "a good job of making her various characters integrate their personalities to communal life."[9]

Other of Jordan's writings at this time were more explicit in their relation to war. "Zita Begins Life Over," published in the *Chicago Tribune* in mid-December 1941, was set in a night school that Zita von Gumpert, an Austrian refugee, attends. But she is pursued by an enemy who is trying to force her and her mother to return to Austria, where they will be under German rule. The story focuses on how the teacher tries to save Zita from deportation.

At seventy-six, Jordan could not participate in as many of the activities to support the war and US soldiers as she had during World War I. As she noted, "I am necessarily confining my aid to this war to such checks as I can afford to send out in response to hundreds of appeals."[10] But writing was also a way in which she contributed. She, Harriet, and Martha hunkered down to do what they could and ride out what they must "for the duration."

Chapter 28

The Final Years

THE PSYCHOLOGICAL PRESSURE OF THE WAR ERA WAS OVERWHELMING. Jordan tried to maintain a steady work schedule to afford herself as much peace of mind as she could manage, and in March 1942 her impressive body of work over her lifetime was recognized when she was elected to membership in P.E.N., an international organization of literary artists devoted to human rights. A dinner was held at the Ambassador Hotel to honor the newly inducted members, who included Jordan, playwright Susan Glaspell, biographer Lyman Beecher Stowe, author and actor Cornelia Otis Skinner, and Jordan's longtime friend, author and labor activist Mary Heaton Vorse.[1]

The following month, Jordan published *Young John Takes Over*, a novel about civic corruption in a small town and the young lawyer who inherits his father's firm, which has an antagonistic relationship to corrupt politicians. John Campbell IV decides to carry on his father's crusades against the speakeasies and gambling houses run by a domineering politician. While an interesting subject for exploration, the novel was not up to Jordan's usual standard. It was slow paced and would have benefited from editing out much of the repetition of the early chapters.

The reviews were mixed. The *Herald Tribune*, for instance, declared, "Here is a story of warfare in which there is never any peace—the eternal skirmish between honest citizens and graft and corruption in municipal government." While the romance elements of the story would be "satisfactory to Miss Jordan's readers," the reviewer noted, "the pattern of the story is a bit obvious, however, and the development of the love story not as subtle as this author has managed in some of her novels."[2]

One of the joys of Jordan's life in these war years was seeing the continued growth of Clothilde Reo. Having graduated from Smith and completed her apprentice teaching, Clothilde was now a full-fledged teacher in Northampton, Massachusetts. Even more rewarding for Jordan was the happiness Clothilde had found in life, not only in her career but also in the man she loved. In 1943, Clothilde married Joseph Murray Devine. At the time Joseph was on active duty in the US Naval Reserve. The ceremony was held in St. Patrick's Cathedral in New York City.

Another joy for Jordan still centered on attending the theater and writing reviews for *America* magazine. War themes were now more notable on the stage, and she praised the relatively new Studio Theatre for its ensemble production of *Winter Soldiers*, "which showed the superb fight of oppressed peoples under Nazi attacks and domination." Most impressive, however, was Sidney Kingsley's *The Patriots*. Jordan noted that the play forced people to consider what constitutes a patriot in time of war.[3]

In March 1943, Jordan published *Herself*, a mystery advertised as "a story of horror and heartbreak." It was a least-likely-suspect mystery; this subgenre went back to Poe and was used by Agatha Christie in her first mystery as well as by Ellery Queen and others. Although a slow-burn mystery, much more so than Jordan's usual fast-paced stories, *Herself* spoke to the moment in which select groups—Jews and homosexuals—were being singled out as dangers to the state. In Jordan's story, a mysterious plague moves through a community, killing several people, and select groups—working-class citizens and immigrants—become the target of those who suspect them of carrying the disease and infecting others. The story is a study of the kind of desperation engendered when a mysterious illness, "an epidemic," attacks a community and the way in which rumors about who brought this taint on the community tear people apart. The shocking ending was pure Jordan.

It had been some years since Jordan produced a mystery, and reviewers loved the return to form. The *Chicago Tribune* called it "an extraordinarily developed mystery drama." Similar praise came in newspapers across the country. The *Herald Tribune* noted that Jordan had a "preference for slow beginnings, nothing ominous or sinister in sight. But if you are acquainted with her method, you recognize the purpose behind it—to build up a lull of calm before the storm of drama. It is applied very effectively in [*Herself*]. . . . Miss Jordan keeps you guessing right up to a tense climax."[4] It was a delightful comeback, especially since this was the last mystery she published.

In 1944, the impact of Jordan's age on her productivity became evident. For the first time in decades, she did not publish her annual novel and produced only one short story. As much as she loved the theater, age

Cover of *Herself*, Jordan's final mystery

and worsening health made attending productions increasingly difficult. She managed to go to the theater for a few months, but in April she published her last column for *America*. She offered no sign-off; she simply laid down her pen after nearly twenty-two years as their drama critic.

However poor her health was becoming, she would never forgo the right to cast her ballot at the election box. She had fought too hard for too many decades to give women the opportunity to vote, and she proudly cast her ballot for Franklin Delano Roosevelt.[5]

Jordan published her final novel in 1945, *Miss Warren's Son*. Unfortunately, the most exciting aspect of the book was its title. The premise—a young single woman, Alicia, finds a lost little boy at the park and takes him home to care for him. There are moments in the plot that could have developed into exciting reading, such as when the boy is kidnapped, but he is quickly found and the story drains off into a mundane romance.

Early in 1945, Jordan fell, and her health declined rapidly thereafter.[6] With her low productivity in these years, her income had diminished significantly, but Martha Cutler, who retained a good portion of her inheritance even after the stock market crash, helped Jordan through these final years, and Harriet aided her personally in every way she could. The bond that had been formed so long ago remained until the end.

In April 1946, Jordan published a two-part story, "Remington's Easter Gift," in the *Boston Globe*, and that ended her sixty-year writing career. She had come so far since those early days of editing the women's page for *Peck's Sun* and freelance work for the *Milwaukee Sentinel* and other papers. A lifetime of exceptional accomplishments as a journalist, editor, author, columnist, suffragist, drama critic—and beloved friend to so many—came to an end on February 24, 1947, when she died of arteriosclerotic heart disease and bronchopneumonia at her home at Gramercy Park.[7] The funeral, held in her apartment, was attended by Harriet and Martha and a handful of other surviving friends, including Mary King.[8]

Long, appreciative obituaries appeared in every major newspaper. Most of them indicated her age at death as seventy-nine; Jordan would have appreciated that they were still shaving two years off her real age. The *New York Times* was typical in its thorough coverage of her life's work, from her early days on Milwaukee newspapers to her "True Stories" column in the *World* to her long list of published books and her commitment to suffrage.[9] Interestingly, almost all the obituaries referred to her as a journalist. The impact she made on the nation as an early woman journalist had not been forgotten. Nor had her influence on so many young journalists and authors.

But equally important was the influence she had on the development of mystery writing in America. Her fifteen mysteries helped establish classic genres, demonstrated that gender was not a factor in the ability to write exciting mysteries, and revealed the genre as an excellent vehicle for cultural critiques. For more than twenty years, she was considered one of America's top mystery writers, with good cause. An outstanding writer, a visionary in terms of genre, and an astute critic of contemporary American culture, she earned her place in the forefront of early twentieth-century mystery writing.

Notes

Chapter 1: Life in Milwaukee

1. Elizabeth Jordan [hereafter "EJ"], *Three Rousing Cheers* (New York: D. Appleton-Century Company, 1938), 23.
2. "Mrs. William Francis Jordan," *New York Herald Tribune* (July 28, 1931), 13.
3. EJ, *Three Rousing Cheers*, 10.
4. EJ, *Three Rousing Cheers*, 2, 5.
5. EJ, "Elizabeth Jordan," in *The Book of Catholic Authors*, ed. Walter Romig (Detroit: Walter Romig & Co., 1943), 151.
6. EJ, "Elizabeth Jordan," *Catholic Authors*, 152–53.
7. EJ, *Three Rousing Cheers*, 57–58.
8. EJ, "Elizabeth Jordan," *Catholic Authors*, 152–53.
9. EJ, *Three Rousing Cheers*, 19.
10. *Notre Dame Convent, Motherhouse of the School Sisters of Notre Dame, Milwaukee, Wis., U.S.A.* (Milwaukee: P. M. Abbelen, 1894), n.p.
11. Michael Tkach, "Notre Dame Convent Created a 'City unto Itself' in Milwaukee," On Milwaukee, https://onmilwaukee.com.
12. Tkach, "Notre Dame Convent."
13. "Find a Grave," Ancestry.com.
14. EJ, foreword, *May Iverson Tackles Life* (New York: Harper and Brothers, 1912), viii.
15. EJ, *Three Rousing Cheers*, 4–5.
16. EJ, "Elizabeth Jordan," *Catholic Authors*, 152.
17. EJ, "Elizabeth Jordan," in *My Maiden Effort*, ed. Gelett Burgess (Garden City, NY: Doubleday, Page, 1921), 123–24; EJ, *Three Rousing Cheers*, 6–8.
18. EJ, "Elizabeth Jordan," *My Maiden Effort*, 125.
19. EJ, *Three Rousing Cheers*, 7–8.
20. EJ, "Elizabeth Jordan," *My Maiden Effort*, 125.
21. EJ, "Olive's First Story," *Harper's Magazine* 126 (April 1913), 788–95.
22. EJ, *Three Rousing Cheers*, 2.
23. EJ, *Three Rousing Cheers*, 5.
24. EJ, *Three Rousing Cheers*, 6.
25. EJ, "Elizabeth Jordan," *Catholic Authors*, 151.
26. "Meaning of 'Cross of Honor,'" *Washington Times* (February 16, 2002), col. 3.

Chapter 2: The Plan

1. EJ, *Three Rousing Cheers*, 8.
2. EJ, *Three Rousing Cheers*, 12.
3. Lida Rose McCabe, "Practical Outcome of Higher Education for Women," *Independent* (August 3, 1893), 7; "The Best Known Women Writers," *Advance* (May 4, 1905), 565.
4. William George Bruce, *History of Milwaukee, City and County* (Milwaukee: S. J. Clarke Publishing Co., 1922), 2:813.
5. Bruce, *History of Milwaukee*, 13.
6. Advertisement, *The Meridional* (May 8, 1886), 1.
7. EJ, *Three Rousing Cheers*, 14.
8. EJ, *Three Rousing Cheers*, 14–15, 17; Helen M. Winslow, "Some Newspaper Women," *Arena* 1 (June 1897), 139–40; Margherita Arlina Hamm, "New York Newspaper Women," *Peterson Magazine* 5 (April 1895), 403; "Gazette des Dames," *Weekly Wisconsin* (June 20, 1891), 3.
9. EJ, *Three Rousing Cheers*, 17.
10. Paul Prescott, *New Journalism, New Critics, 1890–1910* (Cambridge: Cambridge University Press, 2013), 57.
11. Quoted in James McGrath Morris, *Pulitzer: A Life in Politics, Print, and Power* (New York: HarperCollins, 2011), 271.
12. EJ, "Elizabeth Jordan," *Catholic Authors*, 153; EJ, *Three Rousing Cheers*, 20.
13. Kim Todd, *Sensational: The Hidden History of America's "Girl Stunt Reporters"* (New York: HarperCollins, 2021), 24.
14. Todd, *Sensational*, 23.
15. Todd, *Sensational*, 4–8.
16. Todd, *Sensational*; on detection, see chapter 3.
17. Todd, *Sensational.*
18. Todd, *Sensational*, 110.

Chapter 3: A New Kind of Education

1. EJ, "Elizabeth Jordan," *Catholic Authors*, 153.
2. EJ, *Three Rousing Cheers*, 23.
3. James D. Livingston, *Arsenic and Clam Chowder: Murder in Gilded Age New York* (Albany: State University of New York Press, 2010), 13.
4. Quoted in Milton Rugoff, *The Gilded Age* (New York: New Word City, 2018), 131.
5. Karen Roggenkamp, "Elizabeth Jordan, 'True Stories,' and Newspaper Fiction in Late-Nineteenth-Century Journalism," in *Literature and Journalism: Inspirations, Intersections, and Inventions from Ben Franklin to Stephen Colbert*, ed. Mark Canada (New York: Palgrave Macmillan, 2013), 120–21; Paul Collins, *The Murder of the Century: The Gilded Age Crime That Scandalized a City and Sparked the Tabloid Wars* (New York: Broadway Books/Random House, 2011), 17; Alice Fahs, *Out on Assignment: Newspaper Women and the Making of Modern Public Space* (Durham: University of North Carolina Press, 2011), 4, 10, 93–99.

6. Morris, *Pulitzer*, 273; Art M. Blake, *How New York Became American, 1890–1924* (Baltimore: Johns Hopkins University Press, 2020), 53.
7. EJ, *Three Rousing Cheers*, 26.
8. EJ, *Three Rousing Cheers*, 73.
9. EJ, *Three Rousing Cheers*, 27.
10. EJ, *Three Rousing Cheers*, 27–29.
11. EJ, *Three Rousing Cheers*, 28.
12. EJ, *Three Rousing Cheers*, 27–28.
13. EJ, *Three Rousing Cheers*, 28–31.
14. EJ, *Three Rousing Cheers*, 33.
15. EJ, *Three Rousing Cheers*, 33.
16. EJ, *Three Rousing Cheers*, 33–35.

Chapter 4: Making Her Way

1. EJ, *Three Rousing Cheers*, 17, 19, 28, 31.
2. Morris, *Pulitzer*, 215.
3. EJ, *Three Rousing Cheers*, 37.
4. "Mr. Maugham Sobs Aloud," *America* (May 27, 1933), 184–85.
5. EJ, *Three Rousing Cheers*, 36–39.
6. EJ, *Three Rousing Cheers*, 38–39.
7. Sharon M. Harris, *Rebecca Harding Davis: A Life Among Writers* (Morgantown: West Virginia University Press, 2018), 239ff.
8. EJ, *Three Rousing Cheers*, 40.
9. EJ, "Elizabeth Jordan," *Catholic Authors*, 153–54.
10. EJ, *Three Rousing Cheers*, 39–48; EJ, "The Newspaper Woman's Story," *Lippincott's Magazine* 51 (March 1893), 344–46.

Chapter 5: True Stories

1. EJ, *Three Rousing Cheers*, 72.
2. EJ, *Three Rousing Cheers*, 51.
3. See, for example, [EJ], "A Shatchen's Work," *World* (December 5, 1890); "A Natural Criminal," *World* (November 28, 1890).
4. Roggenkamp, "Elizabeth Jordan," 125.
5. Collins, *The Murder of the Century*, 17.
6. Morris, *Pulitzer*, 287.
7. Collins, *The Murder of the Century*, 17.
8. [EJ], "A Psychological Study," *World* (January 21, 1891).

Chapter 6: Sections Editor

1. EJ, *Three Rousing Cheers*, 86.
2. Fahs, *Out on Assignment*, 13–14, 87; Jane Johnson Lewis, "Sorosis: Professional Women's Club," February 27, 2019, https://www.thoughtco.com; Dustin Harp,

Desperately Seeking Women Readers: U.S. Newspapers and the Construction of a Female Readership (Lanham, MD: Lexington Books, 2007), 23.

3. EJ, *Three Rousing Cheers*, 97.

4. Helen M. Winslow, "Some Handsome Newspaper Women," *Godey's* 134 (March 1897), 242–47.

5. "Her Political Status," (Washington, DC) *Evening Star* (February 26, 1891), 6.

6. Hamm, "New York Newspaper Women," 404.

7. Ishbel Ross, *Ladies of the Press: The Story of Women in Journalism by an Insider* (New York: Harper & Brothers, 1936), 9.

8. EJ, *Three Rousing Cheers*, 33.

9. "Women Newspaper Writers," *New-York Tribune* (October 19, 1899), 7; Fahs, *Out on Assignment*, 23–24. For an excellent study of early women journalists, see Brooke Kroeger, *Undaunted: How Women Changed American Journalism* (New York: Alfred A. Knopf, 2023), Parts I and II.

10. Joan Cashin, *First Lady of the Confederacy: Varina Davis's Civil War* (Cambridge, MA: Belknap Press, 2006).

11. EJ, *Three Rousing Cheers*, 86–87.

12. Bayard Veiller, *The Fun I've Had* (New York: Reynal & Hitchcock, 1941), 311.

13. Letter, Zona Gale to EJ, October 10, no year (EGJ Papers, NYPL).

14. EJ, *Three Rousing Cheers*, 73–74; Eliza Archard Conner, "Woman's World in Paragraphs," *Worcester Spy* (November 14, 1892), 7.

15. "Harper's Bazar's New Editor," *Los Angeles Herald* (January 14, 1900), 11. The cache of letters to Jordan from Field are not extant.

16. Veiller, *The Fun I've Had*, 311–14.

17. Veiller, *The Fun I've Had*, 311–14.

18. EJ, "Elizabeth Jordan," *Catholic Authors*, 153–54.

19. EJ, "Elizabeth Jordan," *Catholic Authors*, 153–54.

20. EJ, *Three Rousing Cheers*, 100.

21. [EJ], "Ready with Bail," *Evening World* (March 21, 1891), 1, 3.

22. EJ, *Three Rousing Cheers*, 100–103; EJ, "Elizabeth Jordan," *Catholic Authors*, 154.

Chapter 7: Lizzie Borden's Trial and a Shocking Aftermath

1. William F. Hanna, "Lizzie Borden and the Taunton Jail," Old Colony History Museum (August 3, 2020), ochm.medium.com.

2. Kate McGuirk, "In a New Light," *New York Recorder* (September 20, 1892), n.p.

3. Quoted in Hanna, "Lizzie Borden and the Taunton Jail."

4. EJ, *Three Rousing Cheers*, 116. This is the only time Jordan mentions being asked to lead readers to a certain conclusion. We have no sense of whether this directive was the norm or if she minded doing so.

5. Morris, *Pulitzer*, 298.

6. EJ, *Three Rousing Cheers*, 116.

7. Cara Robertson, *The Trial of Lizzie Borden* (New York: Simon & Schuster, 2019), 25.

8. EJ, "The Case of Lizzie Borden," *World* (June 4, 1893), 1.

9. EJ, "Last Edition: Borden Trial Begins," *World* (June 5, 1893), 1.

10. EJ, *Three Rousing Cheers*, 117.
11. Robertson, *The Trial of Lizzie Borden*, 79, 82; [EJ], "Borden Jury Chosen," *World* (June 6, 1893), 1.
12. [EJ], "Borden Jury Chosen," *World* (June 6, 1893), 1.
13. EJ, "Is Lizzie Borden Innocent?" *World* (June 11, 1893), 20.
14. EJ, "Going Lizzie's Way," *World* (June 13, 1893), 1.
15. EJ, *Three Rousing Cheers*, 120.
16. Robertson, *The Trial of Lizzie Borden*, 177; EJ, *Three Rousing Cheers*, 119.
17. EJ, "You Gave Me Away!" *World* (June 15, 1893), 3.
18. EJ, *Three Rousing Cheers*, 119.
19. EJ, "Lizzie's Side Heard," *World* (June 16, 1893), 14.
20. Advertisement, "To-Morrow," *World* (June 17, 1893), 6.
21. EJ, "This Is the Real Lizzie Borden," *World* (June 18, 1893), 15.
22. EJ, "Lizzie Borden Free," *World* (June 21, 1893), 1, 7.
23. EJ, *Three Rousing Cheers*, 122.
24. Letter, EJ to Alexander Woollcott, April 16, 1938 (EGJ Papers, NYPL). In her autobiography, Jordan had referred to Emma as having gone insane (*Three Rousing Cheers*, 121).
25. Veiller, *The Fun I've Had*, 314.

CHAPTER 8: ASSISTANT EDITOR

1. Morris, *Pulitzer*, 301–2.
2. Fahs, *Out on Assignment*, 3.
3. Hamm, "New York Newspaper Women," 404.
4. Ishbel Ross, "Elizabeth Garver Jordan," in *Notable American Women: A Biographical Dictionary*, eds. Edward T. James et al. (Cambridge, MA: Radcliffe College, 1971), 2:294.
5. EJ, *Three Rousing Cheers*, 94–96.
6. Frances E. Willard, *Glimpses of Fifty Years: The Autobiography of an American Woman* (New York: Woman's Christian Temperance Union, 1889), 642.
7. EJ, *Three Rousing Cheers*, 144.
8. EJ, *Three Rousing Cheers*, 144, 147.
9. EJ, "Approaching the Editor," *The Writer* 5 (November 1891), 243–44.
10. Although there were several references to this book when it was published, no copy is extant.
11. EJ, "The Newspaper Woman's Story," 340–47.
12. Item, *Los Angeles Herald* (April 16, 1893), n.p. The reporter who wrote "A New York Newspaper Woman" noted that Jordan had begun publishing fiction under the pen name of "Jean Memy" in 1893; unfortunately, I have been unable to find any publications under that name. Well into her late years, the family called her "Aunt Jean" from this early use of a pen name (email from Betsy Devine to author, October 3, 2019).
13. EJ, *Three Rousing Cheers*, 104.
14. EJ, *Three Rousing Cheers*, 93ff.
15. EJ, *Three Rousing Cheers*, 99–103; EJ, "Elizabeth Jordan," *Catholic Authors*, 153.
16. Gertrude Atherton, *Adventures of a Novelist* (New York: Liveright, 1932), 220.

17. Atherton, *Adventures of a Novelist*, 220–21.

18. Rose O'Neill, *Rose O'Neill: An Autobiography*, ed. Miriam Formanek-Brunell (Columbia: University of Missouri Press, 1997), 72.

19. O'Neill, *Rose O'Neill*, 72.

20. O'Neill, *Rose O'Neill*, 106–7.

21. O'Neill, *Rose O'Neill*, 127.

22. S. J. Wolfe, "Arthur Brisbane—Fifty Years in Journalism," *Literary Digest* (October 21, 1933), 29.

23. EJ, *Three Rousing Cheers*, 111.

24. Lauren C. Santangelo, "The Merry War Goes On: Elite Suffrage in Gilded Age Manhattan," *New York History* 98 (Fall 2017), 353.

25. "Gilded suffragists" is Johanna Neuman's term; see Johanna Neuman, *Gilded Suffragists: The New York Socialites Who Fought for Women's Right to Vote* (New York: New York University Press, 2017).

26. EJ, *Three Rousing Cheers*, 130–31.

27. EJ, *Three Rousing Cheers*, 128–29.

28. EJ, *Three Rousing Cheers*, 129.

29. Elizabeth Jordan, "Kittie's Sister Josephine," in *Different Girls* (Harper's Novelettes), eds. William Dean Howells and Henry Mills Alden (New York: Harper and Brothers, 1895), 19–40.

30. Rugoff, *The Gilded Age*, 134.

31. Livingston, *Arsenic and Clam Chowder*, 13.

32. Livingston, *Arsenic and Clam Chowder*, 13.

33. Rugoff, *Gilded Age*, 134–35; W. A. Swanberg, *Citizen Hearst* (New York: Macmillan, 1961), 93–193.

34. Kenneth Whyte, *The Uncrowned King: The Sensational Rise of William Randolph Hearst* (New York: Penguin Random House, 2009).

35. Livingston, *Arsenic and Clam Chowder,* 67.

36. [EJ], "Mrs. Fleming and the Sunday World's Woman Jury," *World* (June 21, 1896), 21.

37. [EJ], "The Sunday World's Woman Jury in the Fleming Case," *World* (June 28, 1896), n.p.

Chapter 9: Transitioning

1. Fahs, *Out on Assignment*, 4; Frank Luther Mott, *American Journalism: A History, 1690–1960* (New York: Macmillan, 1962), 546; Collins, *The Murder of the Century*, 35.

2. "Frederick A. Duneka, Manager of Harper's, Dead," *New York Tribune* (January 25, 1919), 13.

3. EJ, *Three Rousing Cheers*, 112.

4. "Book Talk," *Nassau Literary Magazine* 33 (March 1898), 438.

5. "Women in Journalism," *Dover Express* (April 8, 1898), 3.

6. Jean Marie Lutes, *Front-Page Girls: Women Journalists in American Culture and Fiction, 1880–1930* (Ithaca, NY: Cornell University Press, 2006), 104.

7. Doug Underwood, *Literary Journalism in British and American Prose: An Historical Overview* (Jefferson, NC: McFarland, 2019), 104.
8. Collins, *Murder of the Century*, 246–48; Livingston, *Arsenic and Clam Chowder*, 23.
9. Morris, *Pulitzer*, 346.
10. EJ, *Three Rousing Cheers*, 166.

CHAPTER 10: *HARPER'S BAZAR*

1. "Harper and Brothers Reorganize," *New York Times* (November 17, 1899), 1.
2. June Howard, "'Her Very Handwriting Looks as If She Owned the Earth': Elizabeth Jordan and Editorial Power," in *Women in Print: Essays in the Print Culture of American Women from the Nineteenth and Twentieth Centuries*, eds. James P. Danky and Wayne A. Wiegand (Madison: University of Wisconsin Press, 2006), 69–70.
3. "Frederick A. Duneka, Manager of Harper's, Dead," 13.
4. EJ, *Three Rousing Cheers*, 173, 174–75, 195; EJ, "Elizabeth Jordan," *Catholic Authors*, 154.
5. "Both Ends of the Plank," *Fame* (February 1900), 68.
6. See, for example, "Miss Elizabeth Jordan, the Catholic Editor of Harper's Bazar," *Catholic Advance* (April 25, 1903), 3.
7. "Harper's Bazar's New Editor," *Los Angeles Herald* (January 14, 1900), 11.
8. EJ, *Three Rousing Cheers*, 264.
9. *One Hundred Year Biographical Directory of Mount Holyoke College, 1837–1934* (Bulletin Series 30, no. 5) (South Hadley, MA: Mount Holyoke College, 1935), n.p.; Jane R. Siegel, "Women in the Stacks," www.womeninthestacks.wordpress.com.
10. EJ, *Three Rousing Cheers*, 170.
11. EJ, *Three Rousing Cheers*, 146.

CHAPTER 11: FASHIONING LITERATURE

1. "Mostly about Women," *Advance* (March 9, 1905), 307.
2. "Elizabeth Jordan, Editor," *Harper's Bazaar*, www.pressreader.com.
3. Note, J. Henry Harper to EJ, July 6, 1900 (EGJ Papers, NYPL).
4. EJ, *Three Rousing Cheers*, 171ff, 181ff.
5. EJ, *Three Rousing Cheers*, 189.
6. Letter, William Dean Howells to EJ, January 6, 1900 (EGJ Papers, NYPL).
7. Letter, William Dean Howells to EJ, January 25, 1900 (EGJ Papers, NYPL).
8. See, for example, Letter, William Dean Howells to "Gentlemen," May 24, 1900 (EGJ Papers, NYPL).
9. Letter, Ida Tarbell to EJ, April 9, 1900 (EGJ Papers, NYPL).
10. Letter, Stephen Crane to EJ, February 5, no year (EGJ Papers, NYPL).
11. See, for instance, [EJ], *Harper's Bazar* editorials: "Women as War Barometer" (May 12, 1900), "To End the Boer War" (May 26, 1900), "The Cry of India" (June 2, 1900), "The Army Canteen" (June 9, 1900), and "When Johnny Comes Marching Home" (July 7, 1900).
12. [EJ], "When Johnny Comes Marching Home," 642.
13. [EJ], "When Johnny Comes Marching Home," 642.

Chapter 12: Editor and Author

1. Madame Wu, "Chinese and American Women Contrasted," *Harper's Bazar* (July 21, 1900), 729–31.

2. Letter, Josephine Daskam (Bacon) to EJ, October 29, no year (EGJ Papers, NYPL).

3. Philip Horne, "Henry James and the Economy of the Short Story," in *Modernist Writers and the Marketplace*, eds. Warren Chernaik et al. (New York: Springer, 1996), 10.

4. EJ, *Three Rousing Cheers*, 184.

5. EJ, *Three Rousing Cheers*, 182–85.

6. In later May Iverson books, she changed the convent's title to St. Catherine's.

7. Charles A. Johanningsmeier, *Fiction and the American Literary Marketplace: The Role of Newspaper Syndicates in America, 1860–1900* (Cambridge, MA: Cambridge University Press, 2002), chapter 4.

Chapter 13: Retreats

1. EJ, *Three Rousing Cheers*, 104, 180, 185.

2. "New Books," *Outlook* (October 19, 1901), 420; "Other New Fiction," *Current Literature* 31 (November 1901), 625; "Within Convent Walls," *Evening World* (August 30, 1901), 5.

3. EJ, *Three Rousing Cheers*, 195–96.

4. EJ, *Three Rousing Cheers*, 195–96.

5. "Miss Elizabeth Jordan, the Catholic Editor of Harper's Bazar," *Catholic Advance* (April 25, 1903), 3.

6. Carole Klein, *Gramercy Park: An American Bloomsbury* (Baltimore: Johns Hopkins University Press, 1987).

7. Theodore Roosevelt, *The Strenuous Life* (New York: The Century Co., 1900).

8. Henry Van Dyke, "The Strenuous Life for Girls," *Harper's Bazar* (July 1902), 575–78.

9. "Books and Writers," *Harper's Bazar* 36 (August 1902), 731.

10. "Books," *Chicago Tribune* (June 28, 1902), 18; "Some New Books," *Literary World* (August 1, 1902).

11. Mrs. John A. Logan, *The Part Taken by Women in American History* (Wilmington, DE: Perry-Nalle Publishing Co., 1912), 835.

12. EJ, *Faith Desmond's Last Stand* (Chicago: Extension Press, 1924), 205.

13. Anne O'Hagan, "The Shop Girl and Her Wages," *Munsey's Magazine* 50 (November 1913), 252–59.

14. Letter, Frances Hodgson Burnett to EJ, April 22, 1903 (EGJ Papers, NYPL).

15. Letter, Margaret Deland to EJ, February 20, 1904 (EGJ Papers, NYPL).

Chapter 14: The Whole Darn Family

1. Letter, William Dean Howells to EJ, June 6, 1904 (EGJ Papers, NYPL).

2. Letter, Henry James to EJ, July 5, 1904 (EGJ Papers, NYPL).

3. Norman Page, ed., *Mark Twain: Interviews and Reminiscences* (New York: Springer, 1984), 45.

4. EJ, *May Iverson Tackles Life*, viii.

5. EJ, *May Iverson—Her Book* (New York: Harper and Brothers, 1904), 8.

6. [Jeannette Gilder], "The Lounger," *Critic* 45 (November 1904), 398; "May Iverson," *Literary World* 35 (December 1904), 381. For other reviews that suggest Jordan created a new type in American literature, see "Books and Their Makers," *New York Sun* (October 12, 1904), 7, and "Life in a Convent," *Town Talk* (January 7, 1905), 7.

7. EJ, "Van Dorn's Home," *Smart Set* (October 1, 1905), 83.

8. EJ, *Three Rousing Cheers*, 208–16.

9. "Celebrate Mark Twain's Seventieth Birthday," *New York Times* (December 6, 1905).

10. Initially, the "Grandmother" chapter was to be at the beginning of the novel, but the order was rearranged to allow Howells's chapter "The Father" to come first.

11. EJ, *Three Rousing Cheers*, 258.

12. Letter, Alice Brown to EJ, June 1, 1906 (EGJ Papers, NYPL).

13. EJ, *Three Rousing Cheers*, 261; Letter, Margaret Deland to EJ, June 5, 1906 (EGJ Papers, NYPL).

14. Letter, William Dean Howells to EJ, June 18, 1906 (EGJ Papers, NYPL).

15. Letter, Kate Douglas Wiggin Riggs to EJ, June 22, 1906 (EGJ Papers, NYPL).

16. Letter, Mary E. Wilkins Freeman to EJ, July 24, 1906 (EGJ Papers, NYPL).

17. EJ, *Three Rousing Cheers*, 267.

18. Letter, Henry James to EJ, Oct. 31, 1906 (EGJ Papers, NYPL).

19. Letter, Frederick Duneka to EJ, December 19, 1906 (EGJ Papers, NYPL).

20. Letter, EJ to Edith Wyatt, December 26, 1906 (EGJ Papers, NYPL).

21. Letter, Henry James to EJ, January 2, 1907 (EGJ Papers, NYPL).

22. Letter, Henry James to EJ, August 13, 1907 (EGJ Papers, NYPL).

23. Letter, Henry James to EJ, October 2, 1907 (EGJ Papers, NYPL).

24. Letters, Henry Van Dyke to EJ, November 23 and December 31, 1907, and January 2, 1908 (EGJ Papers, NYPL).

25. "Polish Sympathizers," *New York Times* (February 25, 1908), 6.

26. "As to 'The Whole Family,'" *Harper's Bazar* 42 (February 1908), 210.

27. EJ, *Three Rousing Cheers*, 280.

28. EJ, *Three Rousing Cheers*, 281–83.

29. "Stories by Elizabeth Jordan," *Philadelphia Inquirer* (November 23, 1908).

30. "A Book of Episodes," *New York Times* (December 4, 1908), 720.

31. EJ, *Three Rousing Cheers*, 312–13.

32. EJ, *Three Rousing Cheers*, 312–13.

33. "'Harper's Bazar' in New Form," *Brooklyn Eagle* (January 18, 1910), 25.

Chapter 15: The Progressive Era and the Playwright

1. Max Shulman, *Performing the Progressive Era* (Iowa City: University of Iowa Press, 2019).

2. Mark Whalan, *American Culture in the 1910s* (Edinburgh: Edinburgh University Press, 2010), 91–93.

3. Letter, Kate Douglas Wiggin Riggs to EJ, March 28, 1910 (EGJ Papers, NYPL).

4. Letter, Mary E. Wilkins Freeman to EJ, April 11, 1910 (EGJ Papers, NYPL).
5. "Last Glimpse Here of Mark Twain," *New York Times* (April 24, 1910), quoted in www.twainquotes.com, accessed January 16, 2023.
6. EJ, *Three Rousing Cheers*, 219.
7. "Lady from Oklahoma," *Baltimore American* (May 17, 1911), 10; *New York Times* (May 16, 1911), 13.
8. Advertisement, *Harper's Bazar* 46 (February 1912), 99.
9. See, for example, Letter, Effie Shannon to EJ, May 1, 1911 (EGJ Papers, NYPL).
10. EJ, "May Iverson Writes a Play," included in *May Iverson Tackles Life* (New York: Harper and Brothers, 1912), 45.
11. Quoted in EJ, *Three Rousing Cheers*, 245.
12. "Lady from Oklahoma," *Chicago Tribune* (December 9, 1911), 9.
13. EJ, *Three Rousing Cheers*, 245–50.
14. EJ, *May Iverson Tackles Life*, 244.
15. "Life in Convent School," *Boston Globe* (September 14, 1912), 7.
16. Quoted in advertisement in *New York Sun* (September 2, 1912), 6; *Louisville Courier-Journal*, quoted in "Mary [*sic*] Iverson Tackles Life," *Sun* (September 7, 1912), 12.
17. EJ, *Three Rousing Cheers*, 222–23.
18. "The Folks That Write Our Books," *Evening World* (November 12, 1912), 20.
19. For a study of Heterodoxy, see Joanna Scutts's *Hotbed: Bohemian Greenwich Village and the Secret Club that Sparked Modern Feminism* (New York: Seal Press, 2022).
20. "Elizabeth Jordan, Playwright," *Buffalo Inquirer* (January 24, 1913), 6.
21. "Miss Jordan Objects," *Brooklyn Eagle* (March 30, 1913), 34.
22. "The Lady from Oklahoma," playbill.com (accessed September 13, 2022).
23. "Oklahoma Lady Lacks Fresh Theme," *New York Times* (April 3, 1913), 9; advertisement, *Sun* (April 4, 1913), 11.
24. EJ, *Three Rousing Cheers*, 239–41.
25. Theodore Peterson, *Magazines in the Twentieth Century* (Champaign-Urbana: University of Illinois Press, 1956), 206–7.
26. EJ, *Three Rousing Cheers*, 306.
27. Unfortunately, I have been unable to locate any of these letters.
28. EJ, *Three Rousing Cheers*, 287; Gretchen Holbrook Gerzina, *Frances Hodgson Burnett: The Unexpected Life of the Author of* The Secret Garden (New Brunswick, NJ: Rutgers University Press, 2004), 293.
29. EJ, *Three Rousing Cheers*, 325.
30. EJ, *Three Rousing Cheers*, 287.

Chapter 16: Harper's Publishing

1. Atherton, *Adventures of a Novelist*, 537.
2. EJ, *Three Rousing Cheers*, 342; Letter, Sinclair Lewis to EJ, March 11, 1938 (EGJ Papers, NYPL).
3. Undated biographical notes (Betsy Devine Collection).
4. Neuman, *Gilded Suffragists*, chapter 1.
5. Neuman, *Gilded Suffragists*, chapter 1.

6. EJ, *Three Rousing Cheers*, 307.
7. EJ, *Three Rousing Cheers*, 308.
8. EJ, *Three Rousing Cheers*, 308–10.
9. EJ, *Three Rousing Cheers*, 315–16.
10. Burnett's autobiographer, Gretchen Holbrook Gerzina, refers to their relationship as "a romantic friendship"; I do not believe that term does justice to the love they had for one another.
11. Atherton, *Adventures of a Novelist*, 484–85.
12. Atherton, *Adventures of a Novelist*, 484–85.
13. "Stars Draw 1,500 to Suffrage Fete," *New York Times* (February 17, 1914), 6.
14. "The Grand Woman of America," *McAlpin Pibroch* 1 (April 1914), 9–13.
15. EJ, *Three Rousing Cheers*, 330–31.
16. EJ, *Three Rousing Cheers*, 331.
17. EJ, *Three Rousing Cheers*, 330–36.
18. "Fighters Who Win Success against Odds," *New York Times Book Review* (September 26, 1915), 346.
19. Betsy Devine Collection.
20. David Blanke, *The 1910s* (Westport, CT: Greenwood Press, 2002), 3.
21. Quoted in EJ, *Three Rousing Cheers*, 225.
22. EJ, *Three Rousing Cheers*, 223–25; "The Crosby's Rest Cure" (IMDb).
23. "Have Motion Pictures with Your Tea," *New York Times* (May 17, 1914), 10.
24. EJ, *Three Rousing Cheers*, vi–vii.
25. Letter, Frances Hodgson Burnett to EJ, July 14, 1914 (EGJ Papers, NYPL).
26. Letter, Frances Hodgson Burnett to EJ, undated [1914] (EGJ Papers, NYPL).
27. EJ, *Three Rousing Cheers*, 290–91.
28. EJ, *Three Rousing Cheers*, 292; EJ, "Liner's Passengers Thrilled When 'Captured' by British," *New York Evening World* (September 3, 1914), n.p. [clipping from Library of Congress].
29. EJ, *Three Rousing Cheers*, 292–93, 295.
30. EJ, *Three Rousing Cheers*, 294.
31. EJ, *Three Rousing Cheers*, 305.
32. "Wilson Starts Gold Mercy Flood," *New York Tribune* (October 26, 1914), 5.
33. See, for example, Letter, Gertrude Atherton to EJ, undated (EGJ Papers, NYPL).
34. Letter, Gertrude Atherton to EJ, undated [October 1914] (EGJ Papers, NYPL).
35. Letter, Gertrude Atherton to EJ, November 8, [1914] (EGJ Papers, NYPL).
36. Jordan was not the only female journalist to discuss such issues. Contemporaries such as Miriam Michelson and Ida B. Wells also addressed this subject. See Lori Harrison-Kahan, "The Seeds of #MeToo Started Growing 100 Years Ago," CNN Opinion, https://www.cnn.com/2019/11/02/opinions/me-too-movement-history-jordan-michelson-harrison-kahan.
37. "Latest Fiction," *New York Times* (November 22, 1914), 516; "May Iverson's Career," *San Francisco Chronicle* (December 7, 1914), 8; "The Recent Books," *Continent* (January 21, 1915), 82.
38. Letter, Frances Hodgson Burnett, undated [c. November 1914] (EGJ Papers, NYPL).

39. See Melissa J. Homestead, *The Only Wonderful Things: The Creative Partnership of Willa Cather and Edith Lewis* (New York: Oxford University Press, 2021).
40. Letter, Frances Hodgson Burnett to EJ, December 1, 1914 (EGJ Papers, NYPL).
41. Letter, Frances Hodgson Burnett to EJ, April 7, 1915 (EGJ Papers, NYPL).

Chapter 17: A Second Composite Novel

1. EJ, *Three Rousing Cheers*, 149–52.
2. EJ, *Three Rousing Cheers*, 152–54.
3. EJ, *Three Rousing Cheers*, 368–70.
4. "Elizabeth Jordan's Escape from Drowning," *Trenton Evening News* (September 5, 1915), 4.
5. Letter, Frances Hodgson Burnett to EJ, September 15, 1915 (EGJ Papers, NYPL).
6. Quoted in Jordan, *Three Rousing Cheers*, 343.
7. EJ, *Three Rousing Cheers*, 342.
8. EJ, *Three Rousing Cheers*, 342.
9. James M. Hutchinson, *The Rise of Sinclair Lewis, 1920–1930* (University Park: Pennsylvania State University Press, 2010), 249n.
10. Quoted in Ruth Dunbar, "How America Reacts to Edith Cavell's Death," *New York Tribune* (October 31, 1915), 5.
11. Letter, Frances Hodgson Burnett, November 15, 1915 (EGJ Papers, NYPL).
12. Regent of the League award (NYPL mssfiles 1597-6043).
13. Letter, Vira Boarman Whitehouse to EJ, February 26, 1916 (EGJ Papers, NYPL).
14. Leslie Petty, *Romancing the Vote: Feminist Activism in American Fiction, 1870–1920* (Athens: University of Georgia Press, 2006), 143.
15. Letter, Frances Hodgson Burnett to EJ, April 1916 (EGJ Papers, NYPL).
16. Letter, Frances Hodgson Burnett to EJ, April 11, 1916 (EGJ Papers, NYPL).
17. "Suffrage Novel to Be Most Novel Thing in Book Form," *Chicago Tribune* (April 29, 1916), 15.
18. Letter, Vira Whitehouse to EJ, May 5, 1916 (EGJ Papers, NYPL).
19. Letter, EJ to Whitehouse, May 15, 1916, and Letter, Whitehouse to EJ, May 15, 1916 (EGJ Papers, NYPL).
20. Letter, Kathleen Norris to EJ, undated [c. July 3, 1916] (EGJ Papers, NYPL); Letter, EJ to Norris, July 5, 1916 (NYPL mssfiles 1597-6035).
21. Letters, Frances Hodgson Burnett to EJ, May 15 and May 18, 1916 (EGJ Papers, NYPL) and May [no day], 1916 (quoted in *Three Rousing Cheers*, 319–20).
22. Martha deB. Beaver, "Spreadwings," *Hampshire Gazette* (June 2, 1998), n.p.
23. Quoted in Mary Jo Buhle and Paul Buhle, eds., *The Concise History of Woman Suffrage* (Champaign-Urbana: University of Illinois Press, 2005), 430ff.
24. "Latest Works of Fiction," *New York Times Book Review* (October 29, 1916), 460; "Lovers' Knots," *Duluth News-Tribune* (January 14, 1917), 12C; "Books," *New York Sun* (October 28, 1916), 9.
25. Letter, Frances Hodgson Burnett to EJ, December 28, 1916 (EGJ Papers, NYPL).

CHAPTER 18: GOLDEN APPLES

1. Blanke, *The 1910s*, xxvi; Whalan, *American Culture in the 1910s*, xvi.

2. Letter draft, undated, EJ to newspaper editors (NYPL mssfile 1597-6041).

3. Brooke Kroeger, *Fannie: The Talent for Success of Writer Fannie Hurst* (New York: Random House, 1999), 39.

4. Letter, EJ to Vira Whitehouse, May 18, 1917 (NYPL, mssfiles 1597-6039).

5. Letter, EJ to Vira Whitehouse, May 21, 1917 (NYPL, mssfiles 1597-6039).

6. "Writers Demand War," *Washington Times* (April 4, 1917), 3.

7. Letter, Edith Œ. Somerville to EJ, May 1, 1917 (EGJ Papers, NYPL).

8. Letter, Roland Holt to EJ, July 18, 1917 (NYPL, mssfiles 1597-6039).

9. "Gotham Gleanings," *New York Tribune* (June 10, 1917), 3.

10. Oliver Carlson, *Brisbane: A Candid Biography* (New York: Stackpole Sons, 1937), chapter 9.

11. Quoted in EJ, *Three Rousing Cheers*, 360.

12. EJ, *Three Rousing Cheers*, 361.

13. "Plays and Players," *Washington Post* (December 23, 1917), 4.

14. EJ, *Three Rousing Cheers*, 363.

15. EJ, *Three Rousing Cheers*, 358–63.

16. "Latest Works of Fiction," *New York Times* (November 11, 1917), 42–43.

CHAPTER 19: GOLDWYN PICTURES

1. Letters, Sinclair Lewis to EJ, January 4 and January 15, 1918 (Sinclair Lewis Papers, Yale Collection of American Literature, Beinecke Rare Book and Manuscript Library, Yale University, New Haven, CT).

2. Letters, EJ to Eleanor H. Porter, January 17 and January 30, 1918 (Papers of Eleanor H. Porter, Albert and Shirley Small Special Collections Library, University of Virginia, Charlottesville, VA).

3. Item, *The Editor* (March 11, 1918), 171.

4. "Books," *Brooklyn Eagle* (June 8, 1918), 8; "Books," *Oregonian* (March 31, 1918), 79; "Wings of Youth," *Catholic World* 107 (September 1918), 839.

5. *Fort Lee: Birthplace of the Motion Picture Industry* (Charleston, SC: Arcadia Publishing, 2006).

6. EJ, *Three Rousing Cheers*, 364.

7. EJ, "Elizabeth Jordan," *Catholic Authors*, 156.

8. Jan Cohn, *George Horace Latimer and the Saturday Evening Post* (Pittsburgh: University of Pittsburgh Press, 1989), 103.

9. Fahs, *Out on Assignment*, 56–58.

10. On the history of advice columns, see Julia Golia, *Newspaper Confessions: A History of Advice Columns in a Pre-Internet Age* (New York: Oxford University Press, 2021).

11. EJ, *Three Rousing Cheers*, 379.

12. Fahs, *Out on Assignment*, 370.

13. 1920 Census; Edward Beyer's occupation was simply listed as "Own Account."

14. Letters, Frances Hodgson Burnett to EJ, February 15, June 16, 1918 (EGJ Papers, NYPL).

15. Letter, Frances Hodgson Burnett to EJ, October 15, 1918 (EGJ Papers, NYPL).
16. Letter, Frances Hodgson Burnett, December 19, 1918 (EGJ Papers, NYPL).
17. EJ, *Three Rousing Cheers.*

CHAPTER 20: MYSTERY WRITING

1. EJ, "Elizabeth Jordan," *Catholic Authors*, 156.
2. Letter, Harriet Beardslee Prescott to Clothilde Reo, undated (Betsy Devine Collection).
3. Clothilde Reo Devine interviews (Betsy Devine Collection).
4. 1910 Census. For more on Leda Carpentier's background, see Betsy Devine's blog: *Betsy Devine: Funny ha-ha and/or funny peculiar* (betsydevine.com/blog/).
5. Letter, Charles Hanson Towne, editor of *McClure's*, to EJ, March 26, 1919 (EGJ Papers, NYPL); the story was reprinted in the *Tribune* on June 8, 1919.
6. Quoted in EJ, *Three Rousing Cheers*, 24.
7. "Activity of Members," *Journal of the National Institute of Social Sciences* 5 (1919), 216–17; "Jordan, Elizabeth," *Who's Who* (1918–1919), 1478.
8. Letter, Frances Hodgson Burnett to EJ, undated [c. summer 1919] (EGJ Papers, NYPL).
9. Letter, Frances Hodgson Burnett to EJ, undated (EGJ Papers, NYPL).
10. EJ, *May Iverson Tackles Life*, 75.
11. EJ, *Three Rousing Cheers*, 24.
12. "Personal Gossip about Writers," *Writer* 32 (November 1919), 171.
13. "The Latest Books," *Life* (January 22, 1920), 156; "Books and the Book World," *The Sun* (September 7, 1919), 5; "The New Books," *Outlook* (November 12, 1919), 306; "Latest Works of Fiction," *New York Times Review of Books* (August 24, 1919), 78–79.
14. Materials description, *Chicago Tribune* Papers, University of Oregon Library; "Mary Patterson, Ex-News Editor," *New York Times* (December 28, 1975), 33.
15. Advertisement, *New York Times* (October 1, 1919), 2.
16. Gerzina, *Frances Hodgson Burnett*, 296, 51.
17. Letters, Frances Hodgson Burnett to EJ, December 10 and December 17, 1919 (EGJ Papers, NYPL).
18. Erica Ryan, *When the World Broke in Two: The Roaring Twenties and the Dawn of America's Cultural Wars* (Santa Barbara, CA: Praeger, 2018), 42–47; Whalan, *American Culture in the 1910s*, 3–5.

CHAPTER 21: THE ROARING TWENTIES

1. EJ, *Three Rousing Cheers*, 114–15.
2. See, for example, the full-page advertisement, *Wheeling Intelligencer* (July 27, 1920), 8.
3. EJ, "Women in the Presidential Campaign," *Ladies' Home Journal* 37 (October 1920), 3–4, 138; "New Women Leaders in Politics," *Ladies' Home Journal* 37 (December 1920), 6–7, 192–93; "The Big Little Things for Women in Politics: Employ the Ballot Early and Often for Your Community's Betterment," *Ladies' Home Journal* 38 (January 1921), 20, 78; "Education for Citizenship," *Ladies' Home Journal* 38 (February 1921).

4. Gerzina, *Frances Hodgson Burnett*, 296.

5. Letters, Frances Hodgson Burnett to EJ, December 8, 1920, and undated (EGJ Papers, NYPL).

6. Gerzina, *Frances Hodgson Burnett*, 297.

7. Clothilde Reo Devine interviews (Betsy Devine Collection).

8. Email to author from Betsy Devine, March 21, 2020.

9. Clothilde Reo Devine interviews (Betsy Devine Collection).

10. Letter, Frances Hodgson Burnett to EJ, May 24, 1921 (EGJ Papers, NYPL).

11. Letter, Frances Hodgson Burnett to Martha Cutler, undated [July 1921] (EGJ Papers, NYPL).

12. Gerzina, *Frances Hodgson Burnett*, 300.

13. "Gold Tournament for Country Club at Atlantic City," *New York Herald* (October 2, 1921), 3.

14. Letter, Frances Hodgson Burnett to EJ, [1921] (EGJ Papers, NYPL).

15. EJ, *Three Rousing Cheers*, 328.

Chapter 22: *America*'s Theater Critic

1. Willa Cather, *Not under Forty* (New York: Alfred A. Knopf, 1922), 3.

2. EJ, *The Blue Circle* (New York: Century Co., 1922), 15.

3. EJ, *The Blue Circle*, 17.

4. "Fiction," *Buffalo Courier* (May 21, 1922), 92; "Elizabeth Jordan's 'The Blue Circle,'" *Century* (May 1922), 964; "Few Good Mystery Stories by Women," *Philadelphia Inquirer* (June 11, 1922), 20.

5. "Social Notes," *New York Times* (June 9, 1922), 12.

6. Clothilde Reo Devine interviews (Betsy Devine Collection).

7. Clothilde Reo Devine interviews (Betsy Devine Collection).

8. Letter, Frances Hodgson Burnett to EJ, October 24, 1921 (EGJ Papers, NYPL).

9. EJ, "Drama," *America* (December 9, 1922), 184–85.

10. Gerzina, *Frances Hodgson Burnett*, 301.

11. Letter, Mary King to EJ, September 12, 1923 (EGJ Papers, NYPL).

Chapter 23: Rebuilding from Loss

1. Letter, Mary King to EJ, April 22, 1924 (EGJ Papers, NYPL).

2. EJ, "Automobile Accidents," *Saturday Evening Post* (January 2, 1926), 16–17, 94, 96.

3. "Miss Elizabeth Jordan Better," *Boston Globe* (August 8, 1924), 11A; Item, *Dayton News* (August 9, 1924), 35; "Jordans in Auto Crash," *New York Herald* (August 6, 1924), 11; EJ, "Automobile Accidents," 4.

4. Letter, EJ to Frances Hodgson Burnett, October 14, 1924 (EGJ Papers, NYPL).

5. Letter, Frances Hodgson Burnett to EJ, undated (EGJ Papers, NYPL).

6. Letter, Frances Hodgson Burnett to EJ, "Saturday night" (EGJ Papers, NYPL).

7. "Mrs. Frances H. Burnett Buried Near Loved Home," *New York Herald* (November 2, 1924), 19.

8. Letter, Vivian Burnett to EJ, December 19, 1924, quoted in Jordan, *Three Rousing Cheers*, 322–23.

9. EJ, *Three Rousing Cheers*, 322–23.

10. "Mystery and Love," *Ephraim Enterprise* (December 19, 1924), 2. Jordan was not actually admitted as an official member to P.E.N. until 1942, but she participated in so many of their events that it was an unsurprising error.

11. "Latest Works of Fiction," *New York Times Book Review* (May 24, 1925), 17.

12. "Church Activities," *New York Age* (March 21 and 25, 1925), 5, 5.

13. Gerzina, *Frances Hodgson Burnett*, ix–xxiv, 304.

14. Gerzina, *Frances Hodgson Burnett*, ix; "Will Honor Memory of Mrs. Burnett," *New York Times* (May 31, 1925), S13.

15. EJ, "Lonely and Poor, But She Knew It Not," *Philadelphia Inquirer* (October 2, 1925), 16.

16. EJ, *Three Rousing Cheers*, 312.

17. Jordan, "On Being a Spinster," *Saturday Evening Post* (April 10, 1926), 35, 214, 217–18.

18. John H. Lewy, "Thrilling Sin Plus," *Brooklyn Eagle* (March 30, 1927), 17; "Young Girl's Quest," *Democrat and Chronicle* (April 10, 1927), 75; Eleanor Harley, "'Black Butterflies' and Our Studiously Shocking Youngsters," *Philadelphia Inquirer* (May 28, 1927), 15.

19. Lucy Worsley, *Agatha Christie: An Elusive Woman* (New York: Pegasus Crime, 2022), chapters 19–21.

20. Worsley, *Agatha Christie*, 135.

21. "Miss Nobody, Nowhere," *Oakland Tribune* (April 29, 1928), 40; Elmira Gordon, "Miss Nobody from Nowhere," *New York Herald-Tribune* (August 12, 1928), K8.

22. EJ, "Mary Riordan's Lesson," *Messenger of the Sacred Heart* 63, no. 8 (1928), 27–35.

23. EJ, *Three Rousing Cheers*, 323.

24. EJ, *The Devil and the Deep Sea* (New York: Century Co., 1929), 164.

25. "Reviews of Summer Books," *Sunday Star* (August 4, 1929), 4.

26. "Book Notes," *Brooklyn Times Union* (January 12, 1930), 8A.

27. "Book Notes," 8A; Siegel, "Women in the Stacks."

28. EJ, *Three Rousing Cheers*, 377–81.

29. EJ, *Three Rousing Cheers*, 382.

CHAPTER 24: NEW DIRECTIONS

1. Anthony Young, *New York Café Society: The Elite Meet to See and Be Seen, 1920s–1940s* (Jefferson, NC: McFarland, 2015), 3–8, 126; Terry A. Cooney, *Balancing Acts: American Thought and Culture in the 1930s* (Ann Arbor: University of Michigan, 1995), 1–15.

2. 1930 Census.

3. *The Roaring 20s* (*Life* magazine Special Issue, February 7, 2020), 78.

4. "Less Blood and More Mystery Is Author's Plea," (Mansfield, OH) *News-Journal* (April 27, 1930), 17; "Real Murder Here," (Rochester, NY) *Democrat and Chronicle* (March 29, 1930), 12; "The Night Club Mystery," *Atlanta Constitution* (June 15, 1930), 28.

5. "Notes on Social Activities," *New York Times* (April 16, July 16, 1930), 24; 31; "Personal Intelligence," *New York Herald-Tribune* (July 16, 1930), 15.

6. Cooney, *Balancing Acts*, 2–9.
7. "Book Chat," *Burlington Free Press* (May 30, 1931), 6.
8. EJ, *Three Rousing Cheers*, 383–84.

Chapter 25: Writing against the Odds

1. Martin Edwards, *The Golden Age of Murder* (London: HarperCollins, 2015), 187.
2. "Man Takes Heroine's Role in Novel," *Detroit Free Press* (March 13, 1932), 40.
3. M. D., "Brief Reviews," *Chicago Tribune* (May 27, 1933), 13; "Satisfying New Mystery Is by Elizabeth Jordan," *Boston Globe* (February 25, 1933), 13; "Young Mr. X," *New York Herald Tribune* (January 29, 1933), 110.
4. EJ, *Three Rousing Cheers*, 385–88.
5. EJ, *Three Rousing Cheers*, 385–88.
6. EJ, *Three Rousing Cheers*, 385–88.
7. "Mystery and Adventure," *New York Herald-Tribune* (March 18, 1934), F18; "Mysteries," *New Yorker* (March 17, 1939), 103–4.
8. EJ, *Three Rousing Cheers*, 388–89.
9. EJ, *Three Rousing Cheers*, 389–94.

Chapter 26: Three Rousing Cheers!

1. Letter, EJ to Mr. Stevens, April 24, 1935 (EGJ Papers, NYPL).
2. EJ, *Life of the Party* (New York: D. Appleton-Century Co., 1936), 85–86.
3. EJ, *Life of the Party*, 108.
4. EJ, *Life of the Party*, 106.
5. This subgenre was popularized by the British author R. Austin Freeman around 1910 (Martin Edwards, *The Life of Crime: Detecting the History of Mysteries and Their Creators* [London: Collins Crime Club, 2022], chapter 10).
6. EJ, *Three Rousing Cheers*, 338–39.
7. "New Mystery Stories," *New York Times* (August 1, 1937), 95; "Mystery and Adventure," *New York Herald Tribune* (July 18, 1937), 12.
8. Gerzina, *Frances Hodgson Burnett*, 305.
9. EJ, *Three Rousing Cheers*, 186, 307.
10. EJ, *Three Rousing Cheers*, 310–11.
11. EJ, *Three Rousing Cheers*, 125.
12. EJ, *Three Rousing Cheers*, 185.
13. "Harriet Monroe's Life and Elizabeth Jordan's," *Philadelphia Inquirer* (March 19, 1938), 26; "Miscellaneous Brief Reviews," *New York Times* (March 20, 1938), 105.
14. Letters, Sinclair Lewis to EJ, March 11 and March 29, 1938 (Harrison Smith Papers, Yale Collection of American Literature, Beinecke Rare Book and Manuscript Library, Yale University, New Haven, CT).
15. Letter, Margaret Deland to EJ, March 15, 1938 (EGJ Papers, NYPL).
16. Letter, Charles Hanson Towne to EJ, March 27, 1938 (EGJ Papers, NYPL).

Chapter 27: Passages

1. Evelyn Page, "In Grim Earnest," *Washington Post* (May 21, 1939), B10; "'Flower of Smoke' and Some Other Recent Works of Fiction," *New York Times* (April 9, 1939), BR4.
2. Siegel, "Women in the Stacks."
3. Hutchinson, *The Rise of Sinclair Lewis*, 18–19.
4. Mary King had married Joseph Medill Patterson, publisher of *The Daily News*, in 1938, but she still published under "Mary King."
5. "Her Novel Unusual," *Chicago Tribune* (April 17, 1940), 16.
6. Letter, Otis Skinner to EJ, April 24 [1940] (EGJ Papers, NYPL).
7. "Catholics Appeal for Aid to Britain," *New York Times* (October 28, 1940), 5.
8. Item, *New York Times* (January 29, 1941), 14; Letter, Fannie Hurst to EJ, January 21, 1941 (EGJ Papers, NYPL).
9. "Island Dwellers Eventually Get on Each Other's Nerves," *Oakland Tribune* (June 1, 1941), 20; "Fiction in a Lighter Vein," *New York Times Book Review* (August 3, 1941), 19.
10. EJ, *Three Rousing Cheers.*

Chapter 28: The Final Years

1. "Book Notes," *New York Herald Tribune* (March 31, 1942), 21.
2. "Civic Corruption," *New York Times Book Review* (June 7, 1942), 23; "Young John Takes Over," *New York Herald Tribune* (April 26, 1942), 16.
3. EJ, "Theater," *America* (January 2, 1943); EJ, "Theater," *America* (February 13, 1943).
4. "'Herself,'" *Chicago Tribune* (March 28, 1943), 133; Audrey E. Lee, "Herself," *Sioux City Journal* (May 16, 1943), 36; "Herself," *New York Times Book Review* (April 11, 1943), 14; Lisle Bell, "New Popular Novels," *New York Herald Tribune* (March 28, 1943), 22.
5. Letter, Alice Brown to EJ, undated [1944] (EGJ Papers, NYPL). Brown, a diehard Republican, lamented Jordan's vote for Roosevelt, but Jordan was a lifelong Democrat and admired him.
6. Letters, Alice Brown to EJ, January 10, 1945, and April 24, 1946 (EGJ Papers, NYPL).
7. Death certificate #4786, New York City (ancestry.com). No will survives.
8. Scrap of paper listing attendees (Betsy Devine Collection).
9. "Elizabeth Jordan, Journalist, Dead," *New York Times* (February 25, 1947), 25.

Selected Secondary Bibliography

Blake, Art M. *How New York Became American, 1890–1924*. Baltimore: Johns Hopkins University Press, 2020.

Edwards, Martin. *The Golden Age of Murder*. London: HarperCollins, 2015.

———. *The Life of Crime: Detecting the History of Mysteries and Their Creators*. London: Collins Crime Club, 2022.

Fahs, Alice. *Out on Assignment: Newspaper Women and the Making of Modern Public Space*. Durham: University of North Carolina Press, 2011.

Gerzina, Gretchen Holbrook. *Frances Hodgson Burnett: The Unexpected Life of the Author of* The Secret Garden. New Brunswick, NJ: Rutgers University Press, 2004.

Golia, Julia. *Newspaper Confessions: A History of Advice Columns in a Pre-Internet Age*. New York: Oxford University Press, 2021.

Harrison-Kahan, Lori. "The Seeds of #MeToo Started Growing 100 Years Ago." CNN Opinion. https://www.cnn.com/2019/11/02/opinions/me-too-movement-history-jordan-michelson-harrison-kahan.

Homestead, Melissa J. *The Only Wonderful Things: The Creative Partnership of Willa Cather and Edith Lewis*. New York: Oxford University Press, 2021.

Howard, June. *Publishing the Family*. Durham, NC: Duke University Press, 2001.

Kroeger, Brooke. *Fannie: The Talent for Success of Writer Fannie Hurst*. New York: Random House, 1999.

———. *Undaunted: How Women Changed American Journalism*. New York: Alfred A. Knopf, 2023.

Livingston, James D. *Arsenic and Clam Chowder: Murder in Gilded Age New York*. Albany: State University of New York Press, 2010.

Lutes, Jean Marie. *Front-Page Girls: Women Journalists in American Culture and Fiction, 1880–1930*. Ithaca, NY: Cornell University Press, 2006.

Neuman, Johanna. *Gilded Suffragists: The New York Socialites Who Fought for Women's Right to Vote*. New York: New York University Press, 2017.

Petty, Leslie. *Romancing the Vote: Feminist Activism in American Fiction, 1870–1920*. Athens: University of Georgia Press, 2006.

Prendergast, Catherine. *The Gilded Age: Two Audacious Women and the Cyanide Love Triangle That Shook America*. New York: Dutton, 2021.

Prescott, Paul. *New Journalism, New Critics, 1890–1910*. Cambridge: Cambridge University Press, 2013.

Robertson, Cara. *The Trial of Lizzie Borden*. New York: Simon & Schuster, 2019.

Roggenkamp, Karen. "Elizabeth Jordan, 'True Stories,' and Newspaper Fiction in Late-Nineteenth-Century Journalism." In *Literature and Journalism: Inspirations, Intersections, and Inventions from Ben Franklin to Stephen Colbert*, edited by Mark Canada, 32–51. New York: Palgrave Macmillan, 2013.

Rugoff, Milton. *The Gilded Age*. New York: New Word City, 2018.

Ryan, Erica. *When the World Broke in Two: The Roaring Twenties and the Dawn of America's Cultural Wars*. Santa Barbara, CA: Praeger, 2018.

Scutts, Joanna. *Hotbed: Bohemian Greenwich Village and the Secret Club that Sparked Modern Feminism*. New York: Seal Press, 2022.

Todd, Kim. *Sensational: The Hidden History of America's "Girl Stunt Reporters."* New York: HarperCollins, 2021.

Young, Anthony. *New York Café Society: The Elite Meet to See and Be Seen, 1920s–1940s*. Jefferson, NC: McFarland, 2015.

Index